THE JOHN HARVARD LIBRARY

BERNARD BAILYN

Editor-in-Chief

THE JOHN HARVARD LIBRARY

THE SPIRIT OF
AMERICAN GOVERNMENT

J. ALLEN SMITH

Edited by Cushing Strout

THE BELKNAP PRESS OF
HARVARD UNIVERSITY PRESS

CAMBRIDGE, MASSACHUSETTS

1965

CONTENTS

The Spirit of American Government

INTRODUCTION

Alexis de Tocqueville wrote in 1835: "A new science of politics is needed for a new world." [1] Yet, apart from *The Federalist,* the new world stimulated among its own citizens remarkably little sustained attention to the theory of political problems. Americans saw themselves as an ideology incarnate, and therefore, not needing abstract philosophers, they could leave reflective problems of government, under a written constitution with a heritage of the ideals expressed in the Declaration of Independence, in the safe hands of practical statesmen and Supreme Court Justices. Poor by European standards in political philosophy, the nation was living out its commitment to the large ideas embedded in its major public documents. The intellectual inheritance of the Republic was kept alive mainly by party disputes over its meaning.

In the first decade of the twentieth century a generation of reformers began to question the inheritance itself. The Founding Fathers had become the idols of the established powers in business and politics, and the reformers began to seek elsewhere for the democratic wisdom to deal with the corruption, privilege, monopoly, and exploitation which characterized urban and

[1] Author's Introduction, *Democracy in America,* ed. Phillips Bradley (New York, 1946), I, 7.

industrial life. Perhaps the saving wisdom had somehow been lost—lost ever since it had first been glimpsed
by the American rebels of 1776. It might even be that
the Founding Fathers and their Constitution were
themselves at the root of the evils. This twist of thought
in a country whose people and heroes had long vener-
ated the framers of the Constitution was a somersault
of perspective that enthralled a powerful group of
Progressive reformers and still survives in the writings
of some influential historians.

The original prophet of this new political vision was
James Allen Smith, and *The Spirit of American Government* vividly illustrated the reversal of perspective
in 1907. Smith was a teacher of political economy, but
his theory was as much a polemic, addressed to the particular situation which had provoked it, as any of the
classical political theories of American statesmen. In recent years scholars even more influential, such as
Charles A. Beard and Vernon L. Parrington, whose
work made Smith's appear to be a precursor, have been
subjected to substantial reappraisal. A tide of historical
change left Smith's thesis beached and largely ignored,
though many of his favorite reforms had been achieved
by the Progressives. His theory about the aristocratic
spirit of American government escaped the direct fire
of historical criticism until the mid-1950's, if only because he himself was forgotten, and his ideas survived
as a commonplace, a piece of mental furniture placed
in a corner and neglected while the rest of the furnish-

ings were done over in a new style. "Cribbing and confining the popular spirit that had been at large since 1776," wrote Richard Hofstadter in 1948, for example, "were essential to the purposes of the new Constitution."[2] Hofstadter's widely read book perpetuated much of Smith's image of the framers for a new public, while the more detailed and lengthy analysis of Merrill Jensen in *The New Nation* (1950), addressed to scholars, carried on Smith's thesis of an antidemocratic reaction against the Articles of Confederation.

Smith's career was that of the academic rebel, admired by the young, feared by regents and trustees, and a worry for the college president. He was born on May 5, 1860, in Pleasant Hill, Missouri, of homesteading parents from Virginia. At the University of Missouri he was a student of the first rank, majoring in the arts and discovering the democratic case for reform in Henry George's *Progress and Poverty,* which students had been warned not to read. After obtaining a law degree from the university in 1887, he went into practice, but found, at a time when bench and bar were deeply committed to the interests and outlook of the business community, that "it did not offer a suitable opportunity for one who was mainly interested in political and economic reforms."[3] Brooking the disfavor of

[2] *The American Political Tradition* (New York, 1948), p. 4.

[3] Letter to the Chautauqua Institute, quoted by Thomas C. McClintock, "J. Allen Smith and the Progressive Movement: A Study in Intellectual History," unpub. diss., University of Washington, 1959, p. 21. For the

his mother, Smith married a stenographer, Doris J. Lehmann, who encouraged him in 1892 to take the risk of graduate study in political economy at the University of Michigan.

The attraction at Michigan was Henry Carter Adams, a leader of the new economics, inspired by Germany's "historical school," and critical of classical *laissez-faire* theory. Adams was himself an academic rebel, once forced out of Cornell University for defending trade unionism. Under his guidance Smith studied finance and comparative constitutional law. Characteristically Smith wrote a dissertation on the money question, a topic so controversial as to worry his teacher about its acceptance by conservative colleagues. The Populists had agitated for a more flexible currency throughout the nineties by attacking the gold standard for its hardship on rural debtors in the cotton and wheat country of the South and West. Smith in fact had lost his savings in the panic of 1893, and his thesis, "The Multiple Money Standard," was published in 1896, just a few months before William Jennings Bryan brought the cheering Democratic National Convention to its feet with his cry, "you shall not crucify mankind upon a cross of gold." But in effect the Populist's broad, radical, and constructive program was crucified instead

---

facts of Smith's career I have drawn heavily on this judicious and thorough account, based on the J. Allen Smith papers at the University of Washington and on conversations with his widow, colleagues, and former students. The author has kindly given me permission to use it.

on Bryan's cross of silver, the narrow Democratic plank of "the free and unlimited coinage of silver in the ratio of 16 to 1." Though Smith voted for Bryan, the student's argument was much more sophisticated than this free-silver plank.

In the vision of the good society as seen in Smith's thesis the United States would be exempted from the repercussions of financial crises abroad, and an elastic currency of stable purchasing power would ensure an economy of continuously rising wages and falling interest rates. To fulfill these ends Smith made a limited break with *laissez-faire* tradition, while accepting in general the competitive system. His program required fixing railroad rates; establishing a central government bank to regulate the money supply by its lending policy, its purchase of securities, and its control of the price in the home market of gold and silver; and an adjustment of taxation to the contraction or expansion of the volume of money. These policies were tied to his main theme of currency reform to prevent the periodic panics which characterized his time.

The Populists had originally proposed that the government ease their load of debt by issuing paper money up to 80 percent of the value of crops stored in government warehouses. Smith's more sophisticated theory was developed from earlier ideas proposed by eminent English economists, including Stanley Jevons and Alfred Marshall, and by Simon Newcomb, an American scientist. It aimed to stabilize the purchasing power of the dollar by making adjustments in the government price of gold or silver whenever there was a change in the general level of the wholesale prices of certain important commodities. The price of gold or silver, in which government notes could be redeemed, would be varied inversely with the rise and fall of general prices. The government would buy gold and silver above their market price when the currency was appreciated and sell them below that level when money depreciated. This loss would be morally justified, unlike the panic of 1893, as a general tax upon the community.[4]

Prophets with panaceas from Bryan to Ezra Pound have notoriously been attracted by the lure of money theories. The intricacies or merit of Smith's scheme need not be analyzed here; it is enough to emphasize that his purposes were humane and that some of his policies anticipated objectives and methods which modern governments in democratic countries habitually pursue by central banking systems and government spending. In 1932 Irving Fisher, the most persistent and articulate theorist of monetary reform, defended before Congress a proposal very similar to Smith's scheme, and he cited a host of prominent economists and financial leaders who, in principle at least, accepted the objective of stable money.[5]

[4] "The Multiple Money Standard," *Annals of the American Academy of Political and Social Science*, 7 (1896), 173–232.

[5] "Stabilization of Commodity Prices," *Extracts from Hearings before the Subcommittee of the Committee on Banking and Currency*, House of Representatives, 72nd Cong., 1st sess. (March 28, 29, 1932).

After the 1890's Smith did not pursue his money policy further; he concentrated instead on historical and political aspects of the democratic ideal, problems which absorbed and animated his energies for the rest of his life. After 1897 the force of the Populist money argument was weakened anyway by the discovery of new gold supplies and new refining processes which supported a world-wide trend of rising prices. Yet Smith's career was conditioned by his graduate thesis: he had marked himself as a heretic. He would find academic security only in places where the Populists were in favor.

The issue of the gold standard, which McKinley and the Republicans had held high as the sign of political virtue and sanity, remained the most sensitive index of the limits of tolerance in academic life. Reform-minded professors, such as John R. Commons, Edward A. Ross, and George Herron, were dismissed from academic jobs for their heresy on the money question, and in states where the Populists dominated the board of regents the fate of a gold-standard advocate was equally precarious. Colleges and universities had no strongly established traditions of academic freedom; it mattered very much whose ox was being gored. Smith found a job at Marietta College, Ohio, where the president was in sympathy with the Social Gospel movement of liberal Protestantism, and he became a respected and popular teacher. His tenure was shaken when along with the president he and four other faculty members who had voted for Bryan were forced out. Smith's salary came from a fund donated by private benefactors, whose views were expressed by an editorial in a local paper, owned by a trustee, warning that the man who did not advocate "hope and confidence" was "out of joint with the times" and should seek the cloister or "the solitude of banishment." [6] From Smith's point of view the men who ran Marietta College were his natural enemies: "They are partisan Republicans, are interested in gas and other monopolies, and would like to see the teaching in this college subordinated to their own private interests. It is probable that I should have found no difficulty in remaining here had I been willing to defend protection, unregulated private ownership of monopolies, and the gold standard. As it was a case of intellectual prostitution or giving up my position, I preferred the latter." [7] He really was given no choice; under the force of an "economy" policy he was ultimately compelled to look for a new post.

Smith's search for an academic place had its ironies. His wife's father led him to a friend in power—a regent at Kansas State Agricultural College. There, where the Populist majority on the Board of Regents had requested the resignation of the entire faculty, the Populist president knew a good man of his own stripe when

[6] Quoted from *The Industrialist*, 22 (September 2, 1897), p. 180, by McClintock, "Smith," p. 109.

[7] Letter to Frank Docter, May 3, 1897, quoted by Eric F. Goldman, "J. Allen Smith: The Reformer and His Dilemma," *Pacific Northwest Quarterly*, 35 (July 1944), p. 198, n. 19.

he saw one, just as the Marietta trustees had recognized their natural enemy. Accordingly, when the President turned down the chair of history and political science at the Populist-controlled University of Washington, he suggested Smith, among others, as a substitute. The president of the University of Washington picked out Smith because he was a fellow alumnus of the University of Michigan. By this odd turn of events Smith acquired a professorship in 1897. As a defender of academic freedom, he must have reflected wrily on the workings of the market place in the region of the higher learning.

If Smith had found sanctuary, it was not at all a cloister. The University, like Seattle itself, was in a pioneer stage of development. There were poor library resources; and he had to protest in order to get his teaching "load" reduced to what today any self-respecting institution would consider a "sweatshop" level. Smith plunged into local politics with a spirited defense of municipal ownership for street railways, delivered before the city council, and he was later urged, unsuccessfully, to run as a candidate for governor on the Progressive ticket of 1912. Conservatives saw him as a dangerous radical, especially after the publication of *The Spirit of American Government,* but his tenure, though often threatened, was never in real danger. He had countervailing support among the students and faculty, as well as influential allies in some sectors of the professions, the press, and the politicians. He suffered his worst blow in 1917 when the president of his own university, who was determined to emphasize the training of students for work in commerce and industry, established a business school, while simultaneously striking at Smith by cutting his omnibus department of history and political science into three, political science, economics, and sociology, and leaving him with but one junior colleague. This slap in the face was given to a man who had been dean of the graduate school for eight years, a great teacher, and a political writer of national reputation.

Smith's academic life was always animated by a passion for social reform. His old department aimed, as the University of Washington catalogue announced, "to inculcate any worthy social ideals and lay the basis for sound and independent thinking on political and economic questions . . . and at the same time to aid in fitting [the student] for a life of useful citizenship, whatever his vocation may be."[8] A man of limited cultivation, he owned a library exclusively composed of works in the subjects he taught, and he had no taste for serious literature or music. Raised as a Southern Baptist, he early lost his religious convictions and never attended any church as an adult. He had found in scholarship, as others had in scientific medicine or social work, a secular form of selfless dedication which was for his generation, as Donald Fleming has pointed

[8] Quoted by McClintock, "Smith," p. 472.

out, "an exit from the acquisitive struggle" and "a form of internal expatriation from the Gilded Age." [9]

The matrix of Smith's outlook and career lay in the decade of the 1890's, which blasted the hopes of democrats with the harshness of a Marxist nightmare. Industrialists had formed huge monopolies, protected by high tariffs. Government regulation through the Interstate Commerce Commission or the Sherman Antitrust Law was feeble. The rich engaged in the "conspicuous consumption" so acidly and memorably described by Thorstein Veblen. Farmers and workers, living through a period of falling prices, panic, and depression, were effectively excluded from representation in the major political parties. In 1895 three decisions of the Supreme Court seemed to turn the law into a bastion of defense for the vested interests of capitalists against popular control.

The Court ruled *(United States v. E. C. Knight Co.)* that the American Sugar Refining Company, controlling more than ninety percent of the manufacture of all refined sugar in the United States, could not be prosecuted under the Sherman Law because manufacturing was not itself interstate commerce and did not directly influence it.[10] This legalistic decision meant that the government could conduct successful prosecu-

[9] "Social Darwinism," in Arthur M. Schlesinger, Jr., and Morton White, eds., *Paths of American Thought* (Boston, 1963), 132–133.
[10] 156 U.S. 1.

tions only against railroad rate combinations, obviously directly engaged in interstate commerce. But the Court did not find the government helpless to curb labor unions. When several thousand workers at the Pullman Company, organized in the American Railway Union, went out on strike under the leadership of Eugene V. Debs and resorted to a boycott of trains hauling Pullman cars, President Cleveland, over the protests of Governor Peter Altgeld, dispatched federal troops to keep order. The attorney general, a former railroad lawyer, obtained a sweeping injunction against Debs, who was convicted of contempt and imprisoned without trial by jury. In sentencing Debs the district court invoked the Sherman Act on the ground that the strikers had engaged in a conspiracy in restraint of trade within the meaning of the law. The Supreme Court *(In re Debs)* defended the injunction as a proper remedy for securing the protection of commerce and the mails, despite the warning of legal conservatives that the new uses of the injunction procedure constituted dangerous innovations and "a degradation of the judicial process." [11]

The third blow to the reformers was the Court's hair-

[11] Charles C. Allen, "Injunction and Organized Labor," a paper read at the 17th annual meeting of the American Bar Association, quoted by Arnold M. Paul, *Conservative Crisis and the Rule of Law: Attitudes of Bar and Bench, 1887–1895* (Ithaca, 1960), p. 147. Allen's phrase referred to the use of the injunction as a basis for invoking the military, which was the Attorney General's reason for obtaining it. For the case see 158 U.S. 564.

splitting and unprecedented opinion against the income tax. The government had taxed incomes during the Civil War and subsequently until 1872. Responding to the pressure of Populists and other reform groups, Bryan and his supporters in 1893 managed to get an income tax bill attached to a lower tariff measure. The tariff bill was eviscerated by amendment, but the income tax survived to become law, providing for a 2 per cent tax on all incomes over $4,000, including gifts and inheritance, and supplemented by a similar tax, with no exemptions, on net corporation profits. The Constitution limited the tax power of Congress only by the provision that "direct taxes" be apportioned among the states according to population, and by legal tradition as far back as 1796 such taxes were, like poll taxes and land taxes, only those which could reasonably and fairly be so apportioned. In 1881 the Court *(Springer v. United States)* specifically and unanimously held that an income tax was not a direct tax within the meaning of the Constitution, for it could not be fairly apportioned according to population in the states.[12]

Given this background of long-standing precedent, even the conservative Attorney General, Richard Olney, who had obtained the injunction against Debs, protested before the Court that throwing out the income tax would "go far to prove that government by written constitution is not a thing of stable principles, but of

[12] 102 U.S. 586.

the fluctuating views and wishes of the particular period and the particular judges when and from whom its interpretation happens to be called for." [13] Proof of prejudice was not lacking. Eminent counsel for the appellants denounced the income tax as populism, socialism, or communism, and in response to this rhetoric the Chief Justice interpreted the Founding Fathers as deliberately intending "to prevent an attack upon accumulated property by mere force of numbers." [14] By a majority of 6-2 the Court rejected a tax on income from rents or from state and municipal bonds, while dramatically dividing 4-4 on the major tax issues. On a rehearing before the full Court a narrow majority of five, obtained by the change of one anonymous Justice's opinion, struck down the entire income tax proposal. Most Conservatives heaved a sigh of relief, while reformers could take comfort only in the indignant language of dissenting Justice Henry B. Brown, who charged that the outcome was "a surrender of the taxing power to the moneyed class" and might "prove the first step toward the submergence of the liberties of the people in a sordid despotism of wealth." [15]

If the Court seemed to have turned the Sherman Law and the Constitution itself into the service of capitalist power and prejudice, it had also forged the "due process" clause of the 14th Amendment, originally passed

[13] 157 U.S. 502, quoted by Paul, *Conservative Crisis*, p. 189.

[14] 157 U.S. 502, pp. 582–583, quoted by Paul, *Conservative Crisis*, p. 199.

[15] 158 U.S. 695, quoted by Paul, *Conservative Crisis*, pp. 212–213.

for the protection of the freed Negro, into a guardian of the property rights of corporations, which were thus shielded from the regulatory power of every state legislature in the Union. Reading into the Amendment the dogma of an unfettered "freedom of contract," derived from the *laissez-faire* theory which had been popularized by such influential publicists as Herbert Spencer and Prof. William Graham Sumner, the Court transformed the traditional meaning of "due process." Instead of being a standard for law enforcement, it became a check on lawmaking whenever it had a restrictive effect on business interests. Justice Brown, three years after his passionate dissent in the income tax case, wrote a majority opinion in defense of a state's power in the area of health, safety, welfare, or morals to pass a statute setting an eight-hour maximum working day in mines, smelters, or ore refineries in Utah.[16] But by 1905 the new interpretation through *laissez-faire* spectacles had gained such ground that Brown himself joined the majority in *Lochner v. New York,* which struck down a New York statute limiting labor in bakeshops to a ten-hour day. The majority opinion, ignoring all sociological evidence, denied that the state had any reasonable ground for interfering with the right of free contract because neither the safety, morals, nor the welfare of the public were in the slightest degree affected by the act.[17]

[16] Holden v. Hardy 169 U.S. 366.
[17] 198 U.S. 45.

This notorious piece of woolgathering dogmatism aroused Justice Oliver Wendell Holmes, Jr., to his historic protest against judges who found laws unconstitutional merely because they disagreed with the legislature about the wisdom of its social policies: "The Fourteenth Amendment does not enact Mr. Herbert Spencer's *Social Statics*." [18] Yet the Court continued to assume that Mr. Spencer had indeed been enacted, and the ground lay open for Smith's assault on judicial review. How, he would ask, could Alexander Hamilton have honestly said that the judiciary has "no direction either of the strength or of the wealth of the society" and is "the weakest of the three departments of power"? [19] Hamilton could cite Montesquieu, but J. Allen Smith could appeal to the course of American history during his own time.

In the context of these events it is understandable why frustrated reformers would be led to a conclusion which the majority opinion in the income tax case had made its own for quite different purposes: that the Founding Fathers deliberately intended to impede popular majorities and had set up a system designed to protect the power of private wealth. Ironically, the conservatives had themselves conjured up an image of the framers which the reformers could turn to their

[18] 198 U.S. 45, pp. 75–76.
[19] Benjamin Fletcher Wright, ed., *The Federalist* (Cambridge, Mass., 1961), No. 78, pp. 490–491.

own advantage. "We have no pure democracy," wrote William Graham Sumner, the apostle of *laissez-faire,* in 1894. "Our democracy is limited at every turn by institutions which were developed in England in connection with industrialism and aristocracy, and these institutions are of the essence of our system." [20] If the conservatives found in this aristocratic and capitalistic version of the framers' work a protection against the winds of doctrine blowing from the Left, the reformers could find in it an insidious reason for the defeat of their efforts at democratic reform. The conservatives saw the Constitution as a sacred Ark of the Covenant; the reformers saw it as a *diabolus ex machina.* But the historical image of the framers as antidemocratic was for both groups rooted not so much in facts as in polemics. Disagreeing on every issue of politics and economics, conservatives and reformers nevertheless agreed on a version of history fraught with profoundly different meaning for both sides.

Lincoln Steffens, the famous "muckraking" journalist, recalled in 1931 that in his college days of the late 1880's he had taken a course in American constitutional history at the University of California. "I hunted far enough to suspect that the Fathers of the Republic who wrote our sacred Constitution of the United States not only did not," he wrote, "but did not want to, establish a democratic government, and I dreamed for a while—

[20] "The Absurd Effort To Make the World Over," *Forum* (1894), reprinted in Perry Miller, ed., *American Thought* (New York, 1954), p. 101.

as I used as a child to play I was Napoleon or a trapper —I promised myself to write a true history of the making of the American Constitution." [21] As Steffens noted, his dream was realized instead by two other men, J. Allen Smith and Charles A. Beard. Smith was the first scholar to develop this theme in an extensive analysis made in the spirit of a bitter protest against what he felt to be a continuing betrayal of the democratic vision first glimpsed in the American Revolution. His passionate critique contrasted sharply with the main line of American historians, who had written with Federalist-Whig-Republican sympathies.[22]

The credit also belongs to Smith for the originality of boldly pinning his whole case on the idea of the uninhibited expression of the majority will as the essence of the true democratic faith. The classic literature of American political thought had emphasized, on the contrary, the need for proper protection against the dangers of majority action. This familiar point, sacred to Jefferson and Madison, was deeply implicated in Lincoln's firm stand against extension of slavery into the new territories under the standard of "popular sovereignty" raised by Senator Douglas. There had to be necessary limits on majority action if "natural rights" were to be preserved. Smith himself was later to dis-

[21] *The Autobiography of Lincoln Steffens* (New York, 1931), p. 125.

[22] See Douglass Adair, "The Tenth Federalist Revisited," *William and Mary Quarterly*, 8 (1951), 48–67. Such historians would include John Fiske, Paul Leicester Ford, Herman E. von Holst, Andrew C. McLaughlin, John B. McMaster, and James Schouler.

cover the importance of the limiting idea, but in 1907 he wrote with a single-mindedness, almost a mono-mania, that makes his book stand out sharply against the past.

Boiling in Smith's mind for many years, *The Spirit of American Government* was published with superb timing in 1907, when the Progressive movement of Republican Insurgents had captured power in many states and found a national leader in Theodore Roosevelt. Two leaders of Progressive reform had themselves been midwives for the birth of the book. E. A. Ross, once forced out of Stanford University for his views, visited the University of Washington in the summer of 1906. He eagerly read Smith's manuscript and urged him to publish it. Back at his home base in the University of Wisconsin, a center of Progressive ferment, Ross discussed the book with Richard T. Ely, a German-trained exponent of the new "historical school" of reform economics and an ally of Smith's mentor, Henry Carter Adams, in organizing the American Economic Association in 1885. Ely was also enthusiastic and asked Smith to give him the book for The Citizen's Library series which he edited for Macmillan. Macmillan had already accepted the manuscript, and so the arrangement was easily made.

Conceived out of a Jeffersonian democrat's frustration with the procapitalist government of the late nineteenth century and born in the midst of the Progressive movement for a new birth of freedom, equality, and community, *The Spirit of American Government* was a tract for the times, cast in the form of a scholarly study. It expressed with relentless repetition an idea whose time had come: The Founding Fathers represented a reactionary movement against the democratic idealism of the Revolution. Fearful for their privileges as representatives of a loosely defined "well-to-do" class, they constructed a document with checks and balances exquisitely designed to inhibit the popular will, and their techniques had been copied by the states and the cities to the benefit of the selfish interests of the commercial and industrial leaders of the country. Diluting for the sake of expediency and appearance the extreme centralized and undemocratic features of Hamilton's plan for the new government, the framers had, however, achieved his ends through the amendment procedure, the presidential veto, the Senate, and the Supreme Court. Once in power, they had added judicial review as a capstone to their solid barrier against, as Smith put it, the "only recognized source of legitimate authority"—the expression of majority opinion. What could be done about it? Put into effect Progressive reforms: the direct primary, the initiative, the referendum, and recall, including that of judges; the direct election of Senators; municipal home rule; pitiless publicity for the financing of parties and candidates; and enforcement of the antitrust laws. Above all, Americans would have to give up their attachment to "checks and balances," judicial review, and an outmoded *laissez-*

faire theory of governmental noninterference with industrial life. Only then could democracy come into its own, after over a century of frustration at the throttling hands of the framers, the Supreme Court, and the leaders of the business community.

This powerful indictment was well received in Progressive circles, particularly among the admirers of Wisconsin's Robert M. La Follette. Though the book sold only some 13,000 copies between 1907 and 1920, it had a much better sale than Herbert Croly's influential Progressive book *The Promise of American Life* (1909), which was written in the very different spirit of sympathy with the Federalists and energetic centralization rather than with Jefferson or direct democracy.[23] One of Smith's students, John Kingsbury, a New York City social worker, sent his master's message directly to Theodore Roosevelt and Woodrow Wilson. The disciple later reported back with pardonable exaggeration: "your book has had a tremendous influence on 'Teddy.' "[24] It is hard to believe that it did, for in 1912 Roosevelt praised Croly, who emphasized the need for vigorous executive action, for understanding "as no other literary man does" what the ex-President had been striving for in politics.[25] Yet if he was ideologically much closer to Croly, Roosevelt's political ambition at

[23] I have analyzed Croly's complicated position in my introduction to the Capricorn edition of *The Promise of American Life* (New York, 1964.)

[24] Letter to Smith, March 23, 1912, quoted in Goldman, "J. Allen Smith," p. 207. For data on the publication, sales, and reactions to Smith's book I have summarized McClintock, "Smith," chap. vii.

[25] Letter to Croly, July 30, 1912, Elting E. Morison, ed., *The Letters of Theodore Roosevelt* (Cambridge, 1951–1954), VII, 582.

the time he encountered *The Spirit of American Government* was leading him toward measures of direct democracy—such measures as his proposal for the recall of judicial decisions on the state level, which the Progressive Party championed in 1912. Other important Progressives hailed Smith's book at once as a triumphant brief for their cause. Editors like S. S. McClure and William Allen White, journalists like Lincoln Steffens and Walter Weyl, and politicians like La Follette, Hiram Johnson, and Robert L. Owen (who cited Smith in the *Congressional Record*) appealed to the book in support of their own Progressive efforts. Its adoption by the Chautauqua adult educational program gave it an enthusiastic popular audience.

In the house of Progressive reform Smith occupied a room with a Western exposure. For the La Follette wing he provided a view of history which made sense of its hopes, its frustrations, and its program. Frederick C. Howe, a Progressive reformer, expressed a typically enthusiastic response. In his autobiography he recounted the recasting of his beliefs during the Progressive era: "My text-book government had to be discarded; my worship of the Constitution scrapped. The state that I believed in with religious fervor was gone. Like the anthropomorphic God of my childhood, it had never existed. But crashing beliefs cleared the air. I saw that democracy had not failed; it had never been tried. We had created confusion and had called it democracy

. . . In politics we lived a continuous lie." [26] He was attuned with perfect pitch to the message of J. Allen Smith.

In 1938 a symposium in the liberal *New Republic* on "Books That Changed Our Minds" made no mention of J. Allen Smith, except as a dimly recognized precursor of Charles A. Beard and Vernon L. Parrington, acknowledged major shapers of intellectual opinion.[27] But Smith's thesis was partly buried by incapsulation in their more famous works. He had said of the Constitution, without developing or documenting the statement, that "its significance was mainly economic." Beard's *An Economic Interpretation of the Constitution* (1913), which briefly acknowledged Smith, was a full-scale, nonpartisan application of the theory of economic determinism to the Founding Fathers. Parrington, who had joined the University of Washington in 1908, dedicated his *Main Currents in American Thought* (1927) to the memory of Smith, and as a close friend he also edited Smith's posthumous second book, *The Growth and Decline of Constitutional Government* (1930). Parrington warmly noted in his introduction the importance of Smith's earlier work: "It provided the leaders of the La Follette 'Insurgent group' with an interpretation of American constitutional history congenial

[26] *The Confessions of a Reformer* (New York, 1925), p. 176.
[27] See Malcolm Cowley and Bernard Smith, eds., *Books That Changed Our Minds: A Symposium* (New York, 1939), pp. 153, 187.

to their temper; it gave them a convincing explanation of the reasons for the failure of democracy in American political practice; and it was drawn upon freely in Congressional debates."[28] Parrington's dualistic Jeffersonian analysis of American literature and politics was itself a three-volume elaboration and variation of Smith's philosophy, as stated in *The Growth and Decline of Constitutional Government:* "From the very beginning of our political history, there has been a constant struggle between conservatism and liberalism ... fundamentally it has been a struggle between those who would limit and diffuse political power and those who would centralize and extend governmental authority."[29]

The linkage of these men was complex. Smith was no economic determinist, nor was he interested in American literature, and he entirely lacked Beard's admiration for the framers and respect for judicial review as an instrument of government. Smith treated politics from an ideological point of view, and he characteristically saw the dialectic of American history not so much in terms of specific economic group conflicts, in the style of Beard and Parrington, but rather as a struggle of doctrine between aristocrats and democrats, "between the advocates of centralization and decentralization, of class and mass rule." Later scholars easily

[28] Introduction, J. Allen Smith, *The Growth and Decline of Constitutional Government* (New York, 1930), p. xv.
[29] *Growth and Decline,* p. 94.

assimilated him with Beard and Parrington because all three shared a powerful tendency to polarize American history as a running fight of opposing forces, whether seen by Smith as aristocrats and democrats, by Beard as capitalists and agrarians, or by Parrington as literary liberal "realists" and conservative "romantics."

In academic circles Smith's work made little positive impression until Beard and Parrington had, in retrospect, made it seem to fall into place.[30] By then, however, the work of Beard and Parrington was much more interesting to scholars, and eventually Smith's thesis seemed almost too obvious to discuss. In 1937 the *Encyclopaedia of the Social Sciences,* discounting the "Machiavellian" overtones of Smith's explanation, found his case fundamentally "unshakable," while it dismissed his second book as merely "commonplace" because of the extent to which other scholars had carried forward the sort of criticism he had initiated.[31] The good news of 1907 had become stale scholarship. The Supreme

[30] His findings were favorably reflected, for example, in the work of the social historian Arthur M. Schlesinger, the constitutional historian Charles Groves Haines, and the political scientist Charles E. Merriam, a Progressive who established the Social Science Research Council in 1923. Schlesinger, *New Viewpoints in American History* (New York, 1922), pp. 80–81, 83, 101, 115; Haines, *The American Doctrine of Judicial Supremacy* (New York, 1914), pp. 191, 337; and Merriam, *American Political Ideas: Studies in the Development of American Political Thought* (New York, 1920), pp. 141, 221. As McClintock points out, Merriam himself had in 1903 anticipated Smith's thesis without his animus in *A History of American Political Theories* (New York, 1903), pp. 38–95, 98–100.

[31] "James Allen Smith," *Encyclopaedia of the Social Sciences,* 7 (1937), 116.

Court's invalidation of the early New Deal must have seemed to liberal reformers a crushingly obvious example of Smith's point that the Court was an undemocratic barrier to popularly demanded legislation.

The rest of the story is ironic. After "the switch in time that saved nine" in 1937 when Roosevelt's "court-packing" plan was discarded and the Court upheld minimum wage legislation, the National Labor Relations Act, and the Social Security Law, the sting of judicial review was withdrawn by the new "judicial self-restraint." The Court slowly transferred its judicial close scrutiny to the area of free speech and association and so eventually became the target of conservatives and reactionaries. Meanwhile liberals increasingly turned their critical attention to the legislatures, attacking their vulnerability to public opinion, which was easily inflamed by demagogues in a time of "cold war" with the Soviet Union. In the academic community a postwar generation of scholarship raked the oversimplifications and prejudices of Beard and Parrington, while the Founding Fathers, especially James Madison and Alexander Hamilton, were treated by scholars with impressive respect and admiration. The political alignments of J. Allen Smith's world were now reversed, as if the poles of the magnet of history had been interchanged.

By 1955 Smith's case had come under attack in Louis Hartz's indictment of the parochial limitations of Progressive scholarship. Hartz did not try specifically to disprove Smith's argument; he aimed to transcend the debate in the hope of escaping "the pervasive frustration that the persistence of the Progressive analysis of America has inspired." [32] The profound involvement of the United States since 1941 in international politics pointed up, he felt, the Progressive historian's unconscious reflection of the limited social perspectives of the average American. The Progressives, for all their scorn of "pietistic" histories, were nationalistic themselves in their treatment of domestic political strife as a cosmic conflict of "conservative" and "radical" forces. They had ignored Tocqueville's major insight that Americans had arrived at a state of democracy without having to endure a democratic revolution in the European sense. Precisely for this reason internal conflict was, in fact, muted and limited. "Actually there was amid all the smoke and flame of Progressive historical scholarship," Hartz noted, "a continuous and almost complacent note of reassurance. A new Jefferson would arise as he had always arisen before. The 'reactionaries' would be laid low again." [33] An America involved after the second World War to an unprecedented degree in an international world of novel political forces could no longer inspire such comfortable expectations.[34]

[32] Hartz, *The Liberal Tradition in America: An Interpretation of American Political Thought Since the Revolution* (New York, 1955), p. 28.

[33] *Liberal Tradition,* p. 32.

[34] Two other scholars, Edmund Morgan and Benjamin F. Wright, have also deliberately emphasized consensus and continuity in the relation of the Revolution to the Constitutional Convention: Morgan, *The Birth of*

There was, as Hartz suggested, much less iconoclasm to Smith's thesis than meets the eye. Not only did it restate with a different animus a conservative historical argument, but it implied that the traditional basis for democratic aspirations lay in the Revolution. The spirit of American government was not the spirit of '76. There had been a fall from grace. Reformers could in this sense be deeply traditional by reviving a democratic spirit which had animated such heroes as Samuel Adams, Patrick Henry, Thomas Paine, and Thomas Jefferson, whose absence from the Convention Smith underlined. (Smith did not add that both Paine and Jefferson were in Europe, that the latter greatly admired *The Federalist,* or that Henry declined his appointment to the Convention and later became a conservative advocate of church establishment against James Madison.) Smith's argument depended, therefore, upon the assumption that the Revolutionary spirit had been somehow supplanted or transformed. This crucial historical point he rested upon mere supposition: the former Loyalists must have regained power and some former Rebels must have turned Conservative. He did not provide evidence, nor did he face the fact that thirty-nine of the fifty-five members of the supposedly aristocratic Convention had sat in the Continental Congress, the crucible of Independence, which, in his own view, had made "sweeping democratic reforms."

---

the Republic, *1763–1789* (Chicago, 1956); Wright, *Consensus and Continuity—1776–1787* (Boston, 1958).

Smith's image of the Constitution as a straitjacket, even when plausible, was often strained by overstatement. He considered it a "practical impossibility" to overcome the Presidential veto, yet, as he shows, the veto was not widely used until the time of President Johnson, and by 1889 it had been overcome twenty-nine times. He bemoaned the great difficulty of making changes in the Constitution by amendment, yet two Progressive reforms, the direct election of Senators and the income tax, were passed as amendments only six years after his book appeared, even though he did not live to see the elimination of the "lame-duck" Congress (1933) and the abolition of the poll tax (1964). Thousands of amendments proposed to Congress have been rejected, but the great majority of those submitted by Congress to the states have been ratified. Jefferson, the apostle of democratic change, thought it would be wise to periodically repair institutions every eighteen years or so in order that they might "go hand in hand with the progress of the human mind." Since the passage of the first ten Amendments as part of the bargain for ratification of the new Constitution, there have been fourteen amendments. Averaged over the years 1791-1964, there has been an amendment every twelve years. From Smith's perspective of 1907, of course, there had been only five amendments since the first ten. His protest was understandable, but in practice the procedure has not resulted in the massive rigidity he feared. Ironically, in recent years the reactionaries have been the ones most anxious to amend the Constitution, in order to curb the power of the President and the Supreme Court.

In Smith's book there are three villains and one hero —the Revolutionaries of '76. The villains get the lion's share of the play, and they continually win out over the frail hero who may, however, get another chance in an epilogue to be written by the Progressives. The villains are the Hamiltonian idea of a centralized nationalistic scheme of government, the "checks and balances" system of controlling power by dividing it, and the Supreme Court's function of judicial review of legislation. They were linked in his mind as part of an aristocratic conspiracy to graft elements of the British system onto the American. Hamilton's scheme for an executive and senate elected for lifetime terms, an absolute presidential veto, and state governors appointed by the central government did reflect his admiration for the British system, though Hamilton offered his ideas, as he said, "merely as suggestions for consideration." [35] The framers rejected his proposals, and he spent very little time at the Convention, yet Smith claimed that the Constitution really contained "all that was essential in Hamilton's plan." From Smith's point of view the framers hid their Hamiltonian sympathies behind the facade of a frame of government which merely looked more democratic.

[35] Letter to Timothy Pickering, September 15, 1803, in Richard B. Morris, ed., *Alexander Hamilton and the Founding of the Nation* (New York, 1957), p. 159.

The system of "checks and balances" thus became, on this reading, an American version of the old "mixed state" ideal of a blend of monarchy, aristocracy, and democracy. There was no king and no nobility in the American government; their place, therefore, was taken by President, Senate, and Supreme Court. They were not directly elected, and they had veto powers. The division of sovereignty between state and central governments was in reality intended to create a "national" government masquerading as a "federal" one for the sake of popular acceptance. The Constitution itself did not, for expedient reasons, directly authorize judicial review of legislation, but the framers intended by their later mastery of the new government to build this power into the system as a final check on the rule of the majority. A preference for minority control was the ruling passion of the framers. In support of this vision Smith appealed to the Constitution, the debates in the Convention, *The Federalist,* and such European commentators as Emile Gaston Boutmy and William E. H. Lecky.

Since the rise of Communism, conspiracy theories in America have tended to be exploited by right-wing groups, who bitterly protest the changes in American life brought about by the New Deal and by the abandonment of the old policy of diplomatic isolation from Europe. In the 1890's some of the Populists, however, in their fiction or their rhetoric, expressed a bitter sense of being threatened by a malevolent conspiracy of monopolists and bankers, allegedly linked to the counting houses of Great Britain, traditional enemy of America. Smith had come out of the Populist movement, and he had his own more sophisticated conspiratorial legend. It told a dark story of the framers' betrayal of democracy by the disingenuous imitation of the British model. Like all conspiratorial theories, it tended to exaggerate, to oversimplify, and to substitute assertion for evidence. Inevitably, it led him to blur badly the stated position of his opponents.

James Madison and Alexander Hamilton, the chief authors of *The Federalist,* or the letters of "Publius," would not have recognized Smith's version of their own thought. Their own concepts of republicanism, of the separation of powers, and of the nature of the new union were carefully discriminated precisely to meet the objections of those who feared aristocratic influences in the Constitution. For Madison there was no question whatever about the desirability of "popular government." He simply recognized two types: the direct democracy of Greece, where "the people meet and exercise the government in person," and representative republicanism. The second type was not only suitable for a large area like the United States but it was an advance in the art of free government. No example could be found in Europe of "a government wholly popular, and founded, at the same time, wholly on that principle." If Europe discovered the principle of representation, "America can claim the merit of making the discovery the basis of unmixed and extensive republics."[36] This was the novel achievement of the Convention. Smith correctly said that the new government was very far from being " 'a government in which all its acts are performed by the people.' " But, because he put it as a criticism, this observation shows that he entirely missed the distinction Madison made, just as he also failed to see Madison's point that representative popular government was an *unmixed* type.

Smith—like his liberal followers and his conservative enemies—also greatly exaggerated the framers' fear of majorities. The framers did not expect republics to be free of evils, but they hoped to find in "the extent and proper structure of the Union" sufficient relief from "the diseases most incident to republican government." Madison's major theme was that these measures of relief constituted a *"republican* remedy."[37] Hamilton himself criticized the Articles of Confederation precisely because the principle of state equality on which it was erected contradicted "the fundamental maxim of republican government, which requires that the sense of the majority should prevail."[38] Smith also saw the framers as enemies of parties, which were necessary instruments for the expression of majority rule. As evidence he quoted Madison's famous theory of faction. But Madison saw "faction" as a number of citizens with

---

[36] *The Federalist,* No. 14, p. 151.
[37] *The Federalist,* No. 10, p. 136.
[38] *The Federalist,* No. 22, p. 193.

a common passion or interest "adverse to the rights of other citizens, or to the permanent and aggregate interests of the community." Political parties had not yet made their appearance as organizations, and they were not factions in this sense but rather loosely organized combinations of them, structured by ideology. Furthermore, Madison accepted factions as necessary evils of a free society: "But it could not be less folly to abolish liberty, which is essential to political life, because it nourishes faction, than it would be to wish the annihilation of air, which is essential to animal life, because it imparts to fire its destructive agency." [39] For relief from the effects of faction Madison prescribed the majority principle for voting, representation in the legislatures at both the national and local levels, and, above all, the large extent of the Union with its resulting variety of interests, making it probable that "a coalition of a majority of the whole society would seldom take place on any other principles than those of justice and the general good . . ." [40] It is true that Madison specifically cited as evils "a rage for paper money, for an abolition of debts, for an equal division of property, or for any other improper or wicked project," [41] but it was his point that such dangers would tend to occur only in a particular county or district, or at worst in a state. Madison was not expressing grave alarms about the

---

[39] *The Federalist,* No. 10, p. 130.
[40] *The Federalist,* No. 51, p. 359.
[41] *The Federalist,* No. 10, p. 136.

dangers of majority rule; he was, on the contrary, reassuring the voters that they had little reason to fear majorities *if* they accepted the new Constitution. Yet the principal reason for confidence was not refinement of opinion by representation, but the size of the Union itself, certainly not an aristocratic argument.

The Federalist was also concerned about the dangers to the ruled from the rulers. For this problem Madison offered other republican remedies, usually called "checks and balances." They did express a fear of legislative omnipotence—a danger which must have appeared absurd to Smith in 1907, but not to the men of 1787. This scheme comprised a limited, moderate separation of powers into legislative, executive, and judicial, with each department being able to counteract encroachments by the other. In aid of this provision—a commonly accepted principle among Federalists and Jeffersonians alike—the legislature, being the predominant power, would be divided into different branches with different modes of election and of action; the executive would be given a limited veto power; and "a double security" would be provided by the division of state and national power in "the compound republic of America." [42] The system of "checks and balances" was, therefore, not designed, as Smith claimed, to protect the minority against popular majorities *among the ruled;* it was meant instead to protect citizens from the possible tyranny of their officials. Smith (like his con-

[42] *The Federalist*, No. 51, p. 358.

servative enemies) stood Madison's argument on its head.

He also misunderstood Madison's description of the nature of the Union as a new composition of "federal" and "national" principles. Smith described it as a national system masquerading as a "federal" one. But Madison presented it as neither exclusively the one nor the other. The system of the Union was in some respects based upon what its critics favored, the *"federal"* principle of "a *Confederacy* of sovereign states," and in other respects based upon what its critics feared, the principle of "a *national* government, which regards the Union as a *consolidation* of the States." [43] There was no conventional term to describe this hybrid, this American innovation of "a compound republic." Hamilton may have confused Smith on this point by inaccurately describing the new Union in the ninth paper as "a confederacy" in accordance with the traditional notion (derived from Montesquieu) of "the idea of a federal government." [44] This disingenuous argument was Hamilton's strained effort to make the Constitution more palatable to its "federal"-minded critics. If Smith had singled out this essay for rebuke he would have justified in this case his charge that Hamilton did not deal honestly with his readers. With a nice poetic jus-

[43] *The Federalist,* No. 39, p. 282. See the excellent analysis in Martin Diamond, "What the Framers Meant by Federalism," Robert A. Goldwin, ed., *A Nation of States; Essays on the American Federal System* (Chicago, 1963), pp. 24–41.

[44] *The Federalist,* No. 9, p. 128.

tice Hamilton's special pleading recoiled on him, over a hundred years later, in the form of Smith's exaggerated polemic against the conspiratorial aristocratic intentions of the framers.

Smith's case against judicial review of legislation was the strongest part of his whole argument. He exploded the myth that the Supreme Court justices were merely finding law when they struck down legislation, as if the judicial task could be accomplished equally well by a computer. He was, especially in the light of the judicial decisions of his age, thoroughly justified in pointing out that "individual temperament, personal views and political sympathies" influenced the Court's conclusions; and he was undeniably right in saying that the Court had tended to favor the interests of the business community rather than of reformers who were struggling to deal with the abuses and inhumanities of industrial life. Even today, when the Supreme Court no longer naïvely reads Herbert Spencer into the Constitution on economic issues, Smith's point still has force in highlighting the paradox of judicial review. How can the idea of democracy be made consistent with giving a small group of appointed judges the power to rule on questions which inevitably are, to a large degree, matters of public policy? There are subtle answers to this problem, but the question itself deserves respect and Smith raised it for his generation with a great deal of power.

This critique was made, however, in the context of

a dubiously reasoned historical argument flawed by a curious inconsistency. Smith argued that judicial review was never publicly accepted by most of the framers. The evidence against him was impressively marshalled in 1912 by Charles A. Beard, who admired Smith without agreeing with him.[45] The point of real interest, however, is that Smith notes only in passing that Luther Martin, Elbridge Gerry, George Mason, and Patrick Henry were all in favor of the judicial veto in some form. But these men were opponents of the Constitution. Smith ignored the implications of the fact that the enemies of the framers' handiwork were in favor of a judicial veto, a power he condemned as an expression of Hamiltonian aristocratic preference for minority rule. If he had felt the force of this connection he might have been led to discover that the Anti-Federalists were, in fact, even more devoted to "checks and balances" than the framers. The signers of the Constitution were mistrusted for not having provided enough precautions.[46]

He could not have made this discovery without con-

---

[45] See Charles A. Beard, "The Supreme Court—Usurper or Grantee?" reprinted from the *Political Science Quarterly*, 27 (1912) in Robert G. McCloskey, ed., *Essays in Constitutional Law* (New York, 1957), pp. 24–58. As McCloskey points out, the evidence is not conclusive, and it is not clear just when, or how finally, the framers expected judicial review to work. Beard's letter esteeming Smith, written in 1930 to his daughter, is cited in McClintock, "Smith," p. 533.

[46] See Cecilia M. Kenyon, "Men of Little Faith: The Anti-Federalists on the Nature of Representative Government," *William and Mary Quarterly*, 12 (January 1955), 3–43.

fronting the unsettling possibility that his seductively simple polarity of good democrats in conflict with bad aristocrats might only be a convenient fiction, a piece of sentimental historical melodrama, not derived from the evidence but from his own need to make an assault on the framers without giving up a foothold in American tradition. Smith treated the conservative Southern apologist John C. Calhoun with surprising sympathy, and perhaps it was because they shared a similar dilemma—the need to make a powerful case against the government while still taking patriotic ground. Calhoun found his solution by transforming the framers into doctrinaire upholders of "state sovereignty" and the right of secession; Smith found his answer in a highly colored contrast between the democratic Revolutionaries and the aristocratic Founding Fathers. A temperament for this sort of ambiguity may have been formed in part by Smith's upbringing in a Southern family of Confederate sympathies in a state whose loyalties during the Civil War were divided.

Scholarship in recent years has chipped steadily away at the base of Smith's position with its posing of a basic conflict between the Revolution and the Constitution. The Revolution itself is now seen as much less revolutionary than Smith thought. Pre-Revolutionary franchise restrictions turn out to have been not very significant in a land-rich continent; the same wealth of land provided no deep roots for the growth of primo-

geniture and entail which Jeffersonians later lopped off
like dead branches. The Church of England was only
weakly established and but a mild irritant to dissenting
sects. "A century before the Revolution and not as the
result of anti-aristocratic ideas," writes Bernard Bailyn
in a review of the new findings, "the colonial aristocracy had become a vaguely defined, fluid group whose
power—in no way guaranteed, buttressed, or even recognized in law—was competitively maintained and
dependent on continuous, popular support."[47] Seen
from this new perspective the democratic ideas of the
Revolutionary Enlightenment were not the weapons
by which a particular social group destroyed an old
order. They were rather the necessary means of justifying and accelerating forces which had long existed.

By undermining the class-conflict thesis about the
Revolution, scholarship has also cast doubt on the
polarized relationship between the Revolution and the
Constitution. Historical continuity forbids painting the
Founding Fathers in the dark tones of Smith's picture.
But his caricature did catch some recognizable features.
The framers did have fears about the status of private
property, threatened, they felt, by such uprisings as
Shay's Rebellion, and they did mistrust an unbalanced
legislature because it necessarily had predominant
power in a republic. It was necessary to guard against
the future day when the propertyless, outnumbering

[47] "Political Experience and Enlightenment Ideas in Eighteenth-Century
America," *American Historical Review*, 67 (January 1962), 349.

the landed, might show what Madison called a "wicked" tendency to be attracted to "a rage for paper money" or for an abolition of debts. Scholars need not be divided on the question of these fears: they can be documented out of the mouths of the framers themselves. It is not surprising, furthermore, that Madison's list of "wicked" projects would have antagonized Smith. Smith could see in his own time that the desperate economic situation of their crops in the 1890's had given cotton and wheat farmers a justified interest in any measures that might reasonably satisfy their need for an elastic currency of stable value which would make debts fair to both creditor and debtor. These conditions of the new industrial and financial capitalist order were in their scope and depth outside the agrarian and mercantile experience of the framers, and it is no wonder that Smith found no solace in their "republican remedies."

There was more than a grain of truth too in Smith's conception of the framers as spokesmen for a "well-to-do" class. Hamilton openly proclaimed that in the new government *moderate* proprietors of land, merchants, and men of the learned professions would predominate "with too few exceptions to have any influence on the spirit of the government." [48] Hamilton was sure, however, that such representatives would in effect represent all "the different classes of citizens," including the small farmers and artisans who were not present at the Con-

---

[48] *The Federalist,* No. 35, p. 257.

vention. Smith could have no such assurance, having seen with his own eyes an American government which excluded from its councils and its political parties any effective representation of farmers and workingmen. The Progressive movement helped to change this imbalance, and Smith's book made its own contribution to that work. Historians must question the use he made of history to support his sense of frustration. For the frustration itself they ought to extend their imaginative sympathy.

Even after the reforms of Progressivism and the New Deal it remains true that the system of divided power with its later embellishments has resulted in a mechanism which does not easily express or fulfill a clearly defined majority program for which the government can be held responsible. A minority in the Senate can obstruct a treaty; the committee system in Congress is a tower of strength to conservative minority interests bent on frustrating legislation; the loose discipline of American parties tends to adulterate any coherent program; the electoral college can put a President in power without majority support; and rural areas are over-represented in the House. Diffusing responsibility, the system is vulnerable to paralysis, as political scientists have often complained. In this sense a modified version of Smith's critique has continuing relevance.

But did the framers intend their system to work out this way? Modern political theorists can find the very spirit of their protest in the language of Alexander

Hamilton, when he complained of "tedious delays, continual negotiation and intrigue; contemptible compromises of the public good," and urged that "the public business must, in some way or other, go forward." He was attacking in general the principle of "unanimity in public bodies, or of something approaching towards it," and in particular the Articles of Confederation, while he was praising "the regular deliberations and decisions of a respectable majority" as a basic principle of the new Constitution.[49] Smith might have made a much stronger case, without any conspiratorial assumptions, if he had complained that the spirit of American government had become in practice much less energetic than the framers had intended. This interpretation would, however, have required an even greater intellectual somersault for him than his thesis required for the conservatives who conventionally revered the Founding Fathers.

A rebel and a seeming iconoclast, Smith was very much a child of his time and place. His Progressivism was in the grain of American individualism. Ending his book with a sensible attack on *laissez-faire* and the assumptions of social Darwinism, he nevertheless paid his own tribute to the idea of individual success. This theme of the Horatio Alger stories had appeared as well in the social Darwinist defense of monopoly as the necessary outcome of the struggle of existence in which the big corporations justified their power merely by

[49] *The Federalist*, No. 22, pp. 194–195.

their acquisition of it. Smith's simplistic solution to the trust problem was to "make success the unfailing reward of merit." Both Theodore Roosevelt and Woodrow Wilson in defending their antitrust programs essentially said the same thing. It was a sign that the Progressives still kept in touch with the old American idealization of competition and individual success. America with all its Constitutional defects was still for Smith an "example" and a "model" of opportunity, and he appealed to this ancient idea of Jeffersonian mission when he defended legislation for general exclusion of any immigrants who might threaten the American reputation for a "high level of well-being" by working for low wages.[50] A nationalistic democrat, like many Midwestern Progressives, he wanted no part of American intervention in World War I or participation in the League of Nations. In his eyes, the war and the League were both evil products of the power of big business.[51]

The war itself was a sobering experience for a man of his faith in direct democracy. The passions of chauvinism and racial suspicion, the suppression of free speech and assembly, culminating in the "Red Scare," frightened and dismayed the whole liberal movement. Democracy was not safe in the nation that was officially dedicated by a Progressive president to "making the

[50] See "The Relation of Oriental Immigration to the General Immigration Problem," American Economic Association, *Bulletin*, 4th series, no. 2 (April 1911), 237–242.

[51] See *The Growth and Decadence of Constitutional Government*, pp. 221, 248.

world safe for democracy." It was a bitter irony, and it was not lost on an ardent democrat. In the posthumous *Growth and Decadence,* Smith repeated his conspiracy theory of the making of the Constitution and broadened it into a general explanation of American history as a continuous struggle between democratic defenders of local self-government and plutocratic extenders of centralized government. But in one important respect he had changed his own outlook: he could no longer complacently assume that the direct expression of majority opinion was the salvation of the American political soul. The war had forced him to suspect both concentrated power and the wisdom of the people. "It is not the number of votes cast but their quality," he now argued, "that determines the success of democratic government." [52]

Smith was still an ardent progressive reformer—if a chastened one. The overrepresentation of rural areas, the failure to reapportion in every decade, "blue-ribbon" juries, the persistence of monopoly, and the continued abuse of the power of judicial review still defined the work remaining on his democratic agenda. But democrats needed to have a renewed respect for constitutional limits on government powers and to cultivate reservations about public opinion. "Political majorities, no less than public officials," he warned, "are prone to take into their own hands as much power as circumstances permit." And the majority might be "fully as intolerant of

[52] *Growth and Decadence,* p. 53.

dissenting opinion as kings and aristocracies have always been."[53] J. Allen Smith had made his own rendezvous with the Founding Fathers.

The intellectuals of the 1920's would not, however, rendezvous with Smith. When he died on January 30, 1924, he could have pointed in justification of his views to the Supreme Court's Spencerian edict of the previous year against a minimum wage statute for women in the District of Columbia.[54] In the regime of Warren Harding the old pattern of political corruption and favoritism to business had revived, like the recurrence of a bad dream. But now the new postwar generation of reformers, unlike the Progressives, would be drawn toward radical bohemianism, Mencken's genial cynicism, artistic emigration to the Left Bank, radical socialism, or enthusiasm for Soviet Russia. In the election of 1924 La Follette carried only his own state of Wisconsin. For the Progressives the mood of the last act was a dying fall.

Since 1947 the social science building at the University of Washington has been officially named "J. Allen Smith Hall." This honor to an academic rebel came at a time of another crisis in academic freedom. In 1949 national debate raged over the action of the President and regents of the University of Washington in dismissing three radical professors and putting three others on probation, despite a faculty committee's recommen-

---

[53] *Growth and Decadence,* pp. 163, 255.
[54] Adkins v. Children's Hospital 261 U.S. 525.

dation that in five of the cases no adequate grounds for such measures had been presented. Six years later every scientist scheduled to speak at a symposium organized by the university's department of biochemistry refused on principle to attend when the president barred J. Robert Oppenheimer as a guest lecturer in physics. They made a gesture of support for a great scientist with a radical past who had been denounced as a "security-risk" by his political enemies. Surely Smith would have appreciated their action even more than the building. He would have been touched most of all by the tribute of John Kingsbury: "He was the greatest teacher I ever had." [55] Kingsbury had also studied under William James, a passionate individualist, and John Dewey, an ardent democrat—the kind of moral company in which J. Allen Smith would have felt at home.

Direct-democracy techniques did not realize Progressive expectations, and modern political science in an age often characterized as marking "the end of ideology" is far removed from a man who believed that the crisis of his time was the clash of "irreconcilable theories of government." The functional analysis of institutions and the sociological study of political behavior have, however, by their dominance pointed up the need to keep alive the evaluation of politics by political and moral ideas. Smith's treatise sometimes simplistically identifies morality and justice with the will of the

[55] Letter to McClintock, Sept. 20, 1953, quoted by McClintock, "Smith," p. 555.

people, but he belonged, fundamentally, to a tradition of moral criticism which was fast fading in his own period and became very unfashionable during the New Deal. In 1937 Thurman Arnold, a New Deal lawyer and pundit, frankly proposed the substitution of cynical but benevolent political opportunism for the discussion of economic principles because in America ideological debate merely represented disputes about the legal and economic "folklore" of capitalism. The democratic tradition, on the other hand, had become "recognized as a tradition and had ceased to be regarded as a set of guiding principles," he wrote with satisfaction. "All over the world, except perhaps in the Orient," he added, "there was a recognition that popular majorities were necessary for a successful government regardless of what the creed happened to be." The result was salutary: "A strange thing had happened to democracy as a creed. Few believed any more that it was a peculiarly sacred or divine thing. The 'principles' of democracy were not worshiped as they were once, as fundamental truths." [56]

Arnold had traveled a very long distance from J. Allen Smith. Except for their common animus against the folklore of *laissez-faire* capitalism, the New Dealer was as far from the Progressive as Smith was from the Founding Fathers. But the rise of Nazi and Soviet dictatorships made Arnold and his antirationalist point of view, with its cult of the organization and the leader,

[56] *The Folklore of Capitalism* (New Haven, 1937), p. 40.

look even more naïve than the reformers he condemned for obsession with moral attitudes, utopias, and systems. He had dismissed as folklore the principles and forms which distinguish democracies from totalitarian movements. Smith also attacked the folklore of the Constitution, yet he was too ideologically minded to impoverish and reduce the good life, as Arnold did, to "a society which produces and distributes goods to the maximum of its technical capacity."[57] Smith hoped that Progressives would work for a more just distribution of opportunity and for a society which would esteem a more generous, less acquisitive type of successful man. If the Progressive mind was not very philosophical or profound, it had the solid virtue of not priding itself in the name of sophistication on having neither ideas nor principles. It prized instead the determination to realize the humane and democratic ideals it had.

Smith's legacy to modern politics and historians was also ideological, and in this case the term has a different and dubious connotation. Ironically, his image of the framers as deceitful antidemocrats alienated liberals from their heritage and paved the way for the unjustified exploitation of the Founders' prestige by reactionary enemies of democratic reform. His historical thesis challenged the conservatives' piety for the Founding Fathers by turning the framers into conspirators with a secret yearning for the aristocratic system of the British. Historians commonly and properly do make judgments

[57] *Folklore*, 178.

based on moral and political values, but they need to be armed against the temptations of what Herbert Butterfield has called "The Whig Interpretation of History." Looking backward for liberal allies and conservative enemies, such historians find a struggle between heroes and villains as the theme of their story, and they deny their imaginative sympathy to those who are not progressives in their drama. "The fervour of the whig historian very often comes from what is really the transference into the past of an enthusiasm for something in the present," as Butterfield says, "an enthusiasm for democracy or freedom of thought or the liberal tradition." [58] Like Smith, the Whig historian thus repeats the style of partisan melodrama which the political process itself generates, and his story becomes a weapon in the warfare of social ideals.

Since the Second World War several American historians have in different ways tried to transcend this passion for polarity. The revision has recently provoked the charge that it has fallen on the other side into a patriotic and conservative cult of a sacred American consensus. The revisionists are accused of fostering a sentimental ideal of a homogenized community with a blandly successful history.[59] This accusation is a valuable warning and reply to some publicists for "the new conservatism," who celebrate social tradition and

[58] *The Whig Interpretation of History* (New York, 1951), p. 96.
[59] See John Higham, "The Cult of the 'American Consensus': Homogenizing Our History," *Commentary*, 27 (February 1959), 93–100.

social agreement as peculiarly American virtues. But as a generalization it obscures the logical point that historical criticism of the Whig distortion need not entail any bland blurring of actual strife in the past. Tocqueville was the first writer to make significant use of the idea of an American consensus, and he wrote with a detachment and discrimination entirely free of any national feeling of "togetherness" which is alleged to have biased the perspective of recent American historians. The critique of Progressive scholarship which Hartz made in 1955 was a plea for historians to take Tocqueville seriously, instead of merely quoting him with a reverential nod of the head. The idea of consensus was central to Tocqueville's effort to disabuse Europeans of their irrational fears about the consequences of democracy. Society, he felt, could exist "only when a great number of men consider a great number of things under the same aspect, when they hold the same opinions upon many subjects, and when the same occurrences suggest the same thoughts and impressions to their minds." [60] In this respect the United States seemed to him more truly a united society than some nations of Europe living under the same laws and prince. Tocqueville made it clear that the consensus which bound Americans together was not necessarily true; it was simply a set of "American opinions" which gave the republic a stability which Europeans failed to comprehend:

[60] *Democracy in America*, I, 392.

The republicans in the United States set a high value upon morality, respect religious belief, and acknowledge the existence of rights. They profess to think that a people ought to be moral, religious, and temperate in proportion as it is free. What is called the republic in the United States is the tranquil rule of the majority, which, after it has had time to examine itself and to give proof of its existence, is the common source of all the powers of the state. But the power of the majority itself is not unlimited. Above it in the moral world are humanity, justice, and reason; and in the political world, vested rights. The majority recognizes these two barriers; and if it now and then oversteps them, it is because, like individuals, it has its passions and, like them, it is prone to do what is wrong, while it discerns what is right.[61]

Tocqueville's analysis supports a paradoxical conclusion: only a majority of this self-limiting kind could accept the institution of an unelected Supreme Court with the power of judicial review, and only such a majority would not ordinarily need a Court to protect it from itself. This is a paradox which justifies both judicial review and Smith's protest against it when the Court had not yet learned the wisdom of "judicial self-restraint" in the exercise of its own power. Even in the 1830's Tocqueville saw that bench and bar were a sort of quasi-aristocracy in America, but he did not see that they might become an oppressive one to the democratic reformers of Smith's generation. The Frenchman wrote

[61] *Democracy in America*, I, 416.

before either the Negro or the "manufacturing aristocracy" had produced the acute tensions and conflicts
which he prophesied might one day come into American life. Smith and his fellow Progressives could have
cited Tocqueville in their own defense, however, when
he warned of the possible growth of a manufacturing
aristocracy: ". . . the friends of democracy should keep
their eyes anxiously fixed in this direction, for if ever
a permanent inequality of conditions and aristocracy
again penetrates into the world, it may be predicted
that this is the gate by which they will enter." [62] The
basic trouble with Smith's historical thesis is simple: his
eyes were too anxiously fixed on his own society when
he was analyzing the American scene of the late eighteenth century. The anxiety was politically understandable, but historians have no justification for clinging
nostalgically to this historical framework of dramatic
polarity merely out of political and moral admiration
for its architect.

History and politics are neither brothers nor lovers;
they are more like discriminating friends who respect
each other's rights. It has always been hard to maintain
the poise of this relationship in America where the
writing of history has so often grown out of the citizen's
passionate absorption in the American mission of setting a New World example for Old Europe. Just because "a new science of politics" was in fact needed for
a new world, it was difficult to write the New World's

[62] *Democracy in America*, II, 161.

history without distorting the story by trying to justify or fulfill the original vision, whether the mount of transfiguration was located in the Revolution or the Convention. If Smith's use of the historical past illustrates that point, *The Spirit of American Government* still has precious value as one of the most characteristic and influential expressions of the Progressive temper in its intellectual and moral effort to bring itself into vital connection with the national inheritance.

Cushing Strout

A NOTE ON THE TEXT

The text of *The Spirit of American Government* photoreproduced for this edition is the 1911 reprint of the original edition published in New York by Macmillan in 1907. The copyright page of the 1911 printing carries this bibliographic note: "Set up and electrotyped. Printed April, 1907. Reprinted March, August, 1911." One later printing, dated 1912, has been located.

In the preparation of the new edition Smith's references have been checked and are presented with full citation in a separate list following the text. Editorial notes have been keyed to the text by arabic numerals in the margins, and appear as an endnote section on p. 407; these notes are intended to correct the author's factual errors, to question important points of interpretation, and to take account of relevant political changes since 1907.

THE SPIRIT OF AMERICAN GOVERNMENT

A STUDY OF THE CONSTITUTION:
ITS ORIGIN, INFLUENCE
AND RELATION TO DEMOCRACY

BY

J. Allen Smith, LL.B., Ph.D.

Professor of Political Science
University of Washington

PREFACE

It is the purpose of this volume to trace the influence of our constitutional system upon the political conditions which exist in this country to-day. This phase of our political problems has not received adequate recognition at the hands of writers on American politics. Very often indeed it has been entirely ignored, although in the short period which has elapsed since our Constitution was framed and adopted, the Western world has passed through a political as well as an industrial revolution.

In the eighteenth century the majority was outside of the pale of political rights. Government as a matter of course was the expression of the will of a minority. Even in the United States, where hereditary rule was overthrown by the Revolution, an effective and recognized minority control still survived through the property qualifications for the suffrage and for office-holding, which excluded a large proportion of the people from participation in political affairs. Under such conditions there could be but little of what is now known as democracy. Moreover, slavery continued to exist upon a large scale for nearly three-quarters of a century after the Constitution was adopted, and was finally abolished only within the memory of many now living.

It could hardly be expected that a political system set up for a community containing a large slave population and in which the suffrage was restricted, even among the free whites, should in any large measure embody the aims and ideas of present day democracy. In fact the American Constitution did not recognize the now more or less generally accepted principle of majority rule even as applying to the qualified voters. Moreover, it was not until several decades after the Constitution was adopted that the removal of property qualifications for voting allowed the people generally to have a voice in political affairs.

The extension of the suffrage was a concession to the growing belief in democracy, but it failed to give the masses an effective control over the general government, owing to the checks in the Constitution on majority rule. It had one important consequence, however, which should not be overlooked. Possession of the suffrage by the people generally led the undiscriminating to think that it made the opinion of the majority a controlling factor in national politics.

Our political writers have for the most part passed lightly over the undemocratic features of the Constitution and left the uncritical reader with the impression that universal suffrage under our system of government ensures the rule of the majority. It is this conservative approval of the Constitution under the guise of sympathy with majority rule, which has perhaps more than any thing else misled the people as to the real spirit and purpose of that instrument. It was by constantly representing it as the indispensable means of attaining the ends of democracy, that it came to be so generally regarded as the source of all that is democratic in our system of government. It is to call attention to the spirit of the Constitution, its inherent opposition to democracy, the obstacles which it has placed in the way of majority rule, that this volume has been written.

The general recognition of the true character of the Constitution is necessary before we can fully understand the nature and origin of our political evils. It would also do much to strengthen and advance the cause of popular government by bringing us to a realization of the fact that the so-called evils of democracy are very largely the natural results of those constitutional checks on popular rule which we have inherited from the political system of the eighteenth century.

The author acknowledges his indebtedness to his colleague, Professor William Savery, and to Professor Edward A. Ross of the University of Wisconsin, for many pertinent criticisms and suggestions which he has borne in mind while revising the manuscript of this work for publication. He is also under obligation to Mr. Edward Mc Mahon for suggestions and for some illustrative material which he has made use of in this volume.

J. ALLEN SMITH.

Seattle, Washington,
    January, 1907.

THE SPIRIT OF
AMERICAN GOVERNMENT

CHAPTER I

THE ENGLISH GOVERNMENT OF THE EIGHTEENTH CENTURY

Constitutional government is not necessarily democratic. Usually it is a compromise in which monarchical and aristocratic features are retained. The proportion in which the old and the new are blended depends, of course, upon the progress the democratic movement has made. Every step toward democracy has been stubbornly opposed by the few, who have yielded to the popular demand, from time to time, only what necessity required. The constitution of the present day is the outcome of this long-continued and incessant struggle. It reflects in its form and character the existing distribution of political power within the state.

If we go back far enough we find government nearly everywhere in the hands of a King and privileged class. In its earlier stages the constitutional struggle was between monarchy and aristocracy, the King seeking to make his authority supreme and the nobility seeking to limit and circumscribe it. Accordingly, government oscillated between monarchy and aristocracy, a strong and ambitious King getting the reins of government largely in his own hands, while the aristocracy encroached upon the power and prerogatives of a weak and incompetent one. Thus democracy played no part in the earlier constitutional struggles. The all-important question was whether the King or the nobility should control the state. Civil wars were waged to decide it, and government gravitated toward monarchy or aristocracy according as the monarchical or aristocratic party prevailed.

Under William the Conqueror and his immediate successors the government of England was practically an absolute monarchy. Only the highest class was consulted in the Great Council and the advice of these the King was not obliged to follow. Later, as a result of the memorable controversy between King John and his feudal barons, the Great Council regained the power which it had lost. Against the King were arrayed the nobility, the church as represented by its official hierarchy, and the freemen of the realm, all together constituting but a small minority of the English people. The Great Charter extorted from the King on this occasion, though frequently referred to as the foundation of English liberty, was in reality a matter of but little immediate importance to the common people. The benefit of its provisions, while not limited to the nobility, extended, however, only to those classes without whose aid and support the tyrannical power of the

King could not be successfully opposed. The church, by reason of the great wealth which it controlled and the powerful influence which it exerted in a superstitious age over the minds of the people, was a factor that could not be ignored. The freemen also played an important part in the constitutional struggles, since they carried the sword and formed the rank and file of the fighting class. The important provisions of the Great Charter relate exclusively to the rights of the church, the nobility and the freemen. The serfs, while not included within the benefit of its provisions, were an overwhelming majority of the English people. This conclusion is irresistible in view of the fact that the Domesday Survey shows that about four-fifths of the adult male population in the year 1085 were below the rank of freemen.[1]

The Great Charter was, it is true, an important step in the direction of constitutional government, but it contained no element of democracy. It merely converted the government from one in which monarchy was the predominant feature, to one in which the aristocratic element was equally important. The classes represented in the Great Council became a constitutional check on the power of the King, inasmuch as he could not levy taxes without their consent. The important constitutional position which this charter assigned to

[1] Sebohm, English Village Community, Ch. III; Traill, Social England, Vol. I, p. 240; Ashley, English Economic History, Vol. I, p. 17.

the nobility was not maintained, however, without repeated struggles under succeeding Kings; but it laid the foundation for the subsequent development which limited and finally abolished the power of the monarch.

In the course of time the Great Council split up into two separate bodies, the House of Lords, composed of the greater nobility and the higher dignitaries of the church, and the House of Commons, representing all other classes who enjoyed political rights. When the House of Commons thus assumed a definite and permanent form as a separate body, a new check upon the power of the King appeared. The consent of two separate bodies was now necessary before taxes could be imposed. The development of these checks was hastened by the fact that the King found it easier and safer to get the assent of these bodies to measures which involved an exercise of the taxing power, than to attempt the collection of taxes without their support. In this way the right of assenting to all measures of taxation came in time to be recognized as belonging to the two houses of Parliament. But this was a right not easily established. It was claimed and fought for a long time before it finally became a firmly established principle of the English Constitution. Around the question of taxation centered all the earlier constitutional struggles. The power to tax was the one royal prerogative which was first limited.

In time Parliament extended its powers and succeeded in making its assent necessary to all governmental acts which vitally affected the welfare of the nation, whether they involved an exercise of the taxing power or not. The law-making power, however, as we understand it now was seldom employed, the idea of social readjustment through general legislation being a recent growth. But as revenues were necessary, the taxing power was the one legislative function that was constantly exercised. It is not strange then that the earlier constitutional development should have turned mainly upon the relation of the various political classes to the exercise of this power.

That English constitutional development resulted in a parliament composed of two houses may be regarded as accidental. Instead of this double check upon the King there might conceivably have been more than two, or there might, as originally was the case, have been only one. Two distinct elements, the secular nobility and the dignitaries of the church, combined to form the House of Lords. The House of Commons was also made up of two distinct constituencies, one urban and the other rural. If each of these classes had deliberated apart and acquired the right to assent to legislation as a separate body, a four-chambered parliament, such as existed in

Sweden up to 1866 and still survives in Finland, would have been the result.[1]

The essential fact, everywhere to be observed in the development of constitutional government, is the rise to political power of classes which compete with the King and with each other for the control of the state. The monopoly of political power enjoyed by the King was broken down in England when the nobility compelled the signing of Magna Charta. This change in the English Constitution involved the placing of a check upon the King in the interest of the aristocracy. Later, with the development of the House of Commons as a separate institution, the power of the King was still further limited, this time in the interest of what we may call the commercial and industrial aristocracy.

At this stage of its development the English government contained a system of checks and balances. The King still retained legislative power, but could not use it without the consent of both Lords and Commons. Each branch of the government possessed the means of defending itself, since it had what was in effect an absolute veto on legislation. This is a stage in political evolution through which governments naturally pass. It is a form of political organization intermediate between monarchy and democracy, and results from the effort to check and restrain, with-

[1] Lowell, Governments and Parties in Continental Europe, Vol. I, Ch. I; Lecky, Democracy and Liberty, Vol. I, p. 265.

out destroying, the power of the King. When this system of checks was fully developed the King, Lords and Commons were three coördinate branches of the English government. As the concurrence of all three was necessary to enact laws, each of these could defeat legislation desired by the other two.

The development of this system of checks limited the irresponsible power of the King only on its positive side. The negative power of absolute veto the King still retained. While he could not enact laws without the consent of the other two coördinate branches of the government, he still had the power to prevent legislation. The same was true of the Lords and Commons. As each branch of government had the power to block reform, the system was one which made legislation difficult.

The system of checks and balances must not be confused with democracy; it is opposed to and can not be reconciled with the theory of popular government. While involving a denial of the right of the King or of any class to a free hand in political matters, it at the same time denies the right of the masses to direct the policy of the state. This would be the case even if one branch of the government had the broadest possible basis. If the House of Commons had been a truly popular body in the eighteenth century, that fact would not of itself have made the English government as a whole popular in form. While it would have constituted a popular check on the King and the House of Lords, it would have been powerless to express the popular will in legislation.

The House of Commons was not, however, a popular body in the eighteenth century. In theory, of course, as a part of Parliament it represented the whole English people. But this was a mere political fiction, since by reason of the narrowly limited suffrage, a large part of the English people had no voice in parliamentary elections. Probably not one-fifth of the adult male population was entitled to vote for members of Parliament. As the right to vote was an incident of land ownership, the House of Commons was largely representative of the same interests that controlled the House of Lords.

That the House of Commons was not democratic in spirit is clearly seen in the character of parliamentary legislation. The laws enacted during this period were distinctly undemocratic. While the interests of the land-holding aristocracy were carefully guarded, the well-being of the laboring population received scant consideration. The poor laws, the enclosure acts and the corn laws, which had in view the prosperity of the landlord, and the laws against combination, which sought to advance the interests of the capitalist at the expense of the laborer, show the spirit of the

English government prior to the parliamentary reform of 1832. The landlord and capitalist classes controlled the government and, as Professor Rogers observes, their aim was to increase rents and profits by grinding the English workman down to the lowest pittance. "I contend," he says, "that from 1563 to 1824, a conspiracy, concocted by the law and carried out by parties interested in its success, was entered into, to cheat the English workman of his wages, to tie him to the soil, to deprive him of hope, and to degrade him into irremediable poverty."[1]

But it is not in statute law alone that this tendency is seen. English common law shows the same bias in favor of the classes which then controlled the state. There is no mistaking the influences which left their impress upon the development of English law at the hands of the courts. The effect of wealth and political privilege is seen here as well as in statutory enactment. Granting all that can justly be said in behalf of the wisdom and reasonableness of the common law, the fact nevertheless remains, that its development by the courts has been influenced by an evident disposition to favor the possessing as against the non-possessing classes. Both the common and the statute law of England reflected in the eighteenth century the political supremacy of the well-to-do minority.

[1] Work and Wages, p. 398.

CHAPTER II

THE AMERICAN GOVERNMENT OF THE
REVOLUTIONARY PERIOD

The American colonists inherited the common law and the political institutions of the mother country. The British form of government, with its King, Lords and Commons and its checks upon the people, they accepted as a matter of course. In their political thinking they were not consciously more democratic than their kinsmen across the Atlantic. Many of them, it is true, had left England to escape what they regarded as tyranny and oppression. But to the *form* of the English government as such they had no objection. The evils which they experienced were attributed solely to the selfish spirit in which the government was administered.

The conditions, however, were more favorable for the development of a democratic spirit here than in the mother country. The immigrants to America represented the more active, enterprising and dissatisfied elements of the English people. Moreover, there was no hereditary aristocratic class in the colonies and less inequality in the distribution of wealth. This approach to industrial and social equality prepared the mind for the ideas of political equality which needed only the stimulus of a favorable opportunity to ensure their speedy development.

This opportunity came with the outbreak of the American Revolution which at the outset was merely an organized and armed protest against what the colonies regarded as an arbitrary and unconstitutional exercise of the taxing power. As there was no widespread or general dissatisfaction with the *form* of the English government, there is scarcely room for doubt that if England had shown a more prudent and conciliatory spirit toward the colonies, the American Revolution would have been averted. No sooner, however, had the controversy with the mother country reached the acute revolutionary stage, than the forces which had been silently and unconsciously working toward democracy, found an opportunity for political expression. The spirit of resistance to what was regarded as unconstitutional taxation rapidly assumed the form of avowed opposition to the English Constitution itself. The people were ready for a larger measure of political democracy than the English Constitution of the eighteenth century permitted. To this new and popular view of government the Declaration of Independence gave expression. It contained an emphatic, formal and solemn disavowal of the political theory embodied in the English Constitution; affirmed that "all men are created equal;" that governments derive "their just powers from the consent of the governed;" and declared the right of the people to alter or to abolish the form of the government "and to institute new government, laying its foundation on such principles and organizing its powers in such form, as to them shall seem most likely to effect their safety and happiness." This was a complete and sweeping repudiation of the English political system, which recognized the right of monarchy and aristocracy to thwart the will of the people.

To what extent the Declaration of Independence voiced the general sentiment of the colonies is largely a matter of conjecture. It is probable, however, that its specification of grievances and its vigorous arraignment of the colonial policy of the English government appealed to many who had little sympathy with its express and implied advocacy of democracy. It is doubtless true that many were carried along with the revolutionary movement who by temperament and education were strongly attached to English political traditions. It is safe to conclude that a large proportion of those who desired to see American independence established did not believe in thorough-going political democracy.

Besides those who desired independence without being in sympathy with the political views expressed in the Declaration of Independence, there were many others who were opposed to the whole Revolutionary movement. The numerical strength of the Tories can not be accurately estimated; but it is certain that a large proportion, probably not less than one-third of the total population of the colonies, did not approve of the war.[1]

"In the first place, there was, prior to 1776, the official class; that is, the men holding various positions in the civil and military and naval services of the government, their immediate families, and their social connections. All such persons may be described as inclining to the Loyalist view in consequence of official bias.

"Next were certain colonial politicians who, it may be admitted, took a rather selfish and an unprincipled view of the whole dispute, and who, counting on the probable, if not inevitable, success of the British arms in such a conflict, adopted the Loyalist side, not for conscience' sake, but for profit's sake, and in the expectation of being rewarded for their fidelity by offices and titles, and especially by the confiscated estates of the rebels after the rebels themselves should have been defeated, and their leaders hanged or sent into exile.

"As composing still another class of Tories, may be mentioned probably a vast majority of those who stood for the commercial interests, for the capital and tangible property of the country, and who, with the instincts natural to persons who

---

[1] Tyler, The Literary History of the American Revolution, Vol. I, p. 300.

have something considerable to lose, disapproved of all measures for pushing the dispute to the point of disorder, riot and civil war.

"Still another class of Loyalists was made up of people of professional training and occupation —clergymen, physicians, lawyers, teachers—a clear majority of whom seem to have been set against the ultimate measures of the Revolution.

"Finally, and in general, it may be said that a majority of those who, of whatever occupation, of whatever grade of culture or of wealth, would now be described as conservative people, were Loyalists during the American Revolution."[1]

These classes prior to the Revolution had largely shaped and molded public opinion; but their opposition to the movement which they were powerless to prevent, destroyed their influence, for the time being, in American politics. The place which they had hitherto held in public esteem was filled by a new class of leaders more in sympathy with the newly born spirit of liberalism. This gave to the revolutionary movement a distinctly democratic character.

This drift toward democracy is seen in the changes made in the state constitutions after the outbreak of the Revolution. At the close of the colonial period, nearly all the state governments were modeled after the government of Great

[1] Tyler, The Literary History of the American Revolution, Vol. I, p. 301.

Britain. Each colony had its legislative body elected by the qualified voters and corresponding in a general way to the House of Commons. In all the colonies except Pennsylvania and Georgia there was also an upper legislative house or council whose consent was necessary before laws could be enacted. The members composing this branch of the legislature were appointed by the governor except in Massachusetts where they were elected by the lower branch of the legislature, subject to a negative by the royal governor, and in Rhode Island and Connecticut where they were chosen by the electorate.

The governor was elected by the voters only in Rhode Island and Connecticut; in all the other colonies he was appointed by the proprietaries or the Crown, and, though independent of the people, exercised many important powers. He was commander-in-chief of the armed forces of the colony; appointed the judges and all other civil and military officers; appointed and could suspend the council, which was usually the upper branch of the legislature; he could convene and dissolve the legislature and had besides an unqualified veto on all laws; he also had an unrestricted pardoning power.

The possession of these far-reaching powers gave to the irresponsible executive branch of the colonial government a position of commanding importance. This was not the case, however, in

Connecticut and Rhode Island. Although the governor in these two colonies was responsible to the voters, inasmuch as he was elected by them, still he had no veto, and the appointing power was in the hands of the legislature.

The tidal-wave of democracy, which swept over the colonies during the Revolution, largely effaced the monarchical and aristocratic features of the colonial governments. Connecticut and Rhode Island, which already had democratic constitutions, were the only states which did not modify their form of government during this period. All the rest adopted new constitutions which show in a marked degree the influence of the democratic movement. In these new constitutions we see a strong tendency to subordinate the executive branch of the government and confer all important powers on the legislature. In the four New England states and in New York the governor was elected by the qualified voters; in all the rest he was chosen by the legislature. In ten states during this period his term of office was one year; in South Carolina it was two and in New York and Delaware it was three years. In addition to this the six Southern states restricted his re-election. Besides, there was in every state an executive or privy council which the governor was required to consult on all important matters. This was usually appointed by the legislature and constituted an important check on the governor.

The power to veto legislation was abolished in all but two states. In Massachusetts the governor, and in New York the Council of Revision composed of the governor and the chancellor and judges of the Supreme Court, had a qualified veto power. But a two-thirds majority in both houses of the legislature could override the veto of the governor in Massachusetts, or that of the Council of Revision in New York. The pardoning power of the governor was quite generally restricted. In five states he was allowed to exercise it only with the advice or consent of the council.[1] In three states, where the advice or consent of a council was not required, he could, subject to certain restrictions, grant pardons except where "the law shall otherwise direct."[2] The constitution of Georgia in express terms deprived the governor of all right to exercise this power.

The appointing power of the governor was also taken away or restricted. In four of the eleven states adopting new constitutions during this period he was allowed to exercise it jointly with the council.[3] In six states it was given to the legislature, or to the legislature and council.[4] The power of the governor to dissolve the legis-

[1] Massachusetts, New Hampshire, New Jersey, Pennsylvania and Virginia.

[2] Delaware, Maryland and North Carolina.

[3] Massachusetts, New Hampshire, Pennsylvania and Maryland.

[4] Delaware, New York, New Jersey, North Carolina, South Carolina and Virginia.

lature or either branch of it was everywhere abolished.

The supremacy of the legislature under these early state constitutions is seen also in the manner of appointment, the tenure and the powers of the judiciary. In nine states[1] the judges were elected by the state legislature, either with or without the consent of a council. In Maryland, Massachusetts, New Hampshire, and Pennsylvania they were appointed by the governor with the consent of the council. But this really amounted to indirect legislative appointment in Maryland, since both the governor and council in that state were elected annually by the legislature. The legislature also had a voice in the appointment of judges in Pennsylvania, New Hampshire and Massachusetts, since it elected the executive in the first and the council in the others. In nine states, then, the judges were elected directly by the legislature; in one indirectly by the legislature; in the other three the legislature participated in their election through an executive or a council of its own choosing.

In every state the judges could be impeached by the lower branch of the legislature and expelled from office on conviction by the senate or other tribunal, as the constitution prescribed.

[1] Connecticut, Rhode Island, New Jersey, Virginia, North Carolina, South Carolina, Georgia, New York and Delaware.

Moreover, in six states[1] they could be removed according to the English custom by the executive on an address from both branches of the legislature. The term of office of the judges in eight states[2] was during good behavior. In New Jersey and Pennsylvania they were appointed for seven years, and in Rhode Island, Connecticut, and Georgia they were chosen annually.

The legislature under these early state constitutions was hampered neither by the executive nor by the courts. It had all law-making power in its own hands. In no state could the courts thwart its purpose by declaring its acts null and void. Unchecked by either executive or judicial veto its supremacy was undisputed.

From the foregoing synopsis of the state constitutions of this period it is evident that their framers rejected entirely the English theory of checks and balances. The principle of separation of powers as expounded by Montesquieu and Blackstone, found little favor with those who controlled American politics at this time. Instead of trying to construct a state government composed of coördinate branches, each acting as a check upon the others, their aim was to make the legislature supreme. In this respect the early state constitutions anticipated much of the later

[1] Massachusetts, New Hampshire, Maryland, Delaware, South Carolina and Pennsylvania.
[2] Massachusetts, New Hampshire, New York, Delaware, Maryland, North Carolina, South Carolina and Virginia.

development of the English government itself.

The checks and balances, and separation of powers, which characterized the government of England and her American colonies in the eighteenth century, resulted from the composite character of the English Constitution—its mixture of monarchy, aristocracy, and democracy. It is not surprising, then, that with the temporary ascendency of the democratic spirit, the system of checks should have been largely discarded.

This democratic tendency is seen also in our first federal constitution, the Articles of Confederation, which was framed under the impulse of the Revolutionary movement. This document is interesting as an expression of the political philosophy of the Revolution; but like the state constitutions of that period, it has had few friendly critics among later political writers. Much emphasis has been put upon its defects, which were many, while but little attention has been given to the political theory which it imperfectly embodied. That it failed to provide a satisfactory general government may be admitted; but this result must not be accepted as conclusive proof that the principles underlying it were altogether false.

The chief feature of the Articles of Confederation was the entire absence of checks and balances. All the powers conferred upon the general government were vested in a single legislative body called the Continental Congress, which was unchecked by a distinct executive or judiciary. In this respect it bore a striking resemblance to the English government of to-day with its omnipotent House of Commons. But, unlike the English government of to-day, its powers were few and narrowly limited. Its failure was due, perhaps, not to the fact that the powers granted to the confederation were vested exclusively in a single legislative body, but to the fact that the powers thus granted were not sufficient for maintaining a strong and effective central government.

The reason for the weakness of the general government under the Articles of Confederation is obvious to the student of American history. It was only gradually, and as necessity compelled coöperation between the colonies, that the sentiment in favor of political union developed. And though some tendencies in this direction are seen more than a century before the American Revolution, the progress toward a permanent union was slow and only the pressure of political necessity finally brought it about.

As early as 1643 Massachusetts, Plymouth, Connecticut and New Haven formed a "perpetual confederation" under the name of the "United Colonies of New England." The motive for this union was mainly offence and defence against the Indian tribes and the Dutch, though provision was also made for the extradition of servants and fugitives from justice. The management of the common interests of these colonies was vested in a board of eight commissioners—two from each colony—and, in transacting the business of the confederacy, the consent of six of the eight commissioners was required. Any matter which could not be thus disposed of was to be referred to the four colonial legislatures. The general government thus provided for could not intermeddle "with the government of any of the jurisdictions." No provision was made for amending the "Articles of Confederation," and only by the unanimous consent of these colonies could any other colony be admitted to the confederacy. This union lasted for over forty years.[1]

Again in 1754 the pressure of impending war with the French and Indians brought together at Albany a convention of delegates from seven colonies north of the Potomac. A plan of union drafted by Benjamin Franklin was recommended by this convention, but it was not regarded with favor either by the colonies or by the English government. The former regarded it as going too far in the direction of subordinating the separate colonies to a central colonial authority, while for the latter it was too democratic.[2]

The union of all the colonies under the Articles of Confederation was finally brought about through the pressure of military necessity during

[1] Macdonald's Select Charters, Vol. I, pp. 94-101.
[2] Schouler's Constitutional Studies, pp. 70-78, Macdonald's Select Charters, Vol. I.

the Revolution. Nor is it surprising, in view of the history of the American colonies, that they reluctantly yielded up any powers to a central authority. We must bear in mind that the Revolution was in a measure a democratic movement, and that democracy was then found only in local government. The general governments of all countries were at that time monarchical or aristocratic. Tyranny in the eighteenth century was associated in the minds of the people with an undue extension or abuse of the powers exercised by the undemocratic central government. It is not surprising, then, that the Revolutionary federal constitution, the Articles of Confederation, should have failed to provide a general government sufficiently strong to satisfy the needs of the country after the return of peace.

It must not be inferred, however, that the political changes which immediately followed the outbreak of the Revolution were in the nature of sweeping democratic reforms. Much that was thoroughly undemocratic remained intact. The property qualifications for the suffrage were not disturbed by the Revolutionary movement and were finally abolished only after the lapse of nearly half a century. The cruel and barbarous system of imprisonment for debt which the colonies had inherited from England, and which often made the lot of the unfortunate debtor worse than that of the chattel slave, continued in several of the states until long after the Revolution. Marked as was the democratic tendency during the first few years of our independence, it nevertheless left untouched much that the progress of democracy has since abolished.

CHAPTER III

THE CONSTITUTION A REACTIONARY DOCUMENT

The sweeping changes made in our form of government after the Declaration of Independence were clearly revolutionary in character. The English system of checks and balances was discarded for the more democratic one under which all the important powers of government were vested in the legislature. This new scheme of government was not, however, truly representative of the political thought of the colonies. The conservative classes who in ordinary times are a powerful factor in the politics of every community had, by reason of their Loyalist views, no voice in this political reorganization; and these, as we have seen, not only on account of their wealth and intelligence, but on the basis of their numerical strength as well, were entitled to considerable influence.

With the return of peace these classes which so largely represented the wealth and culture of the colonies, regained in a measure the influence which they had lost. This tended strongly to bring about a conservative reaction. There was besides another large class which supported the Revolutionary movement without being in sympathy with its democratic tendencies. This also used its influence to undo the work of the Revolutionary radicals. Moreover, many of those who had espoused democratic doctrines during the Revolution became conservatives after the war was over.[1] These classes were naturally opposed to the new political doctrines which the Revolutionary movement had incorporated in the American government. The "hard times" and general discontent which followed the war also contributed to the reactionary movement; since many were led to believe that evils which were the natural result of other causes were due to an excess of democracy. Consequently ' we find the democratic tendency which manifested itself with the outbreak of the Revolution giving place a few years later to the political reaction which found expression in our present Constitution.

"The United States are the offspring of a long-past age. A hundred years, it is true, have scarcely passed since the eighteenth century came to its end, but no hundred years in the history of the world has ever before hurried it along so far over new paths and into unknown fields. The

[1] "Who would have thought, ten years ago, that the very men who risked their lives and fortunes in support of republican principles, would now treat them as the fictions of fancy?" M. Smith in the New York Convention held to ratify the Constitution, Elliot's Debates, Second Edition, Vol. II, p. 250.

French Revolution and the First Empire were the bridge between two periods that nothing less than the remaking of European society, the recasting of European politics, could have brought so near.

"But back to this eighteenth century must we go to learn the forces, the national ideas, the political theories, under the domination of which the Constitution of the United States was framed and adopted."[1]

It is the general belief, nevertheless, that the Constitution of the United States is the very embodiment of democratic philosophy. The people take it for granted that the framers of that document were imbued with the spirit of political equality and sought to establish a government by the people themselves. Widely as this view is entertained, it is, however, at variance with the facts.

"Scarcely any of these men [the framers of the Constitution] entertained," says Fiske, "what we should now call extreme democratic views. Scarcely any, perhaps, had that intense faith in the ultimate good sense of the people which was the most powerful characteristic of Jefferson."[2]

Democracy—government by the people, or directly responsible to them—was not the object which the framers of the American Constitution had in view, but the very thing which they wished

[1] Simeon E. Baldwin, Modern Political Institutions, pp. 83 and 84.
[2] Critical Period of American History, p. 226.

to avoid. In the convention which drafted that instrument it was recognized that democratic ideas had made sufficient progress among the masses to put an insurmountable obstacle in the way of any plan of government which did not confer at least the form of political power upon the people. Accordingly the efforts of the Constitutional Convention were directed to the task of devising a system of government which was just popular enough not to excite general opposition and which at the same time gave to the people as little as possible of the substance of political power.

It is somewhat strange that the American people know so little of the fundamental nature of their system of government. Their acquaintance with it extends only to its outward form and rarely includes a knowledge of the political philosophy upon which it rests. The sources of information upon which the average man relies do not furnish the data for a correct understanding of the Constitution. The ordinary text-books and popular works upon this subject leave the reader with an entirely erroneous impression. Even the writings of our constitutional lawyers deal with the outward form rather than the spirit of our government. The vital question—the extent to which, under our constitutional arrangements, the people were expected to, and as a matter of fact do, control legislation and public policy, is either not referred to, or else discussed in a superficial and unsatisfactory manner. That this feature of our Constitution should receive more attention than it does is evident when we reflect that a government works well in practice in proportion as its underlying philosophy and constitutional forms are comprehended by those who wield political power.

"It has been common," says a late Justice of the United States Supreme Court, "to designate our form of government as a democracy, but in the true sense in which that term is properly used, as defining a government in which all its acts are performed by the people, it is about as far from it as any other of which we are aware."[1]

In the United States at the present time we are trying to make an undemocratic Constitution the vehicle of democratic rule. Our Constitution embodies the political philosophy of the eighteenth century, not that of to-day. It was framed for one purpose while we are trying to use it for another. Is free government, then, being tried here under the conditions most favorable to its success? This question we can answer only when we have considered our Constitution as a means to the attainment of democratic rule.

It is difficult to understand how anyone who has read the proceedings of the Federal Convention can believe that it was the intention of that

[1] S. F. Miller, Lectures on the Constitution of the United States, pp. 84-85.

body to establish a democratic government. The evidence is overwhelming that the men who sat in that convention had no faith in the wisdom or political capacity of the people. Their aim and purpose was not to secure a larger measure of democracy, but to eliminate as far as possible the direct influence of the people on legislation and public policy. That body, it is true, contained many illustrious men who were actuated by a desire to further what they conceived to be the welfare of the country. They represented, however, the wealthy and conservative classes, and had for the most part but little sympathy with the popular theory of government.

"Hardly one among them but had sat in some famous assembly, had signed some famous document, had filled some high place, or had made himself conspicuous for learning, for scholarship, or for signal services rendered in the cause of liberty. One had framed the Albany plan of union; some had been members of the Stamp Act Congress of 1765; some had signed the Declaration of Rights in 1774; the names of others appear at the foot of the Declaration of Independence and at the foot of the Articles of Confederation; two had been presidents of Congress; seven had been, or were then, governors of states; twenty-eight had been members of Congress; one had commanded the armies of the United States; another had been Superintendent of Finance; a third had repeatedly been sent on important missions to England, and had long been Minister to France.

"Nor were the future careers of many of them to be less interesting than their past. Washington and Madison became Presidents of the United States; Elbridge Gerry became Vice-President; Charles Cotesworth Pinckney and Rufus King became candidates for the Presidency, and Jared Ingersoll, Rufus King, and John Langdon candidates for the Vice-Presidency; Hamilton became Secretary of the Treasury; Madison, Secretary of State; Randolph, Attorney-General and Secretary of State, and James McHenry, a Secretary of War; Ellsworth and Rutledge became Chief-Justices; Wilson and John Blair rose to the Supreme bench; Gouverneur Morris, and Ellsworth, and Charles C. Pinckney, and Gerry, and William Davie became Ministers abroad."[1]

The long list of distinguished men who took part in the deliberations of that body is noteworthy, however, for the absence of such names as Samuel Adams, Thomas Jefferson, Thomas Paine, Patrick Henry and other democratic leaders of that time. The Federal Convention assembled in Philadelphia only eleven years after the Declaration of Independence was signed, yet only six of the fifty-six men who signed that document were among its members.[2] Conservatism

[1] McMaster, With the Fathers, pp. 112-113.
[2] "They [the framers of the Constitution] represented the

3   33

and thorough distrust of popular government characterized throughout the proceedings of that convention. Democracy, Elbridge Gerry thought, was the worst of all political evils.[1] Edmund Randolph observed that in tracing the political evils of this country to their origin, "every man [in the Convention] had found it in the turbulence and follies of democracy."[2] These views appear to reflect the general opinion of that body. Still they realized that it was not the part of wisdom to give public expression to this contempt for democracy. The doors were closed to the public and the utmost secrecy maintained with regard to the proceedings. Members were not allowed to communicate with any one outside of that body concerning the matters therein discussed, nor were they permitted, except by a vote of the Convention, to copy anything from the journals.[3]

conservative intelligence of the country very exactly ; from this class there is hardly a name, except that of Jay, which could be suggested to complete the list." Article by Alexander Johnston on the Convention of 1787 in Lalor's Cyclopaedia of Pol. Science, Pol. Econ. and U. S. Hist.

[1] Elliot's Debates, Vol. V, p. 557.

[2] Ibid., p. 138.

[3] "By another [rule] the doors were to be shut, and the whole proceedings were to be kept secret ; and so far did this rule extend, that we were thereby prevented from corresponding with gentlemen in the different states upon the subjects under our discussion. . . . So *extremely solicitous* were they that their proceedings should not transpire, that the members were prohibited even from taking copies of resolutions, on which the Convention were deliberating, or extracts of any kind from the Journals without formally moving for and obtaining permission, by a vote of the Convention for that purpose." Luther Martin's Address to the Maryland House of Delegates. Ibid., Vol. I, p. 345.

"The doors were locked, and an injunction of strict secrecy

It must be borne in mind that the Convention was called for the purpose of proposing amendments to the Articles of Confederation. The delegates were not authorized to frame a new constitution. Their appointment contemplated changes which were to perfect the Articles of Confederation without destroying the general form of government which they established. The resolution of Congress of February 21, 1787, which authorized the Federal Convention, limited its business to "the sole and express purpose of revising the Articles of Confederation," and the states of New York, Massachusetts, and Connecticut copied this in the instructions to their delegates.[1] The aim of the Convention, however, from the very start was not amendment, but a complete rejection of the system itself, which was regarded as incurably defective.

This view was well expressed by James Wilson in his speech made in favor of the ratification of the Constitution before the Pennsylvania convention.

"The business, we are told, which was entrusted to the late Convention," he said, "was merely to

was put upon everyone. The results of their work were known in the following September, when the draft of the Federal Constitution was published. But just what was said and done in this secret conclave was not revealed until fifty years had passed, and the aged James Madison, the last survivor of those who sat there, had been gathered to his fathers." Fiske, The Critical Period of American History, p. 229. McMaster, With the Fathers, p. 112.

[1] Elliot's Debates, Vol. I, pp. 119-127.

amend the present Articles of Confederation. This observation has been frequently made, and has often brought to my mind a story that is related of Mr. Pope, who, it is well known, was not a little deformed. It was customary with him to use this phrase, 'God mend me!' when any little accident happened. One evening a link-boy was lighting him along, and, coming to a gutter, the boy jumped nimbly over it. Mr Pope called to him to turn, adding, 'God mend me!' The arch rogue, turning to light him, looked at him, and repeated, 'God mend you! He would sooner make half-a-dozen new ones.' This would apply to the present Confederation; for it would be easier to make another than to amend this."[1]

The popular notion that this Convention in framing the Constitution was actuated solely by a desire to impart more vigor and efficiency to the general government is but a part of the truth. The Convention desired to establish not only a strong and vigorous central government, but one which would at the same time possess great stability or freedom from change. This last reason is seldom mentioned in our constitutional literature, yet it had a most important bearing on the work of the Convention. This desired stability the government under the Confederation did not possess, since it was, in the opinion of the members of the Convention, dangerously responsive to

[1] Elliot's Debates, Vol. II, p. 470.

public opinion; hence their desire to supplant it with an elaborate system of constitutional checks. The adoption of this system was the triumph of a skillfully directed reactionary movement.

Of course the spirit and intention of the Convention must be gathered not from the statements and arguments addressed to the general public in favor of the ratification of the Constitution, but from what occurred in the Convention itself. The discussions which took place in that body indicate the real motives and purposes of those who framed the Constitution. These were carefully withheld from the people and it was not until long afterward that they were accessible to students of the American Constitution. The preamble began with, "We, the people," but it was the almost unanimous sentiment of the Convention that the less the people had to do with the government the better. Hamilton wanted to give the rich and well born "a distinct, permanent share in the government."[1] Madison thought the government ought "to protect the minority of the opulent against the majority."[2] The prevalence of such views in this Convention reminds one of Adam Smith's statement, made a few years before in his "Wealth of Nations," that "civil government, so far as it is instituted for the security of property, is in reality instituted for the defence of the

[1] Elliot's Debates, Vol. I, p. 422.
[2] Ibid., p. 450.

rich against the poor, or of those who have some property against those who have none at all."[1] The solicitude shown by the members of this convention for the interests of the well-to-do certainly tends to justify Adam Smith's observation.

The framers of the Constitution realized, however, that it would not do to carry this system of checks upon the people too far. It was necessary that the government should retain something of the *form* of democracy, if it was to command the respect and confidence of the people. For this reason Gerry thought that "the people should appoint one branch of the government in order to inspire them with the necessary confidence."[2] Madison also saw that the necessary sympathy between the people and their rulers and officers must be maintained and that "the policy of refining popular appointments by successive filtrations" might be pushed too far.[3] These discussions, which took place behind closed doors and under pledge of secrecy, may be taken as fairly representing what the framers of our Constitution really thought of popular government. Their public utterances, on the other hand, influenced as they necessarily were, by considerations of public policy, are of little value. From all the evidence which we have, the conclusion is irresistible that

[1]Book 5, Ch. I, Part II.
[2]Elliot's Debates, Vol. V, p. 160.
[3]Ibid., p. 137.

they sought to establish a form of government which would effectually curb and restrain democracy. They engrafted upon the Constitution just so much of the features of popular government as was, in their opinion, necessary to ensure its adoption.

CHAPTER IV

THE SIGNIFICANCE OF THE AMENDMENT
FEATURE OF THE CONSTITUTION

All democratic constitutions are flexible and easy to amend. This follows from the fact that in a government which the people really control, a constitution is merely the means of securing the supremacy of public opinion and not an instrument for thwarting it. Such a constitution can not be regarded as a check upon the people themselves. It is a device for securing to them that necessary control over their agents and representatives, without which popular government exists only in name. A government is democratic just in proportion as it responds to the will of the people; and since one way of defeating the will of the people is to make it difficult to alter the form of government, it necessarily follows that any constitution which is democratic in spirit must yield readily to changes in public opinion.

Monarchical and aristocratic constitutions on the other hand are always extremely conservative. Inasmuch as they express the opinion and guarantee the privileges of a dominant class, they are bulwarks erected against popular change. The privileged classes of any society regard stability as the chief political desideratum. They resist, and if possible prevent, those legal and political readjustments which the general progress of society makes necessary. Their interests are furthered in proportion as the system is one which renders change difficult.

With this distinction in mind let us examine the Constitution of the United States. Was it the intention of the framers of this instrument that it should be merely a check upon the governmental machinery with the view of establishing popular control over it, or was it expected to constitute a check upon the people themselves? That it was not intended that the people should be given direct and complete control over the general policy of the government is clear from the fact that the Constitution was made so difficult to amend; for the right to control the political machinery, implies of necessity the right to make such changes in it from time to time, as are needed to make this control effective. It is evident from the views expressed in the Convention that one object of the Constitution was to secure stability by placing the government beyond the direct influence of public opinion.

Madison, who has been called the "father of the Constitution," thought it "ought to secure the permanent interests of the country against inno-

5   vation."[1]   Hamilton said "all communities divide
themselves into the few and the many.   The first
are the rich and well born, the other the mass of
the people . . . [the latter] are turbulent and
changing; they seldom judge or determine right."
Therefore he advocated a permanent senate which
would be able to "check the imprudence of democracy."[2]   Gouverneur Morris observed that "the
first branch [of the proposed Federal Congress],
originating from the people, will ever be subject
to *precipitancy, changeability,* and *excess. . . .*
This can only be checked by *ability* and *virtue* in
the second branch . . . [which] ought to be composed of men of great and established property—
aristocracy; men who, from pride, will support
consistency and permanency; and to make them
completely independent, they must be chosen *for
life,* or they will be a useless body.   Such an aristocratic body will keep down the turbulence of
democracy."[3]

   This dread of the consequences of popular government was shared to a greater or less extent by
nearly all the members of that Convention.   Their
aim was to find a cure for what they conceived to
be the evils of an excess of democracy.

   "Complaints," says Madison in *The Federalist,*
"are everywhere heard from our most considerate
and virtuous citizens, equally the friends of public
and private faith, and of public and personal lib-

[1] Elliot's Debates, Vol. I, p. 450.
[2] Ibid., pp. 421-422.   [3] Ibid., p. 475.

erty, that our governments are too unstable, that the public good is disregarded in the conflicts of rival parties, and that measures are too often decided, not according to the rules of justice and the rights of the minor party, but by the superior force of an interested and overbearing majority."[1]

This criticism of the American government of the Revolutionary period gives us the point of view of the framers of the Constitution. We should remember, however, that the so-called majority rule to which Madison attributed the evils of that time had nothing in common with majority rule as that term is now understood. Under the laws then in force the suffrage was greatly restricted, while the high property qualifications required for office-holding had the effect in many cases of placing the control of legislation in the hands of the wealthier part of the community. But undemocratic as the system was, it was not sufficiently undemocratic to suit the framers of the Constitution. It was no part of their plan to establish a government which the people could control. In fact, popular control was what they were seeking to avoid. One means of accomplishing this was to make amendment difficult, and this accordingly was done. We need not be surprised that no provision was made for its original adoption, or subsequent amendment by direct popular vote.[2]

[1] No. 10.
[2] In Massachusetts and New Hampshire the constitutions

43

The fact that the people can not directly propose, or even ratify changes in the fundamental law, is a substantial check upon democracy. But in addition to this, another check was provided in the extraordinary majority necessary to amend the Constitution. That it requires a two-thirds majority of both houses of Congress, or an application from the legislature in two-thirds of the states to merely set the machinery for constitutional amendment in motion, and that it requires for ratification of amendments proposed, the assent of legislatures or conventions in three-fourths of the states, ought to give one some idea of the extreme difficulty of changing our Constitution.

Patrick Henry clearly saw that this lack of adequate provision for amendment was destructive of democracy. In the Virginia convention held to ratify the Constitution he said:

"To encourage us to adopt it, they tell us that there is a plain, easy way of getting amendments. When I come to contemplate this part, I suppose that I am mad, or that my countrymen are so. The way to amendment is, in my conception, shut

framed during the Revolutionary period were submitted to popular vote. The Virginia Constitution of 1776 contained the declaration "that, when any government shall have been found inadequate or contrary to these purposes [the purposes enumerated in the Bill of Rights], a majority of the community hath an indubitable, inalienable, and indefeasible right to reform, alter, or abolish it, in such manner as shall be judged most conducive to the public weal." The Revolutionary constitution of Pennsylvania contained a similar declaration. Poore, Charters and Constitutions.

. . . ." After quoting Article V (the amendment feature of the Constitution), he continues:

"Hence it appears that three-fourths of the states must ultimately agree to any amendments that may be necessary. Let us consider the consequence of this. . . . Let us suppose—for the case is supposable, possible and probable—that you happen to deal those powers to unworthy hands; will they relinquish powers already in their possession, or agree to amendments? Two-thirds of Congress, or of the state legislatures, are necessary even to propose amendments. If one-third of these be unworthy men, they may prevent the application for amendments; but what is destructive and mischievous, is, that three-fourths of the state legislatures, or of the state conventions, must concur in the amendments when proposed! In such numerous bodies, there must necessarily be some designing, bad men. To suppose that so large a number as three-fourths of the states will concur, is to suppose that they will possess genius, intelligence, and integrity, approaching to miraculous. . . . For four of the smallest states, that do not collectively contain one-tenth part of the population of the United States, may obstruct the most salutary and necessary amendments. Nay, in these four states, six-tenths of the people may reject these amendments. . . . A bare majority in these four small states may hinder the adoption of amendments; so that we may fairly and justly conclude that one-twentieth part of the American people may prevent the removal of the most grievous inconveniences and oppression, by refusing to accede to amendments. . . . Is this an easy mode of securing the public liberty? It is, sir, a most fearful situation, when the most contemptible minority can prevent the alteration of the most oppressive government; for it may, in many respects, prove to be such."[1]

That such a small minority of the people should have the power under our constitutional arrangements to prevent reform, can hardly be reconciled with the general belief that in this country the majority rules. Yet small as was this minority when the Constitution was adopted, it is much smaller now than it was then. In 1900 one forty-fourth of the population distributed so as to constitute a majority in the twelve smallest states could defeat any proposed amendment. As a matter of fact it is impossible to secure amendments to the Constitution, unless the sentiment in favor of change amounts almost to a revolution. Only at critical times in our history have constitutional amendments been adopted. During sixty-one years from 1804 to 1865, and since 1870, no amendments have been made. The fifteen amendments were all adopted, either during the turbulent period of American politics which immediately followed the ratification of the Con-

[1] Elliot's Debates, Vol. III, pp. 48-50.

stitution, or during the reconstruction period after the Civil War. That it is not possible in ordinary times to change the Constitution is evident from the fact that of some twenty-two hundred propositions for amendment only fifteen have been adopted, and these during the periods above mentioned.[1]

8

"The argument in favor of these artificial majorities," says Professor Burgess, "is that innovation is too strong an impulse in democratic states, and must be regulated; that the organic law should be changed only after patience, experience and deliberation shall have demonstrated the necessity of the change; and that too great fixedness of the law is better than too great fluctuation. This is all true enough; but, on the other hand, it is equally true that development is as much a law of state life as existence. Prohibit the former, and the latter is the existence of the body after

[1] Ames, Proposed Amendments to the Constitution of the United States. This book gives a list of the amendments proposed during the first one hundred years of our history under the Constitution. During the fifteen years from 1889 to 1904, four hundred and thirty-five amendments were proposed. These figures are taken from a thesis submitted for the LL. B. degree at the University of Washington by Donald McDonald, A. B.

It is interesting to observe that this is one of the few important features of the Constitution not copied by the Confederate States at the outbreak of the Civil War. The constitution which they adopted provided an easier method of amendment. Any three states could suggest amendments and require Congress to summon a convention of all the states to consider them. To adopt a proposed amendment ratification by legislatures or conventions in two-thirds of the states was necessary.

the spirit has departed. When, in a democratic political society, the well-matured, long and deliberately formed will of the undoubted majority can be persistently and successfully thwarted, in the amendment of its organic law, by the will of the minority, there is just as much danger to the state from revolution and violence as there is from the caprice of the majority, where the sovereignty of the bare majority is acknowledged. The safeguards against too radical change must not be exaggerated to the point of dethroning the real sovereign."[1]

What Professor Burgess seems to overlook is the fact that the framers of the Constitution deliberately intended to dethrone the numerical majority. The restrictions which they placed upon the exercise of the amending power were not only not inconsistent with the form of government which they established, but as a matter of fact absolutely necessary to ensure its preservation, since without such a limitation of the power to amend, the majority could easily overcome all other checks upon its authority.

This feature of the Constitution, which nominally provides for amendment, but really makes it an impossibility, is perhaps the best proof we could have that the Constitution as framed and adopted represented the views of a minority who intended by this means to perpetuate their in-

[1] Political Science and Constitutional Law, Vol. I, p. 151.

fluence. But, we are told, this can not be the case since the states were free to accept or reject it. Let us not forget, however, that at no stage of the proceedings was the matter referred directly to the people. Bryce says: "Had the decision been left to what is now called 'the voice of the people,' that is, to the mass of the citizens all over the country, voting at the polls, the voice of the people would probably have pronounced against the Constitution."[1] Moreover, "the Convention met," as he observes, "at the most fortunate moment in American History [for securing the adoption of such a constitution]. . . . Had it been attempted four years earlier or four years later at both of which times the waves of democracy were running high, it must have failed."[2] But even under these favoring conditions it was no easy task to get the states to adopt it. The advocates of the Constitution employed every argument and influence that could contribute to the desired result. They appealed with telling effect to the dread of European aggression. This induced many who had little sympathy with the proposed plan of government, to acquiesce in its adoption, believing that some sort of a strong government was necessary for purposes of defence. It was also boldly charged that money was em-

[1] The American Commonwealth, Vol. I, Ch. III.
[2] Second Edition, Vol. I, Appendix, Note on Constitutional Conventions.

ployed to overcome opposition where other means of persuasion failed.[1]

Our natural inclination is to disbelieve anything that reflects on the political methods employed by the founders of our government. Nevertheless, the widespread belief that the politicians and public men of that time were less corrupt than those of to-day is, as Professor McMaster says, a pure delusion. "A very little study of long-forgotten politics will suffice to show that in filibustering and gerrymandering, in stealing governorships and legislatures, in using force at the polls, in colonizing and in distributing patronage to whom patronage is due, in all the frauds and tricks that go to make up the worst form of practical politics, the men who founded our state and national governments were always our equals, and often our masters."[2] Of one thing we may be reasonably certain—the Constitution as adopted did not represent the political views of a majority of the American people—probably not even a majority of those entitled to vote. Universal suffrage, we must remember, did not then exist, and both property and religious qualifications limited the right to hold public office. This of itself is evidence that those who then controlled politics did not believe in the right of the majority to rule. And when we take account of the further fact that

---

[1]Fiske, The Critical Period of American History, p. 328.
[2]McMaster, With the Fathers, p. 71.

this was a time of political reaction, when the government of the country was largely in the hands of those who despised or feared democracy, we can easily see that the natural effects of a restricted suffrage may have been intensified by those methods of "practical politics" which not infrequently defeat the will of the majority even to-day under universal suffrage. That it was the intention of the framers of the Constitution to bring about, if possible, the adoption of a form of government of which the majority of the people did not approve, is clearly established by the record of their proceedings. Hamilton, referring to the plan of government which he had proposed, said: "I confess that this plan, and that from Virginia [the one submitted by Randolph and of which the Constitution as finally adopted was a modification], are very remote from the idea of the people. Perhaps the Jersey plan is nearest their expectation. But the people are gradually ripening in their opinions of government—they begin to be tired of an excess of democracy. . . ."[1]

"The Federal government was not by intention a democratic government. In plan and structure it had been meant to check the sweep and power of popular majorities. The Senate, it was believed, would be a stronghold of conservatism, if not of aristocracy and wealth. The President, it was expected, would be the choice of representa-

[1] Elliot's Debates, Vol. I, p. 423.

tive men acting in the electoral college, and not of the people. The Federal judiciary was looked to, with its virtually permanent membership, to hold the entire structure of national politics in nice balance against all disturbing influences, whether of popular impulse or of official overbearance. Only in the House of Representatives were the people to be accorded an immediate audience and a direct means of making their will effective in affairs. The government had, in fact, been originated and organized upon the initiative and primarily in the interest of the mercantile and wealthy classes. Originally conceived as an effort to accommodate commercial disputes between the States, it had been urged to adoption by a minority, under the concerted and aggressive leadership of able men representing a ruling class. The Federalists not only had on their side the power of convincing argument, but also the pressure of a strong and intelligent class, possessed of unity and informed by a conscious solidarity of material interests."[1]

The Constitution would certainly have been rejected, notwithstanding the influences that were arrayed in favor of its adoption, but for the belief that it would shortly be amended so as to remove some of its more objectionable features. In the large and influential states of Massachusetts, New York, and Virginia it was ratified by very

[1]Woodrow Wilson, Division and Reunion, p. 12.

small majorities,[1] though each of these states accompanied its acceptance of the Constitution with various recommendations for amendment. As a result of these suggestions from the states ratifying it, the first Congress in 1789 framed and submitted the first ten amendments. The eleventh amendment was the outgrowth of the Supreme Court decision in the case of Chisholm v. The State of Georgia. In this case the court held, contrary to the interpretation given to the Constitution by Hamilton when defending it in *The Federalist*,[2] that a private plaintiff could sue a state in the Federal Court. This decision aroused a storm of indignation, and Congress in 1794 proposed the Eleventh Amendment, which counteracted the effect of this decision. The Twelfth Amendment, proposed by Congress in 1803, merely changed the method of electing the President to meet the requirements of the party system which had then come into existence.

These first twelve amendments were all adopted during the infancy of the Constitution, and while it was still regarded as an experiment. But though they had the effect of quieting public opinion and allaying the fears of the people concerning the new form of government, they made no important changes in the Constitution, leaving all its main features as originally adopted. The

[1] The vote in Massachusetts was 187 to 168 in favor of ratification; in New York, 30 to 27; in Virginia, 89 to 79.
[2] No. 81.

same may be said of the last three amendments, which were the result of the Civil War. They were proposed and ratified, as Bryce says, "under conditions altogether abnormal, some of the lately conquered states ratifying while actually controlled by the Northern armies, others as the price which they were obliged to pay for the readmission to Congress of their senators and representatives."[1] These amendments were really carried through, not by the free choice of three-fourths of the states, as the Constitution requires, "but under the pressure of a majority which had triumphed in a great war,"[2] and used military and political coercion to accomplish what otherwise could not have been brought about. Nothing could have been farther from the intention of the victorious Northern states at that time than any important change in the form or character of the government which they had waged a gigantic civil war to defend and enforce. Slavery, it is true, was abolished to remove forever the bone of contention between the North and the South. But the Constitution survived the Civil War, unchanged in all its essential features, and more firmly established than ever.

That the plan of government originally established has undergone no important modification by constitutional amendment can not be ascribed to

[1] The American Commonwealth, Vol. I, Ch. XXXII.
[2] Ibid.

the fact that important changes have not been suggested. With the growth of more liberal views concerning government many attempts have been made to remove the constitutional barriers erected by our forefathers to stay the progress of democracy. Among the political reforms contemplated by this numerous class of proposed amendments may be mentioned a shorter term for United States senators and election by popular vote; direct election of the President and the abolition of his veto power; a shorter term for Federal judges and their removal by the President on the joint address of both houses of Congress. The aim of all these proposed amendments has been the same, viz., to make the Constitution accord better with the democratic spirit of the time. It is interesting to observe, however, that with the single exception of the proposed election of United States senators by popular vote, not one of these had the support of either house of Congress, much less the two-thirds majority in both, or a majority in the legislatures of two-thirds of the states, as required to authorize their submission for ratification or rejection. Even this measure, which has passed the House of Representatives several times by an overwhelming vote, has been entirely ignored by the Senate.

No proposal, then, to make any important change in the Constitution has ever obtained the preliminary two-thirds majority, to say nothing of the majority in three-fourths of the states, necessary for its adoption.

That the majority required to propose an amendment is almost prohibitive of change, is shown by the record of popular elections and the journals of representative bodies. From the presidential election year of 1828, the first for which we have a record of the popular vote, down to 1900, the largest majority ever received by any candidate for the Presidency was that of Andrew Jackson in 1828, when he had less than 56 per cent. of the popular vote.[1] Nine elections since Jackson's time resulted in the choice of a President by less than a popular majority. No candidate in any presidential election from 1876 to 1900 inclusive has carried two-thirds of the states.[2]

It is still more difficult for any important reform measure to secure a two-thirds majority in a representative assembly, as the proceedings of Congress and our state legislatures abundantly prove. This is true for the reason that a wealthy minority can exert an influence over such bodies out of all proportion to its numerical strength at the polls. Hence even a bare majority can seldom be obtained for any measure which interferes with or restricts the privileges of organized wealth. A two-thirds majority under such circumstances is

---

[1] Roosevelt in 1904 received less than 56.4 per cent. of the total popular vote.

[2] In 1904 Roosevelt carried thirty-two states—two more than two-thirds.

practically impossible. And when we remember that any proposed amendment to the Constitution must twice run the gauntlet of representative assemblies, receiving first a two-thirds majority in both houses of Congress and later a majority in both houses of the legislature or in conventions in three-fourths of the states, we readily see that this provision effectually precludes the possibility of any important amendment.

One of the principal objections to the Articles of Confederation—that they lacked a practical amending power—applies, then, with no less force to the Constitution itself. In one respect the Constitution is even more rigid than were the Articles of Confederation, since the Congress of the Confederation was the court of last resort for passing on the constitutionality of its own legislation. This gave to Congress under the Confederation at least a limited power of virtually amending the Articles of Confederation by the ordinary process of law-making—a power possessed by the legislature in all countries where the system of checks and balances is not recognized. Under the Constitution, however, this power to amend the fundamental law can be exercised only to a very limited extent by Congress, since the interpretation of the Constitution by that body for the purposes of law-making is subject to revision at the hands of the Federal Judiciary. The Constitution, then, more effectually prevents changes desired by the majority than did the Articles of Confederation, since the former guards against the possibility of amendment under the guise of ordinary legislation while the latter did not.

Another distinction must be borne in mind. The Articles of Confederation made amendment difficult in order to prevent the general government from encroaching on the rights of the several states. It was not so much a disposition to make change impossible, or even difficult, as, by keeping the general government within established bounds, to leave the several states free to regulate their own affairs and change their institutions from time to time to suit themselves.

This view finds support in the character of the early state constitutions. These were shaped by the same revolutionary movement which produced the Declaration of Independence, and were largely influenced in their practical working by the "self-evident" truths proclaimed in the latter. One of the axioms of political science embodied in the Declaration of Independence was the right of the people to alter or abolish the existing form of government. This principle, however, was expressly recognized in but few of the earlier state constitutions, which, as a rule, contained no provision for future amendment. But such provision was not really necessary, inasmuch as the power of the legislature was limited only by its responsibility to the electorate.   A mere majority of the qualified voters might demand and secure the enactment of laws which would virtually amend the constitution.   From this time on, however, we see a strong tendency to specify in the constitution itself the manner in which it could be changed; and by the time that the framers of the Federal Constitution met in Philadelphia in 1787 a majority of the state constitutions contained provisions of this kind.

According to the Maryland constitution of 1776 it was necessary that an amendment should "pass the General Assembly, and be published at least three months before a new election" and confirmed by the General Assembly in the first session after such election.[1]   The South Carolina constitution of 1778 permitted "a majority of the members of the senate and house of representatives" to adopt amendments after having given ninety days' notice of such intention.   The constitution of Delaware, 1776, required that constitutional amendments should be assented to by five-sevenths of the lower house and seven-ninths of the upper. This check on amendment was largely inoperative, however, for the reason above mentioned, viz., that the legislature was supreme, and could enact by majority vote such laws as it saw fit, whether they were in harmony with the constitution or not.

[1] Poore, Charters and Constitutions.

Five other state constitutions made provision
for the adoption of amendments by conventions.
The Pennsylvania constitution of 1776 provided
for the election every seventh year by the freemen
of the state of a "Council of Censors" to hold
office during one year from the date of their election. This body had the power "to pass public
censures, to order impeachments, and to recom-
mend to the legislature the repealing such laws as
appear to them to have been enacted contrary to
the principles of the constitution." They also
had power to call a convention for amending the
constitution. "But . . . the amendments proposed . . . shall be promulgated at least six
months before the day appointed for the election
of such convention, for the previous consideration
of the people, that they may have an opportunity
of instructing their delegates on the subject."
This provision of the Pennsylvania constitution
of 1776 was copied in the Vermont constitution
of 1777. The constitution of Georgia, 1777, contained the following: "No alteration shall be
made in this constitution without petitions from a
majority of the counties, and the petition from
each county to be signed by a majority of the
voters in each county within this state; at which
time the assembly shall order a convention to be
called for that purpose, specifying the alterations
to be made, according to the petitions preferred
to the assembly by the majority of the counties

as aforesaid." The Massachusetts constitution of 1780 provided that the question of amendment should be submitted to the qualified voters of the state, and if two-thirds of those voting favored amendment, it was the duty of the legislature to order the election of delegates to meet in convention for that purpose. The New Hampshire constitution of 1784 contained a similar provision.

We see, then, that several of the early state constitutions expressly gave, either directly to a majority of the qualified voters, or to their representatives, the right to amend; and even in Massachusetts, New Hampshire, and Delaware, whose constitutions expressly limited the power of the majority, the limitation was not effective, since the majority could push through under the guise of ordinary legislation, measures which virtually amounted to an exercise of the amending power. Such limitations on the power of the majority did not become effective until a judiciary not directly responsible to the people, acquired the right to declare acts of the legislature null and void.

An examination of these features of the various state constitutions in force in 1787 shows clearly the reactionary character of the Federal Constitution. It repudiated entirely the doctrine then expressly recognized in some of the states and virtually in all, that a majority of the qualified voters could amend the fundamental law. And not only did it go farther than any state constitution in expressly limiting the power of the majority, but it provided what no state constitution had done—the means by which its limitations on the power of the majority could be enforced.

A comparison of this feature of our Constitution with the method of amendment in other countries is interesting and instructive. In England no distinction is made between constitutional amendments and other legislation. And since the Crown has lost the veto power and the House of Commons established its right to override the opposition of the House of Lords, the most radical changes may be made without even the checks which impede ordinary legislation in the United States.

In France amendment of the Constitution is almost as easy as in England, though a distinction is made between this and ordinary legislation. When both the Senate and Chamber of Deputies decide by an absolute majority in each that amendment is necessary, they meet in joint session as a National Assembly for that purpose. An absolute majority of the members composing the National Assembly is required to change the Constitution.

Amendments to the Federal Constitution of Australia may be proposed by an absolute majority of both Houses of Parliament. Not less than two nor more than six months after the proposed amendment has been passed by both houses, it must be submitted to the qualified voters in each state. But if either house by an absolute majority passes a proposed amendment which is rejected by the other house, and passes it again by an absolute majority after an interval of three months, the Governor-General may submit the proposed amendment to the qualified voters. A proposed amendment is adopted if it is approved by a majority of all those voting and also by a majority in a majority of the states.

In Switzerland the question whether the Federal Constitution ought to be amended must be submitted to a popular vote whenever demanded by either house of the Federal Assembly or by fifty thousand voters (about one-fifteenth of the voting population). A proposed amendment is adopted if it receives a majority of all the votes cast and at the same time a majority in a majority of the Cantons, a provision copied, as we have seen, in the Federal Constitution of Australia.

These constitutions show the general tendency at the present time to make the majority supreme. In the countries which have been most influenced by democratic ideas constitutional barriers against change have largely or wholly disappeared. A constitution is in no proper sense the embodiment of the will of the people unless it recognizes the right of the majority to amend. Checks which prevent legal and political readjustment are a survival from monarchy and aristocracy and are not found in any full-fledged democracy. Constitutions which are really democratic contain only such checks upon the people, if indeed they can be called checks, as are calculated to insure the deliberate expression of the popular will. Constitutional provisions designed to obstruct amendment are not only an anomaly in popular government, but they are in the very nature of the case inoperative. This follows from the fact that the law-making body, whether it be the people themselves or a representative assembly, is the final interpreter of the constitution and may enact laws which virtually amend it. To make such provisions really effective the constitution must vest the power to prevent legislation in some branch of government not directly responsible to the people. Usually this is a King or hereditary class. Our Constitution, however, provides a substitute for these in its general system of checks and especially in the independence of our national judiciary, which in addition to the exercise of ordinary judicial functions is also practically a branch of the legislature. The constitutional status of the judiciary will be discussed in the following chapter.

CHAPTER V

THE FEDERAL JUDICIARY

No part of our Constitution has received less adverse criticism than that which relates to the powers and tenure of the judiciary. Constitutional writers have almost without exception given it their unqualified approval, claiming that its wisdom is established beyond question by the political experience of the English-speaking race. To express a doubt as to the soundness of this view is to take issue with what appears to be the settled and mature judgment of the American people.

Moreover, the authority of the courts is "the most vital part of our government, the part on which the whole system hinges."[1] This is true for the reason that the Federal judiciary is not only the most important of our constitutional checks on the people, but is also the means of preserving and enforcing all the other checks. To enable the Federal judges to exercise these important and far-reaching powers, it was necessary to make them independent by giving them a life tenure. This provision was in perfect harmony

---

[1] A. Lawrence Lowell, Essays on Government, p. 40.

with the general plan and purpose of the Constitution, a document framed, as we have seen, with a view to placing effectual checks on the power of the majority. As a means to the end which the framers of the Constitution had in view, the independence of the judiciary was an admirable arrangement.

Hamilton says: "Upon the whole, there can be no room to doubt that the Convention acted wisely in copying from the models of those constitutions which have established *good behavior* as the tenure of their judicial offices, in point of duration; and that so far from being blamable on this account, their plan would have been inexcusably defective, if it had wanted this important feature of good government. The experience of Great Britain affords an illustrious comment on the excellence of the institution."[1]

This is quoted with approval by Story in his Commentaries on the Constitution and this same line of argument has been followed by legal and political writers generally. But with all due respect for the eminent authorities who have placed so much stress on the political experience of other countries, we may venture to ask if the parallel which they have assumed really exists. Is the use made of this argument from analogy warranted by the facts in the case? Are we sure that the political experience of England proves

[1] *The Federalist*, No. 78.

the wisdom of an independent judiciary? This can best be answered by referring to the circumstances which gave rise to the doctrine that the judges should be independent.

In England formerly the Crown appointed the judges and could remove them. This power of appointment and removal placed the courts under the control of the King and made it possible for him to use them as a means of oppressing the people. A striking example of the way in which this power could be abused was seen in the career of the notorious Jeffreys, the pliant judicial tool of the cruel and tyrannical James II. To guard against a repetition of this experience it was urged that the judges be made independent of the King.

This was done in 1701 by the Act of Settlement which provided that judges should be removed only on an address from Parliament to the Crown. This deprived the King of the power to remove judges on his own initiative and virtually gave it to Parliament. The object of this provision was to place a check in the interest of the people upon the arbitrary power of the Crown. It made the judges independent of the King, but at the same time established their responsibility to Parliament by giving the latter the right to demand their removal.[1]

[1] "The object of the Act of Parliament was to secure the judges from removal at the mere pleasure of the Crown; but not to render them independent of the action of Parliament." Story, Commentaries on the Constitution, Sec. 1623.

The statement so often made and so generally believed that the American judicial system was modeled after that of Great Britain will not bear investigation. English judges are not and never have been independent in the sense in which that word is used with reference to the Federal judiciary of the United States. In making the judges independent of the King, Parliament had no intention of leaving them free to exercise irresponsible powers. To have made them really independent would have been to create a new political power of essentially the same character and no less dangerous than the power of the King which they were seeking to circumscribe.

"In England," says Jefferson, "where judges were named and removable at the will of an hereditary executive, from which branch most misrule was feared, and has flowed, it was a great point gained, by fixing them for life, to make them independent of that executive. But in a government founded on the public will, this principle operates in an opposite direction, and against that will. There, too, they were still removable on a concurrence of the executive and legislative branches. But we have made them independent of the nation itself."[1]

There is, as a matter of fact, nothing in the political experience of Great Britain to support the belief in an independent judiciary. The

[1] Works (Ford's Edition), Vol. X, p. 38.

judges there do not constitute a co-ordinate branch of the government and can not enforce their opinion in opposition to that of Parliament. Instead of being independent, they are strictly dependent upon Parliament whose supreme power and authority they are compelled to respect.

This being the case, it is hardly necessary to observe that the courts in England do not exercise legislative functions. The power to decide upon the wisdom or expediency of legislation is vested exclusively in Parliament. The courts can not disregard a statute on the ground that it is in conflict with the Constitution, but must enforce whatever Parliament declares to be the law. As the judiciary under the English system has no voice in the general policy of the state, the tenure of judges during good behavior carries with it no power to thwart the popular will.

The provision in the Constitution of the United States for the life tenure of a non-elective judiciary serves, however, an altogether different purpose. It was designed as a check, not upon an irresponsible executive as was the case in England, but upon the people themselves. Its aim was not to increase, but to diminish popular control over the government. Hence, though professing to follow the English model, the framers of the Constitution as a matter of fact rejected it. They not only gave the Federal judges a life tenure, but made that tenure unqualified and absolute, the power which Parliament had to demand the removal of judges being carefully witheld from the American Congress. This reversed the relation which existed between the legislative and judicial branches of government under the English system and raised the judiciary from a dependent and subordinate position to one that made it in many respects supreme. The most important attribute of sovereignty, that of interpreting the Constitution for the purposes of law-making, which belonged to Parliament as a matter of course, was withheld from Congress and conferred upon the Federal judiciary. Not only, then, did the framers of the Constitution depart from the English model in making the Federal judiciary independent of Congress, but they went much farther than this and conferred upon the body whose independence and irresponsibility were thus secured, powers which under the English system were regarded as the exclusive prerogative of a responsible Parliament. This made our Supreme judges, though indirectly appointed, holding office for life and therefore independent of the people, the final interpreters of the Constitution, with power to enforce their interpretation by declaring legislation null and void. A more powerful check upon democratic innovation it would be hard to devise.

The main reason for making the Federal judges independent and politically irresponsible has not been generally recognized. Thus, in a recent work Professor Channing, while expressing some disapproval of this feature of our system, fails to offer a satisfactory explanation of its origin. "Perhaps nothing in the Constitution of the United States is more extraordinary," he tells us, "than the failure of that instrument to provide any means for getting rid of the judges of the Federal courts except by the process of impeachment. In England, in Massachusetts and in Pennsylvania, judges could be removed by the executive upon address by both branches of the legislative body.[1] In none of these cases was it necessary to allege or to prove any criminal act on the part of the judge. In colonial days the tenure of the judicial office had been of the weakest. In the royal provinces, the judges had been appointed by the Crown and had been removable at pleasure. In the charter colonies, the judges had been appointed by the legislature, and their tenure of office was generally for one year. The precariousness of the judicial office in the royal provinces had more than once led to attempts on the part of the colonists to secure greater permanency, because a permanent judiciary would afford them protection against the royal authorities. All attempts of this kind, however, had been defeated by the negative voice of the government of England. Possibly the permanence of judicial tenure which

[1] Cf. supra p. 21.

is found in the Constitution of the United States may be regarded in some sort as the result of this pre-revolutionary contest."[1]

As a matter of fact, however, there is nothing extraordinary or difficult to explain in this permanency of judicial tenure which the Constitution established. It was not in the charter colonies where annual legislative appointment of judges was the rule, but in the royal provinces that efforts were made by the people to secure greater permanency of judicial tenure. They wished to give the judges more independence in the latter, because it would be the means of placing a check upon irresponsible authority, but were satisfied with a short term of office for judges in the colonies where they were elected and controlled by the legislature. Any explanation of the permanent tenure of our Federal judges "as the result of this pre-revolutionary contest" is insufficient. It was clearly a device consciously adopted by the framers of the Constitution, not for the purpose of limiting irresponsible authority, but for the purpose of setting up an authority that would be in large measure politically irresponsible.

Conservative writers while giving unstinted praise to this feature of the Constitution have not explained its real significance. They have assumed, and expect us to take it for granted, that the Federal judiciary was designed as a means of

[1] The Jeffersonian System, pp. 112-113.

making the will of the people supreme; that its independence and exalted prerogatives were necessary to enable it to protect the people against usurpation and oppression at the hands of the legislative branch of the government.

Hamilton tells us, "The standard of good behavior for the continuance in office of the judicial magistracy, is certainly one of the most valuable of the modern improvements in the practice of government. In a monarchy, it is an excellent barrier to the despotism of the prince; in a republic, it is a no less excellent barrier to the encroachments and oppressions of the representative body.

"The complete independence of the courts of justice is peculiarly essential in a limited constitution. By a limited constitution, I understand one which contains certain specified exceptions to the legislative authority. . . . Limitations of this kind can be preserved in practice no other way than through the medium of the courts of justice, whose duty it must be to declare all acts contrary to the manifest tenor of the Constitution void. . . . .[1]

[1] Referring to Hamilton's defence of the judicial veto, Jefferson says "If this opinion be sound, then indeed is our Constitution a complete *felo de se*. For intending to establish three departments, coördinate and independent, that they might check and balance one another, it has given, according to this opinion, to one of them alone, the right to prescribe rules for the government of the others, and to that one too, which is unelected by, and independent of the nation." Ford's Edition of his works, Vol. X, p. 141.

"Some perplexity respecting the rights of the courts to pronounce legislative acts void, because contrary to the Constitution, has arisen from an imagination that the doctrine would imply a superiority of the judiciary to the legislative power. It is urged that the authority which can declare the acts of another void, must necessarily be superior to the one whose acts may be declared void. . . .

"There is no position which depends on clearer principles, than that every act of a delegated authority, contrary to the tenor of the commission under which it is exercised, is void. No legislative act, therefore, contrary to the Constitution, can be valid. To deny this would be to affirm that the deputy is greater than his principal; that the servant is above his master; that the representatives of the people are superior to the people themselves; that men, acting by virtue of powers, may do not only what their powers do not authorize, but what they forbid.

"If it be said that the legislative body are themselves the constitutional judges of their own powers, and that the construction they put upon them is conclusive upon the other departments, it may be answered, that this can not be the natural presumption, where it is not to be collected from any particular provisions in the Constitution. It is not otherwise to be supposed that the Constitution could intend to enable the representatives of the people to substitute their *will* to that of their constituents. It is far more rational to suppose that the courts were designed to be an intermediate body between the people and the legislature, in order, among other things, to keep the latter within the limits assigned to their authority. The interpretation of the laws is the proper and peculiar province of the courts. A constitution is, in fact, and must be, regarded by the judges as a fundamental law. It therefore belongs to them to ascertain its meaning, as well as the meaning of any particular act proceeding from the legislative body. If there should happen to be an irreconcilable variance between the two, that which has the superior obligation and validity ought, of course, to be preferred; in other words, the Constitution ought to be preferred to the statute, the intention of the people to the intention of their agents. . . .

"This independence of the judges is equally requisite to guard the Constitution and the rights of individuals from the effects of those ill humours which the arts of designing men, or the influence of particular conjunctures, sometimes disseminate among the people themselves, and which, though they speedily give place to better information, and more deliberate reflection, have a tendency, in the mean time, to occasion dangerous innovations in the government, and serious oppressions of the minor party in the community."[1]

[1] *The Federalist*, No. 78.

This argument for an independent judiciary, which has been adopted by all writers who have attempted to defend the system, may be summarized as follows:

The Constitution being the solemn and deliberate expression of the will of the people, is the supreme law of the land. As such it enumerates the powers of the several branches of the government and sets limits to their authority. Any act, therefore, on the part of the agents or representatives of the people, which exceeds the authority thus delegated, is in violation of the fundamental law and can not bind those whom they profess to represent.

These checks upon the agents and representatives of the people can not be enforced, however, if each branch of the government is to be permitted to determine for itself what powers the Constitution has conferred upon it. Under such a system Congress would overstep the limits which have been placed upon its authority and substitute its own will for the will of the people. To prevent this the framers of the Constitution placed the courts, in their scheme of government, between the people and the legislature and gave them power to determine and enforce the constitutional limitations on the authority of Congress. This put the Constitution and the rights and liberties of the people under the protection of their natural guardian, the Federal judiciary, and thereby secured the people against the danger of legislative tyranny.

We must not forget the circumstances under which Hamilton wrote this defence of the Federal judiciary. Although the Constitutional Convention had spared no pains to prevent the publication of its proceedings, the feelng was more or less general that the whole movement was a conspiracy against popular government.

"The charge of a conspiracy against the liberties of the people," said Hamilton, "which has been indiscriminately brought against the advocates of the plan [the Constitution], has something in it too wanton and too malignant not to excite the indignation of every man who feels in his own bosom a refutation of the calumny. The perpetual changes which have been rung upon the wealthy, the well-born, and the great, have been such as to inspire the disgust of all sensible men. And the unwarrantable concealments and misrepresentations which have been in various ways practiced to keep the truth from the public eye have been of a nature to demand the reprobation of all honest men."[1]

The evidence now accessible to students of the American Constitution proves that the charges of "concealments and misrepresentations" made with this show of righteous indignation against the opponents of the Constitution might have justly

[1] *The Federalist*, No. 85.

been made against Hamilton himself. But knowing that the views expressed in the Federal Convention were not public property, he could safely give to the press this "refutation of the calumny."

The publication of the debates on the Constitution at that time would have shown that the apprehensions of the people were not entirely without justification. The advocates of the new form of government did not propose to defeat their own plans by declaring their real purpose—by explaining the Constitution to the people as they themselves understood it. For it was not to be supposed that the people would permit the adoption of a form of government the avowed object of which was to limit their power. Therefore the conservatives who framed the Constitution and urged its ratification posed as the friends of democracy. Professing to act in the name of, and as the representatives of the people, they urged them to accept the Constitution as a means of restraining their agents and representatives and thereby making their own will supreme. It was not the aim of these articles, written, as they were, to influence public opinion, to explain the real purpose of the Constitution, but rather to disguise its true character.

In this species of political sophistry Hamilton was a master. It is, to say the least, strange that the misstatement of historical facts, false analogies and juggling of popular catch-words which constitute his defence of the Federal judiciary should have been so often referred to as an example of faultless logic and a complete vindication of the system. Hamilton's interpretation of the Constitution as contained in these articles was merely for popular consumption, and not a frank and unequivocal expression of what he himself really believed. He was an uncompromising opponent of democracy and considered the English government of that day, with its hereditary monarchy and aristocracy, the best form of government ever devised.[1]

He favored therefore as near an approach to the English system as the circumstances of the case would permit. According to the plan which he submitted to the Convention the executive branch of the government was to be placed beyond the reach of public opinion by a method of appointment designed to guard against the choice of a popular favorite and by life tenure. Not only did he wish to make the President independent of the people, but he proposed to give him an absolute veto on all acts of Congress. Moreover, the President was to appoint the governors of the various states, and these, like the royal governors before the Revolution, were to have an absolute veto on the acts of the state legislatures.[2] This would have made the President a monarch in all

[1] Elliot's Debates, Vol I, p. 421.
[2] Ibid., Vol. V, Appendix No. 5.

but name, and though independent of the people, have given him power to thwart legislation which no majority in Congress, however great, could override.

But this did not go far enough in the direction of providing checks on popular legislation to suit Hamilton. The members of the upper house of Congress were, like the President, to be indirectly elected and to hold office for life. And finally over and above Congress was to be placed a Supreme Court whose members, by their mode of appointment and life tenure, were to be independent of the people. This body, which was to be the final interpreter of the Constitution, was designed as an additional safeguard against democratic legislation. The lower house of Congress was the only branch of the government in which any provision was made, under Hamilton's plan, for the representation of public opinion. Through the House of Representatives the people were to have an opportunity to propose legislation, but no power to enact it, or to control the general policy of the government.

The refusal of the Convention to endorse the scheme of government proposed by Hamilton must not be understood as implying lack of sympathy with the political views which it embodied. With his main purpose, that of effectually curbing the power of the majority, nearly all the members of that body were in full accord. They

were, however, shrewd experienced men of affairs
who understood the temper of the people and
knew that their plan of political reorganization
could be carried through only by disguising its
reactionary character and representing it as a
democratic movement. To have submitted the
Constitution in the form in which it was proposed
by Hamilton would have defeated their purpose.
It was too obviously undemocratic, inasmuch as it
provided for a strong centralized government only
one branch of which was to be elected by the people, while the other three were to be placed beyond
the reach of public opinion through indirect election and life tenure. The Constitution as framed
and submitted was more democratic in appearance,
though it really contained all that was essential in
Hamilton's plan. Life tenure for the President
and Senate was discarded, it is true, but indirect
election was expected to ensure their independence. The absolute veto on Federal and state
legislation which Hamilton proposed to give to a
permanent executive was the most serious practical objection to his scheme, since it showed too
clearly the purpose of the Convention to make the
aristocratic element supreme not only in the general government but in the states as well. In form
and appearance the Constitution merely gave the
President a qualified negative on the acts of Congress; but in reality the Convention went much
farther than this and conferred the absolute veto

on federal and state legislation contended for by Hamilton. The power was merely transferred from the President in whose hands he had proposed to place it, and given to the Supreme Court. The end which he had in view was thus attained without arousing the opposition which would have been inevitable had there been anything in the Constitution to indicate that such a power was intended to be conferred.

These facts disclose the true motive for Hamilton's untiring efforts in behalf of the Constitution. He desired its adoption, not because he believed that it would make the will of the people supreme, as his above quoted references to *principal* and *agent* and *master* and *servant* would seem to imply, but for the opposite reason that it would make the government largely independent of public opinion. As a matter of fact, Hamilton had no use whatever for a political system which assumed that the people were a *master* or *principal* and the government merely their *servant* or *agent*. The chief merit of the Constitution from his point of view was not its acceptance, but its repudiation of this principle. Had it been framed on the theory that the will of the people is the supreme law of the land, no one would have been more bitterly opposed to its adoption than Hamilton himself. That he gave it his unqualified support is the best evidence that he did not believe that it would make the will of the people supreme.

No intelligent man who carefully reads Hamilton's argument in defence of the Federal judiciary could be misled as to his real views. His dread of democracy is clearly seen in his desire to exalt the Supreme Court and subordinate Congress, the only branch of the government in which the people were directly represented. His seeming anxiety lest the legislative body should disregard the will of the people was a mere demagogic attempt to conceal his real motive. Had this been what he really feared, the obvious remedy would have been the complete responsibility of Congress to the people. In fact, this was necessarily implied in the doctrine of principal and agent which he pro fessed to accept, but which found no recognition either in the constitution which he himself had suggested, or in the one finally adopted. To this theory of government the system which he defended was in reality diametrically opposed. Under the guise of protecting the people against misrepresentation at the hands of Congress, it effectually limited the power of the people themselves by tying the hands of their responsible agents. It deprived the people of the power to compel the enactment of law by making the consent of the Supreme Court necessary to the enforcement of all legislation, federal and state. This was a substantial compliance with Hamilton's proposal to give an absolute veto to an independent and permanent executive. It was a

matter of but little consequence whether this
power was conferred on a single person, as the
President, or on a body, as the Supreme Court,
provided the manner of appointment and tenure
of those in whose hands it was placed, were such
as to ensure an independent exercise of the power
thus conferred. The result would be the same in
either case: the law-making power would be
placed beyond the reach of popular control.

To allow the legislative body to be "the constitutional judges of their own power," Hamilton
tells us, would be to affirm "that the servant is
above his master." Hence it is necessary, he
argues, to divest Congress of all authority to determine the extent of its own powers. To accomplish this the Supreme Court was made the
constitutional judge of the powers of Congress
and of its own powers as well. Hamilton's argument involves the assumption that, while it is
dangerous to allow a frequently elected and responsible branch of the government to determine
the extent of its own powers, it is at the same time
eminently wise and proper to give, not only this
power, but also the power to determine the
authority of all other branches of government,
to a permanent body whom the people neither elect
nor control. His constant reference to the danger
of legislative oppression was merely a mask for
his hatred of popular government. He was anxious to curb the power of Congress because he

feared that public opinion would too largely influence the proceedings of that body. On the other hand, he saw no danger of executive or judicial tyranny since these branches of the government were expected to be independent of public opinion. Hamilton's purpose was to limit the power of the people by subordinating that part of the government in which they were directly represented and strengthening those parts over which they had no direct control. His defence of the Constitution is thus really an argument against responisble government and a defence of the principles underlying monarchy and aristocracy.

As the English judiciary is really an offshoot from the executive, the power of the court to declare legislation null and void may be regarded as merely a phase of the executive veto. No evidence of this can be found, it is true, in the constitutional history of England during the eighteenth and nineteenth centuries. But if we go back to the period preceding the revolution of 1688, it seems to be clearly established that the English courts claimed, and in a few instances exercised, the power to annul acts of Parliament. As late as 1686, in the case of Godden v. Hales, "the Court of King's Bench actually held that important provisions of the statute of 25 Charles II, cap. 2, were void because conflicting with the King's rightful prerogative."[1]   When we remem-

[1] Brinton Coxe, Judicial Power and Unconstitutional Leg-

ber that the courts were then under the control of the King, it is not surprising that they should have attempted to exercise this power in defence of the royal prerogative. But with the Revolution of 1688, which established the supremacy of Parliament, the last trace of the judicial negative disappeared. From that time on the right of Parliament to be the constitutional judge of its own powers has not been seriously questioned. Even the veto power of the King soon became obsolete, though in theory it for a time survived.

Such was the constitutional status of the English judiciary when the American colonies asserted their independence. The new state constitutions adopted at the outbreak of the war, as has been shown in a previous chapter, represented the more democratic thought of the period and were really revolutionary in character. They abolished the veto power of the governor and failed to abolish the judicial negative only because it did not then exist.[1] This was followed after the Revolution by a conservative reaction which was not, however, a popular movement. It received no general support or sympathy from the masses of the peo-

islation, p. 165. The reader is referred to this work for a discussion of this and other cases.

[1] The constitutions of Massachusetts, Maryland, New Hampshire, North Carolina and Virginia contained provisions expressly declaring that no power of suspending laws, or the execution of laws, should be exercised unless by the legislature, or by authority derived from it. The Vermont constitution of 1786 also contained a similar provision.

ple, but was planned and carried through by those whom we may describe as the ruling class, and who were, for the most part, strongly in sympathy with English political institutions. It was characterized by real, if not avowed, hostility to the new political ideas embodied in the Declaration of Independence and in the Revolutionary state constitutions. Its aim was to reform the state governments by restoring, as far as possible, the checks on democracy which the Revolutionary movement had swept away.

The judiciary was the only branch of the state government in which the principle of life tenure had been retained, and therefore the only one which could be depended on to offer any effectual resistance to public opinion. Evidently, then, the easiest and most practicable method of accomplishing the end which the conservative classes had in view was to enlarge the powers of the judiciary. Accordingly an effort was made at this time in several of the states to revive and develop the judicial veto. A practical argument in favor of this check was doubtless the fact that it required no formal changes in the state constitutions, and, for this reason, was less likely to arouse formidable opposition than any avowed attempt to restore the system of checks.

When the Constitutional Convention met in 1787 the courts in five states were beginning to claim the power to declare acts of the legislature unconstitutional. In a Virginia case as early as 1782 the judges of the court of appeals expressed the opinion "that the court had power to declare any resolution or act of the legislature, or of either branch of it, to be unconstitutional and void."[1] The court, however, did not exercise the power to which it laid claim. It merely declared a resolution of the House of Delegates invalid on the ground that it had been rejected by the Senate. This case is important only as showing that the court was then paving the way for the exercise of the power to annul acts of the legislature.

The case of Trevett v. Weeden, decided by the Superior Court of Judicature of Rhode Island in September, 1786, is said to be the first in which a law was declared null and void on the ground that it was unconstitutional.[2] The court in this case did not expressly say that the law in question was unconstitutional and therefore void, but it refused to recognize its validity. The power which the court exercised to ignore a legislative act was promptly repudiated by the law-making body, and at the expiration of their term of office a few months later, the judges responsible for this decision were replaced by others. In 1786 or 1787 a case was decided in Massachusetts, and

[1] Commonwealth v. Caton, Hopkins and Lamb. Quoted from Coxe, p. 221.
[2] Cooley, Constitutional Limitations, 6th ed., p. 193, n. and Thorpe, A Short Constitutional History of the United States, p. 238.

also one in New Jersey, in which it is claimed that the court declared a legislative act null and void.

The first reported case in which an act of a legislature was held to be contrary to a *written* constitution is that of Bayard v. Singleton, decided by the Superior Court of North Carolina in May, 1787. James Iredell, afterward a member of the North Carolina convention, held to ratify the Constitution, and a judge of the United States Supreme Court, and William R. Davie, one of the framers of the Constitution, were attorneys for the plaintiff, the party in whose interest the law was declared unconstitutional. This decision received much adverse criticism at the time. The judges "were fiercely denounced as usurpers of power. Spaight, afterwards governor, voiced a common notion when he declared that 'the state was subject to the three individuals, who united in their own persons the legislative and judicial power, which no monarch in England enjoys, which would be more despotic than the Roman triumvirate and equally insufferable.' "[1]

Iredell, in a letter to Spaight written August 26, 1787, defended the decision as a means of limiting the power of the majority. "I conceive the remedy of a new election," he says, "to be of very little consequence, because this would only secure the views of a majority. . . ."[2] Iredell expressed

[1] Quoted in Coxe, Judicial Power and Unconstitutional Legislation, p. 252.
[2] *Ibid.*, p. 263.

what was no doubt the real purpose of the judicial veto—the limitation of the power of the majority.

In eight of the thirteen states the doctrine that the judiciary could refuse to enforce laws regularly enacted by the legislative body had not even been asserted by the courts themselves, much less recognized and accepted by the people generally. There is no evidence to warrant the belief that this power was anywhere claimed or exercised in response to a popular demand or that it had at this time become a firmly established or generally recognized feature of any state government.

This being the case, there is no ground for the contention that the power to annul acts of the legislature was necessarily implied in the general grant of judicial authority contained in the Constitution. Moveover, it was not expressly conferred, for the Constitution as submitted and ratified contains no reference to this power.

"There is no provision in the Constitution of the United States . . . which clothes the judiciary with the power to declare an act of the legislature generally null and void on account of its conceived repugnance to the Constitution or on any other account."[1]

It has been claimed that in this respect our general government is even less democratic than the framers of the Constitution intended. This view, however, is not borne out by the facts. The

[1] Burgess, Pol. Sci. and Const. Law, Vol. II, p. 364.

assertion of this far-reaching power by our national judiciary, though not expressly authorized by the Constitution, was nevertheless in harmony with the general spirit and intention of its framers. That the members of the Constitutional Convention declined to confer this power in unequivocal language does not justify the inference that they did not wish and intend that it should be exercised by the courts.

Gouverneur Morris, who claims to have written the Constitution with his own hand, tells us that in framing that part of it relating to the judiciary, "it became necessary to select phrases," which, expressing his own views, "would not alarm others."[1]   There was, it is true, some objection in the Convention to the doctrine that the Supreme Court should have authority to decide upon the constitutionality of Congressional legislation.   Mercer and Dickinson believed that this power should not be exercised by the judiciary.[2] But it was contended on the other hand by Wilson, Luther Martin, Gerry, Mason, and Madison that this power could be exercised without any provision expressly conferring it.[3]

In view of the fact that it was maintained by leading members of the Convention that this power could and should be exercised by the Federal judiciary, it is but reasonable to suppose that

[1] Elliot's Debates, Vol. I, p. 507.
[2] Ibid., Vol. V, p. 429.
[3] Ibid., Vol. V, pp. 151, 344, 345, 346, 347.

a majority of that body wished to confer it; for had this not been the case, the Constitution as submitted would have contained a provision expressly withholding it. But however much the Convention may have desired to give to the judiciary the power to veto legislation, it could not have been done by an express provision of the Constitution. Any such attempt would have disclosed altogether too clearly the undemocratic reactionary character of the proposed government and thus have prevented its adoption. This end was attained indirectly through the general system of checks which the Constitution imposed upon the other branches of the government and upon the people, since it made it possible for the judiciary to assume and exercise this power.

There is nothing to indicate that the people generally appreciated the significance of this feature of the Constitution at the time of its ratification. Outside of the Constitutional Convention the judicial negative appears to have been seldom mentioned. Hamilton, the most courageous and outspoken opponent of popular government, claimed, it is true, that it would be the duty of the Federal courts "to declare all acts contrary to the manifest tenor of the Constitution void."[1] In a few of the state conventions held to ratify the Constitution the power was referred to. Oliver Ellsworth in the Connecticut convention,[2]

[1] *Federalist*, No. 78.
[2] Elliot's Debates, Vol. II, p. 196.

James Wilson in the Pennsylvania convention,[1] and John Marshall in the Virginia convention,[2] expressed the opinion that the Constitution gave the Supreme Court the power to declare acts of Congress null and void.

There is no reason for believing, however, that this was the generally accepted notion at that time. For even Marshall himself a few years later, as attorney in the case of Ware v. Hylton, which involved the validity of an act of the legislature of Virginia, appears to have defended the opposite view before the United States Supreme Court. In that case he said:

"The legislative authority of any country can only be restrained by its own municipal constitution: this is a principle that springs from the very nature of society; and the judicial authority can have no right to question the validity of a law, unless such a jurisdiction is expressly given by the Constitution."[3]   The mere fact that he presented this argument shows that the view which he afterwards held as Chief Justice of the United States Supreme Court was not then generally accepted.   His contention on this occasion that the judiciary can not annul an act of the legislature unless the power be expressly conferred may have been at variance with the opinion which

[1] Elliot's Debates, Vol. II, p. 489.
[2] Ibid., Vol. III, p. 553.
[3] 3 Dallas.

he really held, but it certainly was not opposed to what he regarded as the generally accepted view; otherwise, his argument would have been based on an admittedly false theory of judicial powers. The conclusion is irresistible that at this time the right of the judiciary to declare a legislative act null and void was not generally recognized. The framers of the Constitution clearly understood that this power was not implied in the sense that it was then a recognized function of the judiciary, or one necessarily contained in the Constitution as they interpreted it to the people to secure its adoption. It was by controlling the Executive and the Senate, and through these the appointment of Supreme judges, that they expected to incorporate this power in the Constitution and make it a permanent feature of our political system.[1]

This purpose is evident in the appointments to the Supreme bench made during the twelve years of Federalist rule that followed the adoption of the Constitution. Of the thirteen chief and associate Justices appointed during this period, five had been members of the Constitutional Convention.[2] Eleven had been members of the various

---

[1] 'You have made a good Constitution,' said a friend to Gouverneur Morris after the adjournment of the Convention. 'That,' replied Morris, 'depends on how it is construed.' Gordy, Political Parties in the United States, Vol. I, p. 114. This was clearly understood by the framers of the Constitution and by all the leading Federalists.

[2] Rutledge, Wilson, Blair, Patterson, and Ellsworth.

state conventions held to ratify the Constitution.[1]
Three, as shown by the records of the federal and
state conventions, had unequivocally expressed
themselves in favor of the exercise of this power
by the Supreme Court,[2] while another, James
Iredell, had taken an active part in securing the
first reported decision in which an act of a state
legislature was declared null and void by a court
on the ground that it was contrary to a written
constitution.[3] Only one in this entire list had not
taken part directly in framing or adopting the
Constitution by serving as a delegate to the federal, or a state convention, or both.[4] All had been
ardent supporters of the Constitution and were in
full sympathy with its main purpose.

It is true that Washington in the winter of
1795-6 offered the Chief Justiceship of the United
States Supreme Court to Patrick Henry, who had
been the ablest and most conspicuous opponent of
the Constitution in the Virginia convention.
Henry had, however, as Presidential elector voted
for Washington for President in 1789 and had in
the meantime become reconciled to the Constitution. Moreover, while he had been opposed to
many features of the Constitution, he was from
the first in full sympathy with the judicial veto.

---

[1] Jay, Rutledge, Wilson, Blair, Iredell, Johnson, Chase,
Ellsworth, Cushing, Washington, and Marshall.

[2] Wilson, Ellsworth, and Marshall.

[3] Supra, p. 89.

[4] Alfred Moore.

He thought the Constitution was defective in that it contained no assurance that such a power would be exercised by the courts. In his argument against the ratification of the Constitution in the Virginia convention he said:

"The honorable gentleman did our judiciary honor in saying that they had firmness to counteract the legislature in some cases. Yes, sir, our judges opposed the acts of the legislature. We have this landmark to guide us. They had fortitude to declare that they were the judiciary, and would oppose unconstitutional acts. Are you sure that your Federal judiciary will act thus? Is that judiciary as well constructed, and as independent of the other branches, as our state judiciary? Where are your landmarks in this government? I will be bold to say that you can not find any in it. I take it as the highest encomium on this country, that the acts of the legislature, if unconstitutional, are liable to be opposed by the judiciary."[1]

The fact that only those who were in sympathy with the Constitution were recognized in these appointments becomes the more significant when we remember that several of the leading states ratified it by very slender majorities. In New York, Massachusetts, and Virginia the supporters of the Constitution barely carried the day; yet they alone were recognized in the five appoint-

[1] Elliot's Debates, Vol. III, pp. 324-325.

ments to the Supreme bench from these states made during the period above mentioned. The opponents of the Constitution represented, moreover, not only in these states, but in the country at large, a majority of the people. Nevertheless, true to the purpose of those who founded our Federal government, the popular majority was entirely ignored and the Supreme Court so constituted as to make it represent the minority. Through these appointments the Federalists secured an interpretation of the Constitution in harmony with their political theories and thereby established the supremacy of the judiciary in our scheme of government. The subsequent success of the Supreme Court in asserting and enforcing its right to annul acts of Congress completed the establishment in this country of a form of government which Professor Burgess correctly describes as an "aristocracy of the robe."[1]

The full significance of this annulling power is not generally understood. The Supreme Court claims the right to exercise it only as the guardian of the Constitution. It must be observed, however, that while professing to be controlled by the Constitution, the Supreme Court does, as a matter of fact, control it, since the exclusive right to interpret necessarily involves the power to change its substance. This virtually gives to the aristocratic branch of our government the power to

[1] Political Science and Constitutional Law, Vol. II, p. 365.

amend the Constitution, though this power is, as we have seen, practically denied to the people.

We have become so accustomed to the exercise of this power by the courts that we are in the habit of regarding it as a natural and necessary function of the judiciary. That this is an erroneous view of the matter is shown by the fact that this power "is scarcely dreamed of anywhere else."[1] In other countries the power is unknown whether the Constitution be unwritten as in England or written as in France, Germany, and Switzerland. Nor does it make any difference whether the government be national in character as in England and France, or federal as in Germany, Switzerland, and Australia. In no other important country are the courts allowed to veto the acts of the legislative body. The exercise of this power can be justified here only on the ground that it is indispensable as a means of preserving and perpetuating the undemocratic character of the Constitution.

"This power [the Supreme Court] has the last word in the numberless questions which come under its jurisdiction. The sovereign people after a time conquers the other powers, but this Supreme Court almost always remains beyond its reach. For more than twenty or even thirty years, twice the *grande mortalis aevi spatium*, it

---

[1] Burgess, Political Science and Constitutional Law, Vol. II, p. 365.

may misuse its authority with impunity, may practically invalidate a law voted by all the other powers, or a policy unanimously accepted by public opinion. It may nullify a regular diplomatic treaty[1] . . . by refusing to enforce it by judicial sanction, or may lay hands on matters belonging to the sovereignty of the states and federalize them without one's being able to make any effective opposition, for this Court itself determines its own jurisdiction as against the state tribunals. It is one of Blackstone's maxims that in every constitution a power exists which controls without being controlled, and whose decisions are supreme. This power is represented in the United States by a small oligarchy of nine irremovable judges. I do not know of any more striking political paradox than this supremacy of a non-elected power in a democracy reputed to be of the extreme type. It is a power which is only renewed from generation to generation in the midst of a peculiarly unstable and constantly changing state of things —a power which in strictness could, by virtue of an authority now out of date, perpetuate the prejudices of a past age, and actually defy the changed spirit of the nation even in political matters."[2]

It is a fundamental principle of free government that all legislative power should be under

[1] Infra, pp. 119-122.

[2] Boutmy, Studies in Constitutional Law, pp. 117-118 (Eng. Trans.).

the direct control of the people. To make this control effective all laws must be enacted by the people themselves, or they must at least have what practically amounts to the power of appointing and removing their representatives. Democracy implies not merely the right of the people to defeat such laws as they do not want, but the power to compel such legislation as they need. The former power they possess in any country in which they control one coördinate branch of the legislature, even though the government be a monarchy or aristocracy. This negative power of defeating adverse legislation is merely the first step in the evolution of free government, and is possessed by the people in all countries which have made much constitutional progress. There is a vast difference, however, between a system under which the people constitute a mere check upon the government and one which gives them an active control over legislation. It is the difference between a limited monarchy or aristocracy on the one hand and a government by the people themselves on the other.[1]

If this test be applied to the government of the United States we see that it lacks the essential feature of a democracy, inasmuch as laws can not

[1] Referring to the power of the Supreme Court in our scheme of government, Jefferson said "It is a misnomer to call a government republican, in which a branch of the supreme power is independent of the nation." Works, Vol. X, p. 199.

be enacted without the consent of a body over which the people have practically no control. In one respect at least the American system is even less democratic than was the English government of the eighteenth century. The House of Commons was a coördinate branch of the legislature and as such had a recognized right to interpret the Constitution. No political program, no theory of state functions, could receive legislative sanction without its approval. The House of Commons could enforce its interpretation of the Constitution negatively since it had an absolute veto on all legislation. On the other hand its own views and policies could become law only in so far as they were acquiesced in by the other branches of the law-making authority. Under this system the accepted interpretation of the Constitution was a compromise, one to which each branch of the legislature assented. Each of these coördinate branches of the government was equally the guardian and protector of the Constitution, since it had the right to interpret, and the power to enforce its interpretation, of the legislative authority of the other branches by an absolute veto on their interpretation of their own powers.

This authority to act as final interpreter of the Constitution which under the English system was distributed among King, Lords, and Commons, was under the American scheme of government taken out of the hands of Congress and vested in the judiciary alone. There are certain matters of minor importance, however, concerning which the interpretation placed upon the Constitution by other branches of the government is final. But in interpreting the Constitution for the purpose of legislating, the final authority is in the hands of the Federal Supreme Court. It is the exclusive possession of this most important prerogative of a sovereign legislative body which makes our Supreme Court the most august and powerful tribunal in the world. Through the sole right to exercise this power our Federal judiciary has become in reality the controlling branch of our government. For while it has an absolute veto on the acts of Congress, its own exercise of the highest of all legislative authority—that of interpreting the Constitution and the laws of the land —is unlimited and uncontrolled. It is not surprising, then, that the Constitution as it exists to-day is largely the work of the Supreme Court. It has been molded and developed by, and largely owes its spirit and character to the interpretation which that body has placed upon it.

Our Supreme Court thus has what virtually amounts to the power to enact as well as the power to annul. Congress can legislate only with the consent of the Federal judiciary; but the latter, through its control over the interpretation of the Constitution may in effect legislate without the consent of the other branches of the government, and even in opposition to them. Under the guise of an independent judiciary we have in reality an independent legislature, or rather an independent legislative and judicial body combined. This union of sovereign legislative authority and ordinary judicial functions in the same independent body is a significant and dangerous innovation in government. It has not only deprived the people of the power to make the interpretation of the Constitution and the trend of legislation conform to the public sentiment of the times; it has even taken from them all effectual power to prevent changes which they do not want, but which the judiciary in the exercise of its exclusive right to act as the guardian and interpreter of the Constitution may see fit to make. Under our system, then, the people do not have even the negative power of absolute veto which they possess wherever they control a coördinate branch of the legislature.

In so far as the exercise of legislative power is controlled by the Supreme Court our government is essentially aristocratic in character. It represents the aristocratic principle, however, in its least obtrusive form. But while avoiding the appearance, it provides the substance of aristocratic control.

It is easy to see in the exaltation of the Federal judiciary a survival of the old mediaeval doctrine that the king can do no wrong. In fact, much the same attitude of mind which made monarchy possible may be seen in this country in our attitude toward the Supreme Court. As long as the people reverenced the king his irresponsible power rested on a secure foundation. To destroy the popular belief in his superior wisdom and virtue was to destroy the basis of his authority. Hence all criticism of the king or his policy was regarded as an attack on the system itself and treated accordingly as a serious political crime.

The old view was well expressed by James I of England in a speech made in the Star Chamber on June 20, 1601, in which he said:

"That which concerns the mystery of the King's power is not lawful to be disputed; for that is to wade into the weakness of princes, and to take away the mystical reverence that belongs unto them that sit on the throne of God."[1]

We see this same fact illustrated also in the history of the church, for absolutism was not confined in the Middle Ages to the state alone. As the King was the recognized guardian of the established political order and its final interpreter, so the ecclesiastical hierarchy claimed the right to guard the faith and expound the creed of the people. Criticism and dissent, political and religious, were rigorously repressed. The people were required to accept the political and religious

[1] Lee, Source Book of English History, p. 336.

system imposed on them from above. Implicit faith in the superior wisdom of their temporal and spiritual rulers was made the greatest of all virtues. But with the growth of an intelligent skepticism throughout the western world, the power of king and priest has been largely overthrown.

Yet even in this country something akin to the old system of political control still survives in the ascendency of our Federal judiciary. The exclusive right claimed by this branch of the government to guard and interpret the Constitution is the same prerogative originally claimed by the king. The judiciary, too, is the branch of our government farthest removed from the influence of public opinion and consequently the one in which the monarchical principle most largely survives.

The courts not only claim to be the final arbiters of all constitutional questions, but have gone much farther than this and asserted their right to annul legislative acts not in conflict with any constitutional provision. Story says: "Whether, indeed, independently of the Constitution of the United States, the nature of republican and free government does not necessarily impose some restraints upon the legislative power has been much discussed. It seems to be the general opinion, fortified by a strong current of judicial opinion, that, since the American Revolution, no state government can be presumed to possess the transcendental sovereignty to take away vested rights of property."[1]

The judiciary has thus claimed not only the power to act as the final interpreter of the Constitution, but also the right, independently of the Constitution, to interpret the political system under which we live, and make all legislative acts conform to its interpretation of that system. According to this doctrine the courts are the final judges of what constitutes republican government and need not base their power to annul a legislative act on anything contained in the Constitution itself. If we accept this view of the matter, legislation must conform not only to the Constitution as interpreted by the judiciary, but to the political and ethical views of the latter as well. The President and Congress derive their authority from the Constitution, but the judiciary claims, as we have seen, a control over legislation not conferred by the Constitution itself. Yet, while laying claim to powers that would make it supreme, the judicial branch of our Federal government has, as a rule, been careful to avoid any open collision, or struggle for supremacy, with the other branches of the government. It has retained the sympathy and approval of the conservative classes by carefully guarding the rights of prop-

[1] Commentaries on the Constitution of the United States, sec. 1399; cf. Infra pp. 321-325.

106

erty and, by declining to interfere with the political discretion of Congress or the President, it has largely escaped the hostile criticism which any open and avowed attempt to thwart the plans of the dominant party would surely evoke. But in thus limiting its own authority, the Supreme Court has attempted to make a distinction between judicial and political powers which does not appear to have any very substantial basis. The essential marks of a judicial power, Judge Cooley tells us, are "that it can be exercised only in a litigated case; that its direct force is spent in determining the rights of the parties to that case; and that unless and until a case has arisen for judicial determination, it can not be invoked at all."[1]

"The power given to the Supreme Court," he says, "to construe the Constitution, to enforce its provisions, to preserve its limitations, and guard its prohibitions, is not *political* power, but is judicial power alone because it is power exercisable by that court only in the discharge of the judicial function of hearing and deciding causes in their nature cognizable by courts of law and equity."[2]

In the first place it is to be observed that judicial power as thus defined is practically co-extensive with that of the legislature, since scarcely an exercise of legislative authority could be mentioned which would not affect the rights of per-

[1] Constitutional History as Seen in American Law, p. 80.
[2] *Ibid.*, p. 258.

sons or of property and which could not, therefore, be made the subject of a judicial controversy.

In the second place, it must be remembered that the Federal judiciary in assuming the exclusive right to interpret the Constitution has taken into its keeping a power which, as we have seen, was not judicial in character when the Constitution was adopted, and is not even now considered judicial in any other important country. In declaring a legislative act null and void it is exercising a power which every sovereign law-making body possesses, the power to defeat any proposed legislation by withholding its assent. The mere fact that our Supreme Judges and our legal writers generally have with practical unanimity called it a judicial power does not make it such. That it is in reality a legislative and not a judicial power is amply confirmed by the uniform and time-honored practice of all other nations, even including England, whose institutions until a century and a quarter ago were our own.

There is, however, no difficulty in understanding why those who framed the Constitution and controlled its interpretation exhausted the arsenal of logic in trying to prove that it was a judicial power. This was merely a part of their plan to make the Supreme Court practically a branch of the Federal legislature and thereby secure an effective check on public opinion. As the power could not be expressly given without disclosing too clearly the purpose of the Convention, it was necessary that it should be implied. And it could be held to be implied only by showing that it was a natural, usual and, under the circumstances, proper power for the judiciary to exercise. Unless it could be established, then, that it was essentially a judicial function and not a political or legislative power, its assumption by the Supreme Court could not be defended on any constitutional grounds. This explains the persistent and untiring efforts to convince the American people that the power to set aside an act of Congress is purely judicial—efforts which, though supported by the weight of American authority, are far from convincing.

The Supreme Court has, it is true, time and again expressly disclaimed all right to exercise legislative or political power; yet under the pretext that the authority to annul legislation is purely judicial, it has made use of a power that necessarily involves the exercise of political discretion. The statement, then, that it is the settled policy of this body not to interfere with the political powers of the other departments can not be taken literally, since under the accepted interpretation of the Constitution it has the power to, and as a matter of fact does interfere, whenever it declares an act of Congress null and void.

It would be a mistake, then, to suppose that the Federal judiciary has suffered any loss of influence through its voluntary relinquishment of the veto power in the case of political questions. This self-imposed restriction on its authority merely affords it a convenient means of placing beyond its jurisidiction measures which it may neither wish to approve nor condemn. And since the court must decide what are and what are not political questions, it may enlarge or narrow the scope and meaning of the word *political* to suit its purposes. As a matter of fact, then, the power which it appears to have voluntarily surrendered, it still largely retains.

Upon the whole, the Supreme Court has been remarkably fortunate in escaping hostile criticism. Very rarely have its decisions and policy been attacked by any organized party. In the platform of the Republican party of 1860 the strong pro-slavery attitude of the court was, it is true, severely denounced. But from that time until 1896 no party dared to raise its voice in criticism of the Federal judiciary. Both the Democratic and the Populist platforms of the latter date, however, condemned the Income Tax decision and government by injunction. The Democratic platform also hinted at the possible reorganization of the Supreme Court—the means employed by the Republican party to secure a reversal of the Legal Tender decision of 1869.

This comparative freedom from criticism which the Supreme Court has enjoyed until recent years does not indicate that its decisions have always been such as to command the respect and approval of all classes. It has from the beginning had the full confidence of the wealthy and conservative, who have seen in it the means of protecting vested interests against the assaults of democracy. That the Supreme Court has largely justified their expectations is shown by the character of its decisions.

During the first one hundred years of its history two hundred and one cases were decided in which an act of Congress, a provision of a state constitution or a state statute, was held to be repugnant to the Constitution or the laws of the United States, in whole or in part. Twenty of these involved the constitutionality of an act of Congress. One hundred and eighty-one related to the Constitution or the statute of a state. In fifty-seven instances the law in question was annulled by the Supreme Court on the ground that it impaired the obligation of contracts. In many other cases the judicial veto was interposed to prevent what the court considered an unconstitutional exercise of the power to regulate or tax the business or property of corporations.[1]

These decisions have been almost uniformly advantageous to the capital-owning class in preserving property rights and corporate privileges

[1] For a list of these cases see United States Supreme Court Reports, Vol. 131. Appendix CCXXXV. Banks and Brothers Edition.

which the unhindered progress of democracy would have abridged or abolished. But we need not confine our attention to these comparatively few instances in which laws have actually been declared null and void. There is a much more numerous and more important class of cases in which the Supreme Court, while not claiming to exercise this power, has virtually annulled laws by giving them an interpretation which has defeated the purpose for which they were enacted. The decisions affecting the powers of the Inter-State Commerce Commission may be cited as an illustration. This body, created by Congress for the purpose of regulating the railway traffic of the country, has, as Mr. Justice Harlan observes,[1] "been shorn by judicial interpretation, of authority to do anything of an effective character." Both the general and the state governments in their efforts to grapple with this problem have encountered the restraining arm of the Federal judiciary which has enlarged its jurisdiction until nearly every important case involving corporate interests may be brought before the Federal court.

It is not, however, in the laws which have been annulled or modified by interpretation that we find the chief protection afforded to capital, but rather in the laws which have not been enacted. The mere existence of this power and the cer-

[1] Dissenting opinion Inter-State Commerce Commission, v. Alabama Midland Railway Company, 168 United States, 144.

tainty that it would be used in defence of the existing social order has well-nigh prevented all attacks on vested rights by making their failure a foregone conclusion.

It is but natural that the wealthy and influential classes who have been the chief beneficiaries of this system should have used every means at their command to exalt the Supreme Court and thereby secure general acquiescence in its assumption and exercise of legislative authority. To the influence of these classes in our political, business, and social life must be attributed in large measure that widespread and profound respect for the judicial branch of our government which has thus far almost completely shielded it from public criticism.

There are many indications, however, that popular faith in the infallibility of the Supreme Court has been much shaken in recent years. This is not surprising when we consider the wavering policy of that body in some of the important cases that have come before it. Take, for example, the *Legal Tender* decisions. The court at first declared the legal tender acts unconstitutional by a majority of five to three. Then one of the justices who voted with the majority having resigned and Congress having created an additional judgeship, Justices Strong and Bradley were appointed to fill these vacancies. The former, as a member of the Supreme Bench of the State of Pennsylvania, had rendered a decision upholding the constitutionality of these acts, and the latter was said to hold the same opinion. At any rate the first decision was reversed by a majority of five to four. The point at issue in these two decisions was whether Congress had authority to enact measures of this kind in time of war. The matter coming up again, the Supreme Court decided, and this time by a majority of eight to one, that Congress had this power, not only during war, but in times of peace as well.[1]

Reference should also be made in this connection to the Income Tax decisions of 1895. The first of these was a tie, four to four, Justice Jackson being absent. Six weeks later the second decision was read declaring the Income Tax unconstitutional by a vote of five to four, Justice Shiras, who had voted on the first hearing to uphold the Income Tax, now voting against it. This change in the attitude of a single member of the court converted what would have been a majority for, into a majority against the measure, overruled a line of decisions in which the tax had been sustained and thereby effectually deprived Congress of the power to impose a Federal Income Tax until such time as the court may change its mind. Even more significant are the recent Insular cases in which the division of opinion and

[1] For a discussion of these cases see "The Legal Tender Decisions" by E. J. James, Publications of the American Economic Association, Vol. III.

diversity of grounds for the conclusions reached are, to say the least, surprising. 12

One may well ask, after viewing these decisions, if constitutional interpretation as practiced by the Supreme Court is really a science in the pursuit of which the individual temperament, personal views and political sympathies of the Justices do not influence the result. Have we gained enough under this system in the continuity and consistency of our legislative policy and its freedom from class or political bias to compensate us for the loss of popular control? That these questions are likely to receive serious consideration in the near future we can scarcely doubt, when we reflect that the Supreme Court has, by the character of its own decisions, effectually exploded the doctrine of judicial infallibility, which constitutes the only basis upon which its monopoly of constitutional interpretation can be defended.

The evident lack of sympathy with proposed reforms which has, upon the whole, characterized the proceedings of the Federal courts is rather strikingly illustrated in the address of Judge Taft on "Recent Criticisms of the Federal Judiciary." He makes use of the following language: "While socialism, as such, has not obtained much of a foothold in this country, . . . schemes which are necessarily socialistic in their nature are accepted planks in the platform of a large political party.

The underlying principle of such schemes is that it is the duty of the government to equalize the inequalities which the rights of free contract and private property have brought about, and by enormous outlay derived as far as possible from the rich to afford occupation and sustenance to the poor. However disguised such plans of social and governmental reform are, they find their support in the willingness of their advocates to transfer without any compensation from one who has acquired a large part of his acquisition to those who have been less prudent, energetic, and fortunate. This, of course, involves confiscation and the destruction of the principle of private property."[1] This emphatic condemnation of proposed reforms which had the full sympathy and approval of many thoughtful and conscientious people furnishes the show of justification at least for the very criticisms which it was intended to silence.

With the progress of democracy it must become more and more evident that a system which places this far-reaching power in the hands of a body not amenable to popular control, is a constant menace to liberty. It may not only be made to serve the purpose of defeating reform, but may even accomplish the overthrow of popular rights which the Constitution expressly guarantees. In proof of this statement we need but refer to the

[1] Report of the Am. Bar Association, 1895, p. 246.

recent history of our Federal judiciary. The Sixth Amendment to the Constitution guarantees the right of trial by jury in all criminal prosecutions; but it is a matter of common knowledge that this time-honored safeguard against the tyranny and oppression of ruling classes has been overthrown by the Federal courts. With the ascendency of corporate wealth and influence, government by injunction has become an important feature of our system. The use made of the injunction in recent years in the conflicts between labor and capital has placed a large and important class of crimes beyond the pale of this constitutional provision. Moreover, this particular class of crimes is the one where denial of the right of trial by jury is most likely to result in oppression. Under this mode of procedure the court has virtually assumed the power to enact criminal legislation, and may punish as crimes acts which neither law nor public opinion condemns. It ensures conviction in many cases where the constitutional right of trial by jury would mean acquittal. It places a powerful weapon in the hands of organized wealth which it is not slow to use.[1]

This so-called *government by injunction* is

[1] For a discussion of this recent use of the injunction by our Federal Courts see Annual Address of the President of the Georgia Bar Association, John W. Akin, on "Aggressions of the Federal Courts," 1898; W. H. Dunbar, "Government by Injunction," Economic Studies, Vol. III; Stimson, Handbook of Am. Labor Laws.

merely an outgrowth of the arbitrary power of judges to inflict punishment in cases of contempt. In this respect, as well as in the power to veto legislation, the authority of our courts may be regarded as a survival from monarchy. The right of judges to punish in a summary manner those whom they may hold to be in contempt of their authority has been defended by legal writers generally on the ground that it is the only way in which the necessary respect for judicial authority can be maintained. It is difficult, however, to see why this argument would not apply with equal force to the executive and legislative branches of the government; for there must be some means of enforcing obedience to every lawful authority, legislative, executive, or judicial. The progress toward responsible government has long since deprived the executive of the power to inflict arbitrary punishment, and the legislature, though still retaining in a limited degree the power to imprison for contempt of its authority, seldom uses and almost never abuses it. The question is not whether contempt of authority should be punished, but whether the officer whose authority has been disregarded should also act as judge and jury, should ascertain the guilt and fix the punishment of those whom he as complaining witness has accused of contempt of his authority. This procedure is utterly at variance with the idea of political responsibility, and survives only because the judicial branch of our government has thus far effectually resisted the inroads of democracy. That the exercise of this arbitrary and irresponsible power is necessary in a democratic community, to ensure proper respect for the courts, seems highly improbable. In fact, no course could be suggested which would be more likely in the end to bring them into disrepute.[1]

It is interesting to observe that while the Supreme Court of the United States has not hesitated to veto an act of Congress, "no treaty, or legislation based on, or enacted to carry out, any treaty stipulations has ever been declared void or unconstitutional by any court of competent jurisdiction; notwithstanding the fact that in many cases the matters affected, both as to the treaty and the legislation, are apparently beyond the domain of Congressional legislation, and in some instances of Federal jurisdiction."[2]

Why has the Federal Supreme Court freely exercised the power to annul acts of Congress and

---

[1] "We should like to see the law so changed that any man arrested for contempt of court, for an act not performed in the presence of the court and during judicial proceedings, should have a right to demand trial by jury before another and an impartial tribunal. It is not safe, and therefore it is not right, to leave the liberties of the citizens of the United States at the hazard involved in conferring such autocratic power upon judges of varied mental and moral caliber as are conferred by the equity powers which our courts have inherited through English precedents." Editorial in the *Outlook*, Vol. LXXIV, p. 871.

[2] C. H. Butler, Treaty-Making Power of the United States, Vol. II, p. 347.

at the same time refrained from exercising a like control over treaties? The Constitution makes no distinction between laws and treaties in this respect. It provides that "the judicial power shall extend to all cases, in law and equity, arising under this Constitution, the laws of the United States, and the treaties made, or which shall be made, under their authority."[1] If this provision is to be interpreted as conferring on the Federal courts the power to declare acts of Congress null and void, it also confers the same power in relation to treaties. Moreover, the Supreme Court has claimed, and has been conceded, the right to act as the guardian of the Constitution. The authority thus assumed by the Federal judiciary can be justified, if at all, only on the theory that the Constitution limits all governmental powers, and that it is the duty of the Supreme Court to enforce the limitations thus imposed by declaring null and void any unconstitutional exercise of governmental authority.

Not only in the Constitution itself was no distinction made between laws and treaties in relation to the power of the judiciary, but the same is true of the Judiciary Act of September 24, 1789, which provided that where the highest court in a state in which a decision in the suit could be had decides against the validity of "a treaty or statute of, or an authority exercised under, the United

[1] Art. III, sec. 2.

States," such judgment or decree "may be re-examined, and reversed or affirmed in the Supreme Court [of the United States] on a writ of error." The right of the Federal Supreme Court to declare both laws and treaties null and void was thus clearly and unequivocally recognized in this act. The object here, however, was not to establish judicial control over treaties, but to deprive the state courts of all authority over them.

The failure of the Supreme Court to exercise the right to annul treaties is to be explained in part by the fact that the judicial veto was intended primarily as a check on democracy. From the point of view of the conservatives who framed the Constitution it was a device for protecting the classes which they represented against democratic "excesses" in both the state and Federal government. It was expected that this tendency would be manifested mainly in the legislation of the various states and possibly in some slight degree in Congressional legislation, since the President and Senate would occasionally find it expedient to yield too largely to the demands of the directly elected House. But in the case of treaties made by the President and Senate, both safely removed, as they thought, beyond the reach of popular influence, there was no obvious need of a conservative check. In developing the policy of the Federal courts in pursuance of the purpose of those who framed the Constitution, it was perfectly natural that the judicial veto should not have been used to limit the treaty-making power.

But even if the Federal courts had felt inclined to extend their authority in this direction, the Constitution did not as in the case of congress-sional legislation confer upon them the means of self-protection. In declaring null and void an act of Congress which did not have the support of at least two-thirds of the Senate, the Supreme Court is exercising a power which, if not expressly con-ferred upon it by the Constitution, it can at any rate exercise with impunity, since the majority in the Senate which it thus overrides is not large enough to convict in case of impeachment. All treaties must have the approval of two-thirds of the Senate; and since the majority in this body required to ratify a treaty is the same as that re-quired to convict in impeachment proceedings, it is readily seen that the Senate has the constitu-tional power to prevent judicial annulment of treaties. Two-thirds of the Senate could not overcome judicial opposition, however, unless supported by at least a majority in the House of Representatives. But inasmuch as the Supreme Court is pre-eminently the representative of con-servatism and vested interests, it is likely to dis-approve of the policy of the Senate only when that body yields to the demands of the people. In all such cases the House would naturally support the Senate as against the Supreme Court. It is not surprising, then, that the Federal courts have not attempted to limit the treaty-making power.

Before leaving the subject of the Federal courts one feature of the judicial negative deserves further notice. The fact that it is not exercised until a case involving the law in question is brought before the court in the ordinary course of litigation is often referred to by constitutional writers as one of its chief merits. And yet until a competent court has actually declared a legislative act null and void, it is for all practical purposes the law of the land and must be recognized as such. It may vitally affect industry and commerce and require an elaborate readjustment of business relations. It may even be years after such an act is passed before a decision is obtained from the court of last resort. And if the decision annuls the law, it does so not from the time that the judgment of the court is rendered, but from the time the act in question was originally passed. This retroactive character of the judicial veto is strongly suggestive of the *ex post facto* legislation which the Constitution expressly forbids. By thus invalidating the law from the beginning it may leave a vast body of business contracts without legal protection or support. As a consequence, it is impossible for any one, be he ever so well informed, to know just what legislative acts are valid and what are not. The amount of uncertainty which this introduces into business relations is more easily imagined than described.

America can claim the rather questionable distinction of being the only important country in which we find this uncertainty as to the law, since it is the only one in which the courts have a negative on the acts of the legislature. That we have ourselves realized the disadvantages of the system is shown by the changes made in the constitutions of several states with a view of diminishing the frequency of the judicial veto. These provisions make it the duty of the judges of the supreme court of the state to give their opinion upon questions of law when required by the governor or other branch of the law-making authority.[1]

In so far as constitutional provisions of this sort have been intended to prevent the evils resulting from a deferred exercise of the judicial veto, they have largely failed to accomplish their purpose. This has been due to the attitude of the courts, which have held that an opinion thus given in compliance with a constitutional requirement is not binding upon them when the question is raised again in the ordinary way in the trial of a case.

[1] The constitutions of Maine (since 1820), Rhode Island (since 1842), Florida (since 1875), and Missouri (constitution of 1865, but omitted in constitution of 1875 and since).

A provision of this kind is also found in the Massachusetts constitution of 1780, from which it was copied in the New Hampshire constitution of 1784. Its purpose in these two constitutions, however, was not to guard against the subsequent exercise of the judicial veto, since the latter was then unknown, but to make the judges of the Supreme Court an advisory body to the legislature.

CHAPTER VI

THE CHECKS AND BALANCES OF THE CONSTITUTION

Two features of this system, the difficulty of amendment and the extraordinary powers of the judiciary have been discussed at some length. Both, as we have seen, were designed to limit the power of the popular majority. This purpose is no less evident when we view the Constitution as a whole.

The members of the Federal Convention had little sympathy with the democratic trend of the Revolutionary movement. It was rapidly carrying the country, they thought, to anarchy and ruin. To guard against this impending evil was the purpose of the Constitution which they framed. It was their aim to eliminate what they conceived to be the new and false and bring the government back to old and established principles which the Revolutionary movement had for the time being discredited. They believed in the theory of checks and balances in so far as the system implied the limitation of the right of popular control, and made the Constitution to this extent as complete an embodiment of the theory as the circumstances of the time permitted.

In any evolutionary classification of governments the American system occupies an intermediate position between the old type of absolute monarchy on the one hand and thoroughgoing democracy on the other. Following in a general way the course of political development in England, we may say that there was an early stage in the growth of the state when the power of the king was predominant. Neither the nobility nor the common people exercised any effective control over him. He was what we may call an absolute monarch. His power was unlimited in the sense that there were no recognized checks imposed upon it. He was irresponsible, since no one could call him to account for what he did.

The upper classes, however, were anxious to share with the king the control of the state. Their efforts were directed first toward limiting his power by making their own consent necessary before he could enact any law, carry out any policy, or do any thing of a positive nature. But even after they had been admitted to this share in the government the negative power of the king remained unlimited. The veto power acquired by the upper classes might prevent him from enacting a particular law, or enforcing a given policy, but no one had a veto on his inaction. He might be unable to do what the classes having a voice in the management of the government forbade, but he could decline to do what they wished.

The appearance of a House of Commons did not change essentially the character of the scheme, nor would it have done so, had this body been truly representative of the people as a whole. It placed an additional check on both King and Lords by giving to the representative body the power to negative their positive acts. Both the King and the Lords retained, however, their negative authority unimpaired and could use it for the purpose of defeating any measure which the Commons desired. This is what we may call the check and balance stage of political development. Here all positive authority is limited, since its exercise may be prevented by the negative power lodged for this purpose in the other branches of the government. This negative power itself, however, is absolute and unlimited. The government is in no true sense responsible to the people, or any part of them, since they have no positive control over it.

This complex system of restrictions which is the outgrowth and expression of a class struggle for the control of the government must necessarily disappear when the supremacy of the people is finally established. This brings us to the next and for our present purpose, at least, the last stage of political evolution.

Here the authority of the people is undisputed.

Their will is law. The entire system of checks has been swept away. No irresponsible and insignificant minority is longer clothed with power to prevent reform. The authority of the government is limited only by its direct and complete responsibility to the people.

Corresponding to these three stages of political evolution we have three general types of government:

1. Unlimited and irresponsible.
2. Positively limited, negatively unlimited and irresponsible.
3. Unlimited and responsible.

As shown in a previous chapter, the Revolutionary movement largely destroyed the system of checks. It abolished the veto power, centralized authority and made the government in a measure responsible to the electorate. The Constitution, however, restored the old order in a modified form. In this sense it was reactionary and retrogressive. It went back to the old doctrine of the separation of powers, ostensibly to limit the authority of the government and thereby make it responsible to the people as Hamilton argued in *The Federalist*. That this could not have been the real object is evident to any one who has carefully studied the situation. The unthinking reader may accept Hamilton's contention that the system of checks and balances was incorporated in the Constitution to make the government the servant and agent of the people; but the careful student of history can not be so easily misled. He knows that the whole system was built up originally as a means of limiting monarchical and aristocratic power; that it was not designed to make government in any true sense responsible, but to abridge its powers because it was irresponsible. The very existence of the system implies the equal recognition in the Constitution of antagonistic elements. As it could not possibly exist where monarchy or aristocracy was the only recognized source of authority in the state, so it is likewise impossible where all power is in the people. It is to be observed, then, that what originally commended the system to the people was the fact that it limited the positive power of the king and aristocracy, while the framers of the Constitution adopted it with a view to limiting the power of the people themselves.

There is no essential difference between the viewpoint of the framers of the American Constitution and that of their English contemporaries. Lecky says: "It is curious to observe how closely the aims and standard of the men who framed the memorable Constitution of 1787 and 1788 corresponded with those of the English statesmen of the eighteenth century. It is true that the framework adopted was very different. . . . The United States did not contain the materials for founding a constitutional monarchy or a powerful aristocracy. . . . It was necessary to adopt other means, but the ends that were aimed at were much the same. To divide and restrict power; to secure property; to check the appetite for organic change; to guard individual liberty against the tyranny of the multitude. . . ."[1]

Our Constitution was modeled in a general way after the English government of the eighteenth century. But while the English system of constitutional checks was a natural growth, the American system was a purely artificial contrivance. James Monroe called attention to this fact in the Virginia convention. He observed that the division of power in all other governments ancient and modern owed its existence to a mixture of monarchy, aristocracy, and democracy.[2] This artificial division of power provided for in the Constitution of the United States was intended as a substitute for the natural checks upon the people which the existence of king and nobility then supplied in England.

This idea of government carried out to its logical conclusion would require that every class and every interest should have a veto on the political action of all the others. No such extended application of the theory has ever been made in the actual working of government, nor is it practicable, since no class can acquire, or having

---

[1] Democracy and Liberty, Vol. I, p. 9.
[2] Elliot's Debates, Vol. III, p. 218.

acquired, retain a veto on the action of the government unless it is large and powerful enough to enforce its demands. The attempt on the part of a small class to acquire a constitutional right of this character must of necessity fail. This is why the system which theoretically tends toward a high degree of complexity has not in practice resulted in any very complex constitutional arrangements.

Poland is the best example of the practical working of a system of checks carried to an absurd extreme. The political disintegration and final partition of that once powerful country by its neighbors was due in no small degree to its form of government, which invited anarchy through the great power which it conferred upon an insignificant minority.

The fact that this system can not be carried far enough in practice to confer upon every distinct interest or class the veto power as a means of self defence, has given rise to the doctrine of *laissez faire*. No class in control of the government, or even in possession of the power to negative its acts, has any motive for advocating the let-alone theory. Its veto power affords it adequate protection against any harmful exercise of political authority. But such is not the case with those smaller or less fortunate classes or interests which lack this means of self-protection. Since they do not have even a negative control over the government, they naturally desire to limit the scope of its authority. Viewed in this light we may regard the *laissez faire* doctrine as merely supplementary to the political theory of checks and balances.

It is easy to see that if the idea of checks were carried out in practice to its extreme limits, it would lead inevitably to the destruction of all positive authority by vesting a veto in each class and ultimately in each individual. In fact, John C. Calhoun, the ablest and most consistent expounder of this doctrine, defines a perfect popular government as "one which would embrace the consent of every citizen or member of the community."[1] When this last stage is reached we would have no government in any proper sense; for each individual would be clothed with constitutional power to arrest its action. Indeed the theory of checks and balances, if taken without any qualification and followed out consistently, leads naturally to the acceptance of anarchy as the only scientific system.

The absence of king and aristocracy did not deter the members of the Convention from seeking to follow the English model. In doing this, however, it was necessary to find substitutes for the materials which were lacking. The constitutional devices adopted to accomplish this purpose form the system of checks and are the most

[1] Works, Vol. I, p. 29. Cralle's Ed.

original and interesting feature of our government.

The English model was followed, however, only so far as it served their purpose. In the case of the judiciary, for instance, they declined to follow it; but the reason for this as explained in the preceding chapter was their desire to establish a more effective check on the people. They showed no special preference for the English form where some other method would better accomplish the desired purpose. Hence in many instances they deliberately rejected English precedent, but always with the view of providing something that would impose a more effective check on the public will. An apparent exception to this may be found in the limited term of President and United States senators. But these were the very instances in which lack of king and nobility made departure from the English model a matter of necessity. Moreover, any avowed attempt to provide an effective substitute for the hereditary branches of the English model would have been distasteful to the people generally and for that reason would have ensured the rejection of the Constitution. Theoretically, the nearest approach to the English system possible would have been life tenure, and there were not wanting those who, like Hamilton, contended for it; but the certainty of popular disapproval was an unanswerable argument against it.

It was thought that substantially the same result

could be obtained by indirect election for moderately long periods. Hence we notice a marked departure from the practice of the state constitutions in term of office and mode of election. In every state the governor was elected either by the legislature or directly by the voters, usually for one year and nowhere for as long a period as four years.[1] With only two exceptions[2] the members of the upper legislative chamber were directly elected by the qualified voters, generally for one year and in no state for as long a term as six years.[3]

The desire of the Convention to secure to the President and United States Senators more freedom from popular control than was enjoyed by the corresponding state officials is most clearly seen in the mode of election prescribed.[4] They adopted what Madison called "the policy of refining popular appointments by successive filtrations." They provided that the President should

[1] Supra, p. 18.

[2] Infra p. 239.

[3] Pennsylvania and Georgia had only a single legislative body.

[4] "There was certainly no intention of making the appointment of the Presidential electors subject to popular election. I think it is evident that the framers were anxious to avoid this." Burgess, Political Science and Constitutional Law, Vol. II, p. 219.

According to Fiske, "electors were chosen by the legislature in New Jersey till 1816; in Connecticut till 1820; in New York, Delaware, and Vermont, and with one exception in Georgia, till 1824; in South Carolina till 1868. Massachusetts adopted various plans, and did not finally settle down to an election by the people until 1828." The Critical Period of American History, p. 286.

be chosen by an electoral college, the members of which were not required to be elected by the people. This, it was thought, would guard against the choice of a mere popular favorite and ensure the election of a President acceptable to the conservative and well-to-do classes. It was taken for granted that the indirect method would enable the minority to control the choice. For a like reason they provided that United States senators should be chosen by the legislatures instead of by the people of the several states.

The system as originally adopted did not contemplate, and made no provision for the selection of candidates in advance of a popular election. But this is not surprising when we reflect that it was the very thing they were trying to prevent. They intended that the electoral college should be such in fact as well as in name, that it should have and exercise the power of independent choice instead of merely registering a popular selection already made as it has come in practice to do. They recognized very clearly that there was a distinct line of cleavage separating the rich from the poor. They believed with Hamilton that in this respect "all communities divide themselves into the few and the many,"[1] that the latter will tend to combine for the purpose of obtaining control of the government; and having secured it, will pass laws for their own advantage. This,

[1] Elliot's Debates, Vol. I, p. 421.

they believed, was the chief danger of democracy —a danger so real and imminent that it behooved the few to organize and bring about, if possible, such changes in the government as would "protect the minority of the opulent against the majority."[1] This was the purpose of the system of checks by which they sought to give the former a veto on the acts of the latter. In thus depriving the masses of the power to advance their interests through combination, they thought that the organization of a political party representing the many as opposed to the few would be discouraged. On the other hand, the few while co-operating for a common purpose, could best accomplish it without any visible party organization or any appearance of concerted action. Hence the Constitution as originally adopted made no provision for the party candidate.

In view of the fact that the Constitution was intended to limit the power of the majority, it is perfectly natural that it should have attempted to assign to the popular branch of the government a position of minor importance. This was, of course, in direct opposition to what had been the uniform tendency during the Revolutionary period in the various states. In the latter the lower house had been raised to coördinate rank with the upper and in Massachusetts, Gerry tells us, the people were for abolishing the senate and giving all the

---

[1] Madison, Elliot's Debates, Vol. I, p. 450.

powers of government to the other branch of the legislature.[1]

In the Federal Constitution we see a strong reaction against this policy of enlarging the authority of the lower, and what was assumed to be the more popular branch of the legislative body. The House of Representatives was, it is true, given equal power with the Senate in the matter of ordinary legislation. But here its equality ends. The treaty-making and the appointing power were given to the President and Senate, where, it was thought, they would be safe from popular interference. The effect of this was to make the influence of these two branches of the government greatly preponderate over that of the directly elected House. Through the treaty-making power the President and Senate could in a most important sense legislate without the consent of the popular branch of Congress. They could enter into agreements with foreign countries which would have all the force and effect of laws regularly enacted and which might influence profoundly our whole social, political, and industrial life. The only semblance of a popular check on the exercise of this power was to be found in those cases where appropriations were required to carry treaties into effect. Here the House of Representatives, in theory at least, could defeat the treaty by refusing its assent to the necessary

[1] Elliot's Debates, Vol. V, p. 158.

appropriation. In practice, however, the House has surrendered this power. A treaty is at no stage "submitted to or referred to the House of Representatives, which has no more right to be informed about it than ordinary citizens. The President and the Senate may, for example, cede or annex territories, and yet nothing of the fact will appear in the discussions of the House of Representatives unless the cession involves expenditure or receipt of money. Besides, I must add that even if the treaty contains clauses imposing a charge on the public revenue, it is the rule, since Washington's time, that the House of Representatives should not discuss the terms of the treaty adopted by the Senate, but accept it in silence as an accomplished fact, and simply vote the necessary funds."[1]

The appointing power was in many respects even more important. It meant the right to select those who were to interpret and enforce the laws, and this really involved the power to mold the spirit and character of the government. That this was fully appreciated by those who framed the Constitution we saw in the preceding chapter.

The statement contained in the Constitution that all legislative authority is vested in Congress is far from accurate, not only for the reason above

---

[1] Boutmy, Studies in Constitutional Law, p. 91 (Eng. Trans.).

See also Ford, The Rise and Growth of American Politics, p. 254.

indicated that a portion of it under the guise of treaty-making power is conferred on the President and Senate, and the further reason that the Supreme Court exercises legislative authority of great importance, but for the additional reason that the President, aside from his control over treaties, possesses legislative power co-extensive and co-equal with that of either house. He has been expressly given by the Constitution only a qualified veto, but it is so difficult for Congress to override it by the necessary two-thirds majority that it is in most cases as effective as an absolute negative.[1] Attention has been called to the fact that a two-thirds majority is difficult to secure even under the most favorable circumstances; but here the situation is such as to place practically insurmountable obstacles in the way of its attainment. As an illustration let us suppose that each state is solidly for or against the measure which the President has vetoed and that both Senators and Representatives accurately reflect the sentiment of their respective states. Then taking the population of the forty-five states in 1900 as the basis of our calculation, the smallest

[1] Previous to Andrew Johnson's administration but six measures were passed over the President's veto. Up to 1889 the veto power of the President had been exercised four hundred and thirty-three times, and in but twenty-nine instances had it been overridden by the required two-thirds majority in both houses of Congress. Fifteen measures vetoed by Andrew Johnson were passed over his veto—more than in the case of all other Presidents combined. Mason, The Veto Power. p. 214.

popular majority which would ensure the required two-thirds vote in both houses would be obtained by taking enough of the smaller states to make the necessary majority in the House. But this would mean a popular majority of over 65 per cent. and an eight-ninths majority in the Senate. To obtain the necessary vote in both houses by taking the larger states would require a popular majority of over 93 per cent. and a nine-tenths majority in the House. This gives us some, but by no means an adequate, idea of the President's control over legislation. He may use in support of his veto all the other powers which the Constitution has placed in his hands; and when we consider the immense influence which he can bring to bear upon Congress, especially through his control over appointments, we can readily see the practical impossibility of enacting any measure which he opposes with all the powers at his command. Moreover, the President and Senate would, it was expected, belong to the same class, represent the same interests, and be equally faithful in guarding the rights of the well-to-do. They were to be, therefore, not so much a check on each other, as a double check on the democratic House; and as against the latter, it was the intention that the qualified negative of the President should, in all important matters concerning which the radical and conservative classes disagreed, be fully equivalent to an absolute veto. This follows from the fact that the Senate would in such cases sympathize with the action of the President and refuse to co-operate with the House in overriding it.

It was believed by the framers of the Constitution that the veto power of the President would be seldom used. This was true until after the Civil War. Washington used the power only twice; John Adams, Jefferson, J. Q. Adams, Van Buren, Taylor, and Fillmore did not make use of it at all. During the first seventy-six years of our history under the Constitution the power was exercised only fifty-two times. Andrew Johnson was the first President to use it freely, vetoing as many acts as were vetoed by the first eight Presidents. The largest use of the veto power was by President Cleveland who, during his first term, exercised it three hundred and one times.[1]

In conferring the veto power on the President the members of the Convention were actuated by the desire to strengthen a conservative branch of the government rather than by any desire to copy the English Constitution, or the constitutions of the American states. As a matter of fact, the veto power of the Crown was then obsolete, Hamilton himself remarking in the Convention that it had not been used since the Revolution of 1688,[2]

[1] Mason, The Veto Power, p. 214.

[2] Elliot's Debates, Vol. V, p. 151. Hamilton's statement, which was made in support of a motion to give the President an absolute veto on acts of Congress, was not correct. William III vetoed no less than four acts of Parliament, and his successor used the veto power for the last time in 1707. Medley, English Constitutional History, p. 315.

while in all but two states the last vestige of it had been destroyed.[1]

The position of the President was still further strengthened by discarding the executive council which then existed in every state as a check upon the governor and which was a prominent feature of the English government of that time. In England this council, forming the Ministry or Cabinet, had not, it is true, definitely assumed the form which characterizes it now; but it had deprived the King of all power to act except through ministers who were responsible and could be impeached by Parliament. This, of course, had greatly weakened the executive, a fact which fully explains why the framers of the Constitution rejected it and went back to the earlier English king whose veto power was unimpaired for their model.

As their plan contemplated a strong independent executive who would not hesitate to use the far-reaching powers placed in his hands to defeat measures which he disapproved of, it was necessary to guarantee him against popular removal. In this respect again we see both English and American constitutional practice disregarded, since neither afforded the desired security of tenure. In the various states the governor was liable to be impeached by the lower branch of the legislature and expelled from office when convicted by the senate, which was usually the court

[1] Supra, p. 19.

before which impeachment cases were tried. A mere majority in each house was usually sufficient to convict,[1] and as both houses were directly elected,[2] it virtually gave the majority of the voters the power to remove. This was simply an adaptation of the English practice which allowed a majority of the Commons to impeach and a majority of the Lords to convict. That this had a strong tendency to make the legislative body supreme is evident, since the power, if freely used, would overcome all opposition on the part of either the executive or the judiciary. Any combination of interests that could command a majority in both houses of Parliament could thus enforce its policy. This practically destroyed the executive check in the English Constitution and for that very reason the founders of our government rejected it. They clearly saw that to make the President's veto effective, he would have to be protected in its exercise. To have adopted the English practice and allowed a mere majority of the Senate to convict in impeachment cases would have given Congress power to destroy the President's veto by impeaching and removing from office any executive who dared to use it. This was guarded against by making a two-thirds majority in the Senate necessary to convict any official impeached by the House. And since this two-thirds ma-

[1] Infra, p. 231.
[2] Senate in South Carolina and Maryland (constitutions of 1776) exceptions, Infra p. 239.

jority is one which in practice can not be obtained, the power to impeach may be regarded, like the power to amend, as practically non-existent. Only two convictions have been obtained since the Constitution was adopted. John Pickering, a Federal district judge, was convicted March 12, 1803, and removed from office, and at the outbreak of the Civil War a Federal district judge of Tennessee, West H. Humphreys, who joined the Confederacy without resigning, was convicted. William Blount was acquitted in 1798 on the ground that, as a United States senator, he was not a "civil officer" within the meaning of the impeachment provision of the Constitution, and so not liable to impeachment. Samuel Chase, Associate Justice of the United States Supreme Court, President Andrew Johnson, and Secretary of War, William W. Belknap, would have been convicted but for the extraordinary majority required in the Senate.

The practical impossibility of removing a public official by means of impeachment proceedings has made the executive and the judicial veto thoroughly effective, since it has deprived Congress of all power to punish by removing from office those officials who thwart its purpose. It has made the President and the Supreme Court much stronger than the House of Representatives —a result which the framers of the Constitution no doubt desired.

In addition to the President's qualified veto on laws about to be passed, which, as we have seen, amounts in practice to an unlimited negative, he has what may be called an absolute veto on their execution. This is the necessary consequence of his complete independence, taken in connection with his power of appointment and removal. Controlling the administrative arm of the government, he can execute the laws of Congress or not as he may see fit. He may even fail to enforce an act which he himself signed, inasmuch as his approval in a legislative capacity does not bar his subsequent disapproval as an executive. Of course, it does not follow that this power is openly and avowedly exercised. Usually it is not. An easier and more effective method is the one which obscures the real intention of the executive by a sham attempt at enforcement.

It may be contended that the Constitution makes it his duty to enforce all laws without regard to his own views of their wisdom or expediency. This contention, however, does not appear to be borne out by the purpose of the Constitution itself. It was not the intention of the framers of that instrument to make the President a mere administrative agent of Congress, but rather to set him over against that body and make him in a large measure the judge of his own authority. If it be claimed that it is his duty to enforce all laws that have been regularly enacted, it must at the same time be conceded that the Constitution permits their non-enforcement, since it has given neither to Congress nor to the people any effective power to remove him for neglect of duty. Moreover, his oath of office does not expressly bind him to enforce the laws of Congress, but merely to "execute the office of President . . . and preserve, protect, and defend the Constitution of the United States."[1]

This omission can not be satisfactorily explained as a mere oversight. The Massachusetts constitution of 1780, from which the fathers copied the qualified veto power, required the governor to take an oath in which he obligated himself to perform the duties of his office "agreeably to the rules and regulations of the constitution and the laws of the commonwealth." There was no precedent in any then existing state constitution for expressly binding the executive in his oath of office to defend the Constitution without mentioning his duty to enforce the laws. It is a reasonable inference that the framers of the Constitution intended to impress the President with the belief that his obligation to defend the Constitution was more binding upon him than his duty to enforce the laws enacted by Congress.

In the foregoing discussion it has been shown that political authority was unequally divided between the various branches of the government; to

[1] Constitution, Art. II. Sec. I.

the extent that this was the case the framers of the Constitution did not adhere consistently to the theory of checks. But in this, as in other instances where they departed from precedents which they professed to be following, they were actuated by a desire to minimize the direct influence of the people. If the Constitution had been framed in complete accord with the doctrine of checks and balances, the lower house of Congress as the direct representative of the people would have been given a veto on the entire policy of the government. But this, as we have seen, was not done. The more important powers were placed under the exclusive control of the other branches of the government over which it was believed public opinion would have but little influence. This deprived the people of the unlimited negative to which they were entitled even according to the theory of checks. Richard Henry Lee did not greatly exaggerate then when he said: "The only check to be found in favor of the democratic principle, in this system, is the House of Representatives, which, I believe, may justly be called a mere shred or rag of representation."[1] Nor was Mason entirely mistaken when he referred to the House of Representatives as "the shadow only" and not "the substance of representation."[2]

---

[1] Elliot's Debates, Vol. I, p. 503.
[2] Ibid., p. 494.

It may be thought, even though the Constitution does not give the House of Representatives a direct negative on all the important acts of the government, that it does so indirectly through its control over the purse. An examination of the system with reference to this question, however, reveals the fact that the control of the House over taxation and expenditure is narrowly limited. A revenue law is subject to no constitutional limitation, and when once enacted remains in force until repealed by subsequent legislation. Assuming that a revenue system has been established which is sufficient for the needs of the government, the House can exercise no further control over income. It can not repeal it, or modify it in any way without the consent of the President and Senate.

Turning now to the matter of expenditure, we find that the Constitution allows permanent provision to be made for the needs of the government, with the single exception of the army, for the support of which no funds can be appropriated for a longer period than two years. The policy of permanent appropriations has not yet been applied to the full extent permitted by the Constitution, but it has been carried much further than a consistent adherence to the doctrine of popular control over the budget would warrant. The practice could easily be extended until every want of the government except the expenses of the army, even including the maintenance of the navy, had been provided for by permanent appropriations. And it may be added that with the increasing desire for stability which comes with the development of vast business interests, the tendency is strongly in that direction.

Let us suppose that some political party, for the time being in control of the law-making power of the government, should extend the practice of making permanent appropriations to the extreme limit allowed by the Constitution. This would relieve the administration of all financial dependence upon public sentiment except in the management of the army. And if, as the framers of the Constitution contemplated, the President and the Senate should represent the minority, the administration might for years pursue a policy to which public opinion had come to be strongly opposed. For with the system once adopted its repeal could not be effected without the concurrence of all branches of the law-making authority. The President and Congress could, in anticipation of an adverse majority in the House, guard against the withdrawal of financial support from their policy by simply making permanent provision for their needs. Our present system would permit this to be done even after the party in power had been overwhelmingly defeated at the polls, since the second session of the old congress does not begin until after the members of the new House

of Representatives have been elected.[1]   This
would tie the hands of any adverse popular majority in a succeeding congress and effectually
deprive it of even a veto on the income and expenditure of the government, until such time as it
should also gain control of the Presidency and the
Senate.   But this last could never have happened if the practical working of the Constitution
had been what its framers intended.   Whatever
control, then, the majority may now exercise over
taxation and public expenditure has thus been acquired less through any constitutional provisions
intended to secure it, than in spite of those which
seemingly made it impossible.

Equally significant was the failure of the Convention to make any adequate provision for enforcing publicity.   The Constitution says "a
regular statement of the receipts and expenditures
of public money shall be published from time to
time," and also that "each House shall keep a
journal of its proceedings, and from time to time
publish the same, except such parts as may in their
judgment required secrecy."[2]   That these provisions were of little practical value is evident
from the fact that they contain no definite state-

[1] For a discussion of this feature of our government see
the following chapter.
[2] Under the Articles of Confederation the Congress of the
United States was required to "publish the journal of their
proceedings monthly, except such parts thereof relating to
treaties, alliances, or military operations as in their judgment
require secrecy."   Art. IX.

ment as to when and how often the accounts and journals are to be published. The phrase *from time to time* was susceptible of almost any interpretation that either house of Congress or the President might wish to give it, and could easily have been so construed as to justify a method of publication which gave the people but little information concerning the present state of public affairs. The framers of the Constitution did not believe that the management of the government was in any proper sense the people's business; yet they realized that the people themselves took a different view of the matter, which made some constitutional guarantee of publicity necessary. It was, however, the form rather than the substance of such a guarantee which the Constitution contained.

Neither house of Congress is required by the Constitution to hold open sittings or publish its speeches and debates.[1] Until 1799 the Senate exercised its constitutional right to transact public business in secret; and during that period preserved no record of its debates. This policy did not win for it the confidence of the people, and until after it was in a measure abandoned, the Senate, notwithstanding the important powers

[1] The Revolutionary constitutions of New York and Pennsylvania provided that the doors of the legislature should be kept open at all times for the admission of the public except when the welfare of the state should demand secrecy.

conferred on it by the Constitution, was not a very influential body.

To deny the right of the people to control the government leads naturally to denial of their right to criticise those who shape its policy; since if free and unrestricted discussion and even condemnation of official conduct were allowed, no system of minority rule could long survive. This was well understood in the Federal Convention. The members of that body saw that the constitutional right of public officials to disregard the wishes of the people was incompatible with the right of the latter to drag them before the bar of public opinion. Hence some limitation of the right to criticise public officials was necessary to safeguard and preserve their official independence. This seems to have been the purpose of the Constitution in providing with reference to members of Congress that "for any speech or debate in either House they shall not be questioned in any other place."[1]

This provision may be traced to the English Bill of Rights where it was intended as a means of protecting members of Parliament against imprisonment and prosecution for opposing the arbitrary acts of the Crown. It was at first merely an assertion of the independence of the Lords and Commons as against the King, and a denial of the

[1] Cf. Ford, The Rise and Growth of American Politics, p. 63.

right of the latter to call them to account for anything said or done in their legislative capacity. But after it had accomplished its original purpose and the tyrannical power of the King had been overthrown, it was found to be serviceable in warding off attacks from another direction. It thus came about that the means devised and employed by Parliament to shield its members against intimidation and oppression at the hands of the King was later turned against the people; for Parliament in divesting the King of his irresponsible authority was desirous only of establishing its own supremacy. It jealously guarded its own prerogatives, claimed the right to govern independently, and just as formerly it had resisted the encroachments of royal authority, it now resented the efforts of the people to influence its policy by the publication and criticism of its proceedings.

A standing order passed by the House of Commons in 1728 declared "that it is an indignity to, and a breach of, the privilege of this House for any person to presume to give in written or printed newspapers, any account or minute of the debates or other proceedings; that upon discovery of the authors, printers, or publishers of any such newspaper this House will proceed against the offenders with the utmost severity."[1]

[1] Quoted from Article on Reporting in Encyclopedia Brittanica.

This was the attitude of Parliament down to 1771, when, after a prolonged and bitter struggle, the House of Commons was finally driven by the force of an overwhelming public sentiment to acquiesce in the publication of its proceedings.

There was, however, a small minority in the House that opposed the policy of prosecuting the representatives of the press. The following extract from the Annual Register for 1771 describes the attitude of this minority.

"Some gentlemen however did not rest their opposition on the points of decorum and prudence, but went so far as to deny the authority of the House in this respect, and said that it was an usurpation assumed in bad times, in the year 1641; that while their privileges and authority were used in defense of the rights of the people, against the violence of the prerogative, all men willingly joined in supporting them, and even their usurpations were considered as fresh securities to their independence; but now that they saw their own weapons converted to instruments of tyranny and oppression against themselves, they would oppose them with all their might, and, however they may fail in the first efforts, would finally prevail, and assuredly bring things back to their first principles. They also said that the practice of letting the constituents know the parliamentary proceedings of their representatives was founded upon the truest principles of the

Constitution; and that even the publishing of supposed speeches was not a novel practice, and. if precedent was a justification, could be traced to no less an authority than Lord Clarendon."[1]

"In the early years of the colonial era the right of free speech was not always well guarded. There was frequent legislation, for example, against 'seditious utterances,' a term which might mean almost anything. In 1639 the Maryland assembly passed an act for 'determining enormous offences,' among which were included 'scandalous or contemptuous words or writings to the dishonor of the lord proprietarie or his lieutenant generall for the time being, or any of the council.' By a North Carolina act of 1715 seditious utterances against the government was made a criminal offence, and in 1724 Joseph Castleton, for malicious language against Governor Burrington and for other contemptuous remarks, was sentenced by the general court to stand in the pillory for two hours and on his knees to beg the governor's pardon. A New Jersey act of 1675 required that persons found guilty of resisting the authority of the governor or councillors 'either in words or actions . . . by speaking contemptuously, reproachfully, or maliciously, of any of them,' should be liable to fine, banishment, or corporal punishment at the discretion of the court.

[1] Vol. XIV, p. 62. See also Porritt, The Unreformed House of Commons, Vol. I, pp. 590-596.

In Massachusetts even during the eighteenth century the right of free political discussion was denied by the House of Representatives as well as by the royal governor, though often unsuccessfully."[1]

"The general publication of parliamentary debates dates only from the American Revolution, and even then it was still considered a technical breach of privilege.

"The American colonies followed the practice of the parent country. Even the laws were not at first published for general circulation, and it seemed to be thought desirable by the magistrates to keep the people in ignorance of the precise boundary between that which was lawful and that which was prohibited, as more likely to avoid all doubtful actions. . . .

"The public bodies of the united nation did not at once invite publicity to their deliberations. The Constitutional Convention of 1787 sat with closed doors, and although imperfect reports of the debates have since been published, the injunction of secrecy upon its members was never removed. The Senate for a time followed this example, and the first open debate was had in 1793, on the occasion of the controversy over the right of Mr. Gallatin to a seat in that body. The House of Representatives sat with open doors from the first, tolerating the presence of reporters,—over

[1] Greene, The Provincial Governor, pp. 198-199.

whose admission, however, the Speaker assumed control,—and refusing in 1796 the pittance of two thousand dollars for full publication of its debates.

"It must be evident from these historical facts that liberty of the press, as now understood and enjoyed, is of very recent origin."[1]

Both the original purpose of this parliamentary privilege and its subsequent abuse not only in England but also in the Colonies, were facts well known by those who framed the Constitution. There was no King here, from whose arbitrary acts Congress would need to be protected, but there was a power which the framers of the Constitution regarded as no less tyrannical and fully as much to be feared—the power of the people as represented by the numerical majority. How to guard against this new species of tyranny was the problem that confronted them. The majority was just as impatient of restraint, just as eager to brush aside all opposition as king or aristocracy had ever been in the past. Taking this view of the matter, it was but natural that they should seek to protect Congress against the people as Parliament had formerly been protected against the Crown. For exactly the same reason as we have seen, they made the judges independent of the people as they had been made independent of the King in England. In no other way was it possible to limit the power of the majority.

---

[1] Cooley, Constitutional Limitations, 6th ed., pp. 514-516.

That this provision concerning freedom of speech and debate in the legislative body was not regarded as especially important during the Revolutionary period is shown by its absence from most of the early state constitutions. When the Federal Constitution was framed only three of the original states[1] had adopted constitutions containing such a provision. There was, as a matter of fact, no real need for it in the state constitutions of that time. The controlling influence exerted by the legislature in the state government, and the dependence of the courts upon that body, precluded the possibility of any abuse of their powers in this direction.

The Articles of Confederation contained the provision that "Freedom of speech and debate in Congress shall not be impeached or questioned in any court or place out of Congress."[2] This was designed to protect members of Congress against prosecution in the state courts. Here, as in the English Bill of Rights and in the state constitutions containing a similar provision, reference is made in express terms to prosecution in the courts. The framers of the Constitution, however, left out all reference to the courts. If, as constitutional writers have generally assumed, the framers of the Constitution intended by this provision to protect members of Congress against prosecution

[1] Massachusetts, New Hampshire and Maryland.
[2] Art. V.

in the courts, it is difficult to understand why they should have omitted what had been the main feature and purpose of this provision, not only in the original Bill of Rights, but also in the state constitutions copying it and in the Articles of Confederation. If what they had in mind was the danger of prosecution in the state or Federal courts, why should they have changed completely the wording of this provision by omitting all reference to the very danger which they wished to guard against?

The checks thus far described were intended as a substitute for king and aristocracy; but to make the Constitution acceptable to the people, additional checks were required which the English government did not contain. The division of authority in the latter was solely between different classes or orders, each of which was supposed to represent interests co-extensive with the realm. But while the power of each class was thus limited, their joint and combined action was subject to no constitutional check or limitation whatever. Any policy upon which they agreed could be enforced in any part of the realm, since the Constitution, recognizing no local interests, gave no political subdivision a negative on the acts of the whole. The government of England, then, was purely *national* as opposed to *federal,* that is to say the general government was supreme in all respects and the local government merely its creature.

This was the type of government for which Hamilton contended and which a majority of the delegates in the Federal Convention really favored. But the difficulty of securing the adoption of a Constitution framed on this plan made it impracticable. To merge the separate states in a general government possessing unlimited authority would place all local interests at the mercy of what the people regarded as virtually a foreign power. Practical considerations, then, required that the Constitution should in appearance at least conform to the *federal* rather than to the *national* type. Accordingly the powers of government were divided into two classes, one embracing only those of an admittedly general character, which were enumerated and delegated to the general government, while the rest were left in the possession of the states. In form and appearance the general government and the governments of the various states were coördinate and supplementary, each being supreme and sovereign within its respective sphere. By this arrangement any appearance of subordination on the part of the state governments was carefully avoided; and since the state retained sovereign authority within the sphere assigned to it by the Constitution, the protection of local interests was thereby guaranteed. This understanding of the Constitution seems to have been encouraged by those who desired its adoption and was undoubtedly the only interpre-

ιation which would have found favor with the
people generally. Moreover, it was a perfectly
natural and logical development of the theory of
checks. If the President, Senate, House of Representatives and the Supreme Court were coördinate branches of the general government, and each
therefore a check on the authority of the others,
a like division of authority between the general
government as a whole on the one hand, and the
states on the other, must of necessity imply a
defensive power in the state to prevent encroach-
ment on the authority reserved to it. And since
the government was *federal* and not *national*, and
since the state government was coördinate with
and not subordinate to the general government,
the conclusion was inevitable that the former was
a check on the latter in exactly the same way that
each branch of the general government was a
check on the others.

This view of the Constitution while allowed to
go unchallenged for the time being to secure its
adoption by the states, was not accepted, however,
by those who framed it. For although in outward appearance the Constitution did not provide
for a national government, it at least contained the
germs out of which a national government might
in time be developed. The complete supremacy
of the general government was one important
result which the members of the Convention
desired to bring about. Several plans were pro-

posed by which this supremacy should be expressly recognized in the Constitution. Both Randolph and Charles Pinckney favored giving a negative on state laws to Congress.[1] Madison suggested giving it to the Senate. Hamilton, as we have seen, proposed giving an absolute veto to the governors of the various states, who were to be appointed by the President. According to another plan this power was to be given jointly to the President and the judges of the Supreme Court. All of these proposals to give the general government in express terms the power to annul state laws were finally rejected by the Convention, no doubt for the reason that they indicated too clearly their intention to subordinate the state governments. But while declining to confer this power in express terms, it was not their intention to withhold it. As in the case of the judicial veto on congressional legislation, they relied upon control over the Constitution after its adoption to accomplish their end.

The omission from the Constitution of any provision which clearly and unequivocally defined the relation of the general government to the governments of the various states was not a mere oversight. The members of the Convention evidently thought that to ensure the acceptance of the Constitution, it was necessary to submit it in a form least likely to excite the opposition of the states.

[1] Elliot's Debates, Vol. I, p. 181 and Vol. V, p. 132.

They expected by controlling its interpretation to be able after its adoption to mold it into a shape more in accord with their own views. The choice of this method, though the only one by which it was possible to attain their end, involved consequences more serious and far-reaching than they imagined. It paved the way for a constitutional struggle which lasted for three-quarters of a century and finally convulsed the country in the greatest civil war of modern times. Had the Constitution in so many words expressly declared that the Federal judiciary should have the power to annul state laws, or had it given this power to some other branch of the Federal government in accordance with some one of the suggestions above mentioned, and had it at the same time expressly withheld from the states the power to negative acts of Congress, there would have been no room for doubt that the general government was the final and exclusive judge in all cases of conflict between Federal and state authority.

Such a provision would have left no room for the doctrine of state rights, or its corollary—the power of a state to nullify a Federal law. It would have settled the question of Federal supremacy beyond the possibility of controversy by relegating the states to a strictly subordinate place in our political system. But inasmuch as the Constitution contained no provision of this character it left the states in a position to defend their claim to coördinate rank with the general government.

The adoption of the Constitution was merely the first step in this program of political reconstruction. To carry through to a successful issue the work undertaken by the Federal Convention, it was necessary that the same influences that dominated the latter should also control the new government by which the Constitution was to be interpreted and applied. How well they succeeded may be seen in the impress left upon our system by the twelve years of Federalist rule which followed its adoption. During this period the Constitution was in the hands of those who were in full sympathy with the purpose of its framers, and who sought to complete the work which they had begun.

In shaping the policy of the government during this period the influence of Hamilton was even more pronounced than it had been in the Federal Convention. As Secretary of the Treasury he proposed and brought about the adoption of a financial policy in harmony with his political views. Believing that the government must have the confidence of the conservative and well-to-do classes, he framed a policy which was calculated to gain their support by appealing to their material interests. The assumption by the general government of the state debts incurred during the Revolutionary war was designed and had the effect of detaching the creditor class from dependence upon the governments of the various states and allying them to the general government. The protective tariff system also had far-reaching political significance. It was expected to develop an influential manufacturing class who would look to the general government as the source of their prosperity, and who would therefore support its authority as against that of the states. To unite the moneyed interests and identify them with the general government was one of the reasons for chartering the bank of the United States. The internal revenue system which enabled the general government to place its officials in every community and make its authority directly felt throughout all the states was a political as well as a financial measure. It was prompted partly by the desire to appropriate this field of taxation before it was laid hold of by the states and partly by the desire to accustom the people to the exercise of Federal authority. All these measures which were formulated by Hamilton and carried through largely by his influence were intended to lay a solid basis for the development of national as opposed to state authority.

It was the purpose of the Constitution as we have seen to establish the supremacy of the so-called upper class. To consolidate its various elements and bring the government under their control was the aim of the Federalist party.

That such a policy should have aroused much popular opposition and provoked bitter criticism was to be expected. Criticism, however, was especially irritating to those who accepted the Federalist theory of government. For if the few had a right to rule the many, then the latter, as a matter of course, ought to treat the former with respect; since otherwise the power and influence of the minority might be overthrown.

The Alien and Sedition laws by which the governing class sought to repress criticism were the logical culmination of this movement to limit the power of the majority. This attempt, however, to muzzle the press and overthrow the right of free speech instead of silencing the opposition only strengthened and intensified it. It merely augmented the rising tide of popular disapproval which was soon to overwhelm the Federalist party.

The Constitution, as we have seen, did not expressly subordinate the states. Although framed by those who wished to make the general government supreme, it contained no provision which could not be so construed as to harmonize with the widely accepted doctrine of state rights. It was represented by its framers and understood by the people generally as dividing sovereignty between the general government on the one hand and the states on the other. Within the province assigned to the state, it was to be supreme, which would naturally seem to imply adequate constitutional power in the state to defend itself against federal aggression. This view of the Constitution, if not actually encouraged, was allowed to go unchallenged in order not to endanger its adoption.

The Constitution is and was intended to be rigid only in the sense that it effectually limits the power of the majority. The founders of our government were not averse to such changes in the system which they established as would promote or at least not interfere with their main purpose— the protection of the minority against the majority. Indeed, they intended that the Constitution as framed should be modified, amended and gradually molded by judicial interpretation into the form which they desired to give it, but which the necessity of minimizing popular opposition prevented them from accomplishing at the outset. Amendment by judicial interpretation was merely a means of conferring indirectly on the minority a power which the Constitution expressly denied to the majority. No hint of this method of minority amendment, however, was contained in the Constitution itself. But, on the contrary, any such view of the Constitution would have been negatived by the general theory of checks and balances which, consistently applied, would limit the power of the minority as well as that of the majority. It was not reasonable to suppose that the Constitution contemplated placing in the hands of the minority a power which it was so careful to withold from the majority. In fact, the language of the Constitution warranted the belief that it was intended as a means of checking the general government itself by protecting the states in the exercise of all those powers not expressly denied to them. And since the Constitution, as we have seen, merely marked off the limits of federal and state jurisdiction, without specifying how the general government on the one hand, or the state government on the other, was to be kept within the territory assigned to it, it was natural to suppose that it contemplated giving to each the same means of protecting itself against the encroachments of the other.

Accordingly, when Congress appeared to overstep the limits which the Constitution set to its authority, the states naturally looked for some means of making the checks imposed upon the general government effective. True, the Constitution itself did not specify how this was to be done; but neither could one find in it any provision for enforcing the limitations on the authority of the states. The general government, however, had supplied itself with the means of self-protection by calling into existence the veto power of the Federal judiciary. This made the checks upon the authority of the states operative. But how were those imposed by the Constitution on the general government itself to be enforced?

Not by the Federal government or any of its organs, since this would allow it to interpret the Constitution to suit itself. If the general government should have the right to interpret and enforce the constitutional limitations on the powers of the states, it would for a like reason follow that the states should interpret and enforce the constitutional limitations on the authority of the general government itself. To carry out in good faith what appeared to be the purpose of the Constitution, *i. e.,* to limit the authority of the general government as well as that of the states, it would seem to be necessary to make each the judge of the other's powers. It would devolve then on the state governments to keep the general government within the bounds which the Constitution set to its authority.

This could be accomplished, however, in no other way than by a veto on such acts of the general government as, in the opinion of the state, exceeded its constitutional authority. Those who believed in a federal as opposed to a national government and who therefore wished to enforce the constitutional checks on the general government, were irresistibly impelled toward the doctrine of nullification as the sole means of protecting the rights of the states.

As Von Holst says, "Calhoun and his disciples were not the authors of the doctrine of nullification and secession. That question is as old as the

Constitution itself, and has always been a living one, even when it has not been one of life and death. Its roots lay in the actual circumstances of the time, and the Constitution was the living expression of these actual circumstances."[1]

Madison, in *The Federalist,* refers in a vague and indefinite manner to the power of a state to oppose an unjustifiable act of the Federal government.

"Should an unwarrantable measure of the Federal government," he says, "be unpopular in particular states . . . the means of opposition to it are powerful and at hand. The disquietude of the people; their repugnance, and perhaps refusal, to co-operate with the officers of the union; the frowns of the executive magistracy of the state; the embarrassments created by legislative devices, which would often be added on such occasions, would oppose, in any state, difficulties not to be despised; would form in a large state, very serious impediments; and where the sentiments of several adjoining states happened to be in unison, would present obstructions which the Federal government would hardly be willing to encounter."[2]

Again he says, "The state government will have the advantage of the Federal government, whether we compare them in respect to the immediate dependence of the one on the other; to the weight

---

[1] Constitutional History of the United States, Vol. I, p. 79.
[2] No. 46.

of personal influence which each side will possess; to the powers respectively vested in them; to the predilection and probable support of the people; to the disposition and faculty of resisting and frustrating the measures of each other."[1]

It is doubtful whether Madison, in writing the passages above quoted, had in mind any thing more than a general policy of opposition and obstruction on the part of the states. He certainly intended, however, to convey the idea that under the proposed Constitution the states would have no difficulty in defending their constitutional rights against any attempted usurpation at the hands of the Federal government. We can trace the gradual development of this idea of state resistance to Federal authority until it finally assumes a definite form in the doctrine of nullification.

"A resolution [in the Maryland legislature] declaring the independence of the state governments to be jeopardized by the assumption of the state debts by the Union was rejected only by the casting vote of the speaker. In Virginia the two houses of the legislature sent a joint memorial to Congress. They expressed the hope that the funding act would be reconsidered and that the law providing for the assumption of the state debts would be repealed. A change in the present form of the government of the union, pregnant

[1] No. 45.

with disaster, would, it was said, be the presumptive consequence of the last act named, which the house of delegates had formally declared to be in violation of the Constitution of the United States."[1]

The general assembly of Virginia in 1798 adopted resolutions declaring that it viewed "the powers of the Federal government . . . as limited by the plain sense and intention of [the Constitution] . . . and that, in case of a deliberate, palpable, and dangerous exercise of other powers, not granted . . . , the states . . . have the right, and are in duty bound, to interpose, for arresting the progress of the evil, and for maintaining within their respective limits, the authority, rights, and liberties appertaining to them." These resolutions were drawn by Madison who had now come to oppose the strong centralizing policy of the Federalists.

A more explicit statement of this doctrine is to be found in the Kentucky Resolutions of 1798 which declared "that the several states composing the United States of America are not united on the principle of unlimited submission to their general government; . . . and that whenever the general government assumes undelegated powers, its acts are unauthoritative, void, and of no force; that to this compact each state acceded as a state, and is an integral party; that this government, created by this compact, was not made the exclusive or final judge of the extent of the powers delegated to itself, since that would have made its discretion, and not the Constitution, the measure of its powers; but that as in all other cases of compact among parties having no common judge, *each party has an equal right to judge for itself, as well of infractions as of the mode and measure of redress."*

The Kentucky resolutions of 1799 go one step farther and give definite expression to the doctrine of nullification. They declare "that the several states who formed that instrument [the Constitution], being sovereign and independent, have the unquestionable right to judge of the infraction; and, *that a nullification, by those sovereignties, of all unauthorized acts done under color of that instrument, is the rightful remedy."*

The first clear and unequivocal statement of the doctrine of nullification may be traced to Jefferson. In the original draft of the Kentucky resolutions of 1798, which he wrote, it is asserted that where the Federal government assumes powers "which have not been delegated, a nullification of the act is the rightful remedy; that every state has a natural right in cases not within the compact (*casus non foederis*) to nullify of their own authority, all assumptions of power by others within their limits."[1] This was omitted, how-

[1] Ford's Ed. Jefferson's Works, Vol. VII, p. 301.

ever, from the resolutions as finally adopted, although included in substance, as we have seen, in the Kentucky resolutions of 1799.

Jefferson's authorship of the original draft of the Kentucky resolutions of 1798 is made the basis of Von Holst's contention that he was the father of the doctrine of nullification. This, however, is something of an exaggeration. He is more accurate when he refers to the doctrine as being as old as the Constitution itself and the outgrowth of the circumstances of the time. The prevalent conception of the state as a check upon the Federal government derived support, as we have seen, from the efforts of the framers of the Constitution themselves to give it an interpretation that would remove as far as possible the obstacles to its ratification by allaying the fears and jealousy of the states. The idea that the state government could oppose and resist an unconstitutional exercise of authority by the Federal government was widely accepted as a general principle, although little attention had been given to the practical application of the doctrine. Jefferson merely gave definite form to what had been a more or less vague conception by showing how the constitutional checks upon the Federal government could be made effective.

The best statement of this doctrine, however, is to be found in the works of John C. Calhoun, whose Disquisition on Government and Discourse on the Constitution of the United States are a masterly defense of the system of checks and balances. He had no sympathy with what would now be called popular government. His point of view was essentially aristocratic, and he frankly avowed it.

He recognized the fact that under the existing social organization the interests of all classes are not the same; that there is a continual struggle between them; and that any interest or combination of interests obtaining control of the government will seek their own welfare at the expense of the rest. This, he claimed, made it necessary to so organize the government as to give the minority the means of self-protection. To give to the minority this constitutional power would tend to prevent the selfish struggle to obtain possession of the government, since it would deprive the majority of all power to aggrandize themselves at the expense of the minority. The very essence of constitutional government, according to his view, was the protection afforded to the minority through the limitation of the power of the majority. To accomplish the true end of constitutional government, which is the limitation of the power of the numerical majority, it is necessary, he contended, that the various classes or interests should be separately represented, and that each through its proper organ should have a veto on the acts of the others. In a government so organized no measure could be enacted into law and no policy enforced, unless it had received the assent of each element recognized in the Constitution. This method of taking the sense of the community, which required the concurrence of its several parts, he termed that of the concurrent majority.

This principle of class representation, he maintained, was fundamental in the American Constitution, which recognized for certain purposes the numerical majority as one of its elements, but only for certain purposes. For he tells us, and correctly, that "the numerical majority is, strictly speaking, excluded, even as one of its elements."[1] In support of this statement he undertakes to show that the numerical majority could not even prevent the amendment of the Constitution, since through a combination of the smaller states an amendment desired by the minority could be forced through in opposition to the wishes of the majority. He might have added that it was the intention of those who framed our government to allow the minority a free hand in amending by the method of constitutional interpretation; and also that they intended to deny to the numerical majority a veto on treaties and appointments. This refusal to recognize the numerical majority even as one of the coördinate elements in the government was as hereinbefore shown inconsistent with

[1] Works, Vol. I, p. 169.

the doctrine of checks, and is to be explained on the theory that they wished to subordinate the democratic element in the Constitution.

Calhoun argued that the growth of political parties had broken down our system of constitutional checks. The Constitution as originally adopted made no mention of, and allowed no place for these voluntary political organizations. In fact, the purpose of the political party was diametrically opposed to and subversive of all that was fundamental in the Constitution itself, since it aimed at nothing less than the complete destruction of the system of checks by bringing every branch of the government under its control. To the extent that it had achieved its purpose, it had consolidated the powers of the general government and brought them, he contended, under the direct control of the numerical majority, which was the very thing that the framers of the Constitution wished to guard against.

The complete control which the numerical majority had thus obtained over the Federal government made it supremely important that all constitutional power vested in the several states to resist Federal aggression should be actively employed. That the states had the power under the Constitution to check the general government when it attempted to overstep the limits set to its authority was necessarily implied in the fact that our system of government was federal and not national. His argument proceeded on the theory encouraged by the framers of the Constitution that the general government and the state governments were coordinate. "The idea of coördinates," he tells us, "excludes that of superior and subordinate, and necessarily implies that of equality. But to give either the right, not only to judge of the extent of its own powers, but, also, of that of its coördinate, and to enforce its decision against it, would be, not only to destroy the equality between them, but to deprive one of an attribute,—appertaining to all governments,—to judge, in the first instance, of the extent of its powers. The effect would be to raise one from an equal to a superior, and to reduce the other from an equal to a subordinate."[1]

From this it would follow that neither should have the exclusive right to judge of its own powers—that each should have a negative on the acts of the others. That this was the intention of the framers of the Constitution he argues from the fact that all efforts in the Convention to give the general government a negative on the acts of the states were unsuccessful. The efforts to confer this power, he contends, were made because it was seen that in the absence of such a provision the states would have a negative on the acts of the general government. The failure of these efforts in the Convention was due, he claims, to the fact

[1] Works, Vol. I, p. 242.

that the members of that body wished to make the general government and the state governments coördinate, instead of subordinating the latter to the former as the advocates of a national government desired. The fact upon which Calhoun based this contention would seem to justify his conclusion; but if we consult the debates which took place in that body, it is easily seen that the refusal of the Convention to incorporate such a provision in the Constitution can not be ascribed to any hostility on the part of that body to national government. In fact, as hereinbefore shown, it was for purely practical reasons that they rejected all proposals which contemplated the recognition in the Constitution itself of the supremacy of the general government. While declining to allow a provision of this character to be incorporated in the Constitution, they by no means disapproved of a strong supreme central government, but merely adopted a less direct and therefore easier method of attaining their end.

While Calhoun maintained that in order to make the limitations on the authority of the general government effective it was necessary that a state should have a veto on Federal laws, he did not contend that the verdict of a state should be final. It would still be possible for the general government to override the veto of a state by procuring a constitutional amendment which would remove all doubt as to its right to exercise the power in question. This method of appeal, he argued, was always open to the general government, since it represented and was in the hands of the numerical majority. This would be true, however, only when the party in power had the requisite two-thirds majority in both houses of Congress, or at least controlled the legislatures in two-thirds of the states. Otherwise its control of the general government would not enable it to propose the desired constitutional amendment. With this qualification Calhoun's contention was correct. On the other hand the state could not defend itself against Federal aggression, since, belonging to the minority, it would have no means of compelling the submission of a constitutional amendment involving the point in dispute. The effect of a state veto on an act of Congress would be to compel the latter to choose between abandoning the law in question as unconstitutional and appealing to the constitution-making power in defense of its claim. If it chose the latter alternative and succeeded in having its authority supported by an appropriate constitutional amendment, there was nothing for the state to do but submit, provided that the amendment in question was one clearly within the scope of the amending power. If, as Calhoun assumed, it was the purpose of the Constitution to withhold from a mere majority in control of the general government the power to enact and enforce unconstitutional legislation, the veto of a state would seem to be the only means by which the constitutional rights of a minority of the states could be protected.

Calhoun did not question the right of the Supreme Court of the United States to declare an act of Congress null and void, or its right to pass judgment upon the Constitution or the laws of a state when they were attacked as in conflict with the Federal Constitution in a case before it. This right, he contended, belonged to all courts whether federal or state. A decision of the Supreme Court of the United States adverse to the constitution or law of a state was, however, he maintained, binding only on the general government itself and the parties to the suit. As against the state it had no power to enforce its decision.

His entire argument rests upon the assumption that the Federal and state governments are coequal and not superior and subordinate. This line of argument naturally led to the conclusion that the Federal and state courts were coördinate. It was perfectly natural for the advocate of state rights to take this view of the matter. Moreover there was nothing in the Constitution which expressly contradicted it. The framers of that instrument, as hereinbefore shown, did not wish to make an open attack on the generally accepted doctrine of state sovereignty before the Constitution was adopted. Their purpose was fully disclosed only after they had obtained control of the new government under the Constitution. To carry out their plan of subordinating the states, it was necessary to establish the supremacy of the Federal judiciary. This was accomplished by an act of Congress[1] which provided that "a final judgment or decree in any suit in the highest court . . . . of a state in which a decision in the suit could be had, where is drawn in question the validity of a treaty or statute of, or an authority exercised under, the United States, and the decision is against their validity; or where is drawn in question the validity of a statute of, or an authority exercised under, any state, on the ground of their being repugnant to the Constitution, treaties, or laws of the United States, and the decision is in favor of their validity; or where is drawn in question the construction . . . . of a treaty, or statute of, or commission held under, the United States, and the decision is against the title, right, privilege, or exemption specially set up or claimed by either party, under such clause of said Constitution, treaty, statute, or Commission, may be re-examined, and reversed or affirmed in the Supreme Court of the United States upon a writ of error."

This act, while expressly conferring upon the Supreme Court of the United States the power to veto a state law, at the same time denied to a state court the right to treat as unconstitutional

[1] Sept., 24, 1789. U. S. Statutes at Large, Vol. I.

a statute, treaty, or authority exercised under the general government. The question might properly be asked why this provision was not incorporated in the Constitution itself. Why did not the framers of that document clearly define the relation of the Federal to the state courts? To have included the substance of this act in the Constitution as submitted to the states, would have precluded the possibility of any future controversy concerning the relation of the Federal to the state courts. From the point of view of practical politics, however, there was one unanswerable argument against this plan. It would have clearly indicated the intention of the framers of the Constitution, but in doing so, it would for that very reason have aroused opposition which it would have been impossible to overcome. This is why the matter of defining the relation of the Federal to the state courts was deferred until after the Constitution had been ratified by the states. They chose the only practicable means of accomplishing their purpose. With all branches of the Federal government under their control, they were able to enact a law which virtually amended the Constitution. Calhoun argues that in passing this act Congress exceeded the powers granted to it by the Constitution. What he fails to recognize, however, is the fact that this measure, although at variance with the interpretation placed upon the Constitution by the people generally, was, nevertheless, in entire harmony with the general purpose of its framers and necessary to carry that purpose into effect.

The view of the American Constitution herein presented may not be familiar to the average reader of our political literature. For notwithstanding the overwhelming proof of the aristocratic origin of our constitutional arrangements accessible to the unbiassed student, the notion has been sedulously cultivated that our general government was based on the theory of majority rule. Unfounded as an analysis of our political institutions shows this belief to be, it has by dint of constant repetition come to be widely accepted. It is beyond question that the Constitution was not so regarded by the people at the beginning of our national life. How, then, was this change in the attitude of the public brought about? There has doubtless been more than one influence that has contributed to this result. The abundant natural resources of the country and the material prosperity of the people are a factor that cannot be ignored. To these must in a measure be ascribed the uncritical attitude of mind, the pervailing indifference to political conditions, and the almost universal optimism which have characterized the American people. This lack of general attention to and interest in the more serious and profound questions of government has been favorable to the inculcation and acceptance of ideas of the system utterly at variance with its true character. Still, with all due allowance for these favoring conditions, it is hard to find a satisfactory explanation of the process by which the worshipers of democracy came to deify an undemocratic constitution. The desire of the conservative classes to preserve and perpetuate the system by presenting it in the guise of democracy, and their influence upon the political thought of the people generally must be regarded as the chief factor in bringing about this extraordinary change in public opinion. Hostile criticism of the Constitution soon "gave place to an undiscriminating and almost blind worship of its principles . . . and criticism was estopped. . . . The divine right of kings never ran a more prosperous course than did this unquestioned prerogative of the Constitution to receive universal homage. The conviction that our institutions were the best in the world, nay more, the model to which all civilized states must sooner or later conform, could not be laughed out of us by foreign critics, nor shaken out of us by the roughest jars of the system."[1]

[1] Woodrow Wilson, Congressional Government, p. 4.

CHAPTER VII

UNDEMOCRATIC DEVELOPMENT

It has been shown that the main purpose of the Constitution was to limit the power of the people. The recognition of this fact enables us to understand much of the subsequent development of our political institutions—a development for which the generally accepted theory of our system affords no adequate explanation. The erroneous view of the Constitution so generally inculcated has thus far misled the public as to the true source of our political evils. It would indeed be strange if some of the abuses incident to every form of minority rule had not made their appearance under the operation of a system such as has been described. Where the influence of public opinion has been so restricted, it would be but reasonable to expect that the practical working of the government would reflect something of the spirit of the Constitution itself. As a consequence of these limitations originally placed upon the power of the people, the development of our system has not been wholly in the direction of democracy. The constitutional authority conferred upon the minority has exerted a far-reaching influence upon the growth of our political institutions. The natural effect of subordinating the democratic element would be to render its influence more feeble as the system developed. That this has not been a purely imaginary danger may be easily shown.

The Constitution expressly gave to the qualified voters of the various states the right to contro! the House of Representatives. It was because of this fact, as explained in the preceding chapter, that this body was subordinated in our scheme of government. Even the most perfect control over this branch would have given the people no positive control over the government as a whole. At the most, it conceded to them merely a negative on a part of the acts and policy of the government. Yet popular control over this branch of the government has become less and less effective as our political system has developed.

The Constitution provides that "the times, places, and manner of holding elections for senators and representatives shall be prescribed in each state by the legislature thereof; but the Congress may at any time by law make or alter such regulations, except as to the place of choosing senators."[1]

It also provides that "Congress shall assemble at least once in every year, and such meeting shall be on the first Monday in December, unless they shall by law appoint a different day."

[1] Art. I, Sec. 4.

187

It also requires that the members of the House of Representatives shall be elected every second year; but as originally adopted it does not specify when their term of office shall begin.

After the ratification of the Constitution the Congress of the Confederation on September 13, 1788, designated March 4, 1789, as the time for commencing proceedings under the new régime. This made the term of office of President, Senators, and Representatives begin on that date.

An act of Congress, March 1, 1792, provided that the term of office of President should "in all cases, commence on the fourth day of March next succeeding the day on which the votes of the electors shall have been given."

This date was recognized as the beginning of the President's term of office by the Twelfth Amendment to the Constitution, which went into effect in 1804. By implication this amendment makes the term of representatives begin on the fourth of March of each odd year.

20

Congress, exercising the power vested in it by the Constitution to regulate Federal elections, enacted a law bearing date of February 2, 1872, which requires the election of representatives to be held on the Tuesday next after the first Monday in November of each even year, beginning with the year 1876. By act of March 3, 1875, this was modified so as not to apply to any state whose constitution would have to be amended before the day fixed for electing state officers could be changed in conformity with this provision.[1]

Congress has no power to change the date on which the term of office of a representative begins; but it does have authority to change the time of electing the House of Representatives, and also to determine when its own sessions shall begin, subject to the constitutional limitation that it shall meet at least once each year.

Under the law as it now stands the members of a newly elected House of Representatives do not meet in regular session until thirteen months after their election. Moreover, the second regular session does not begin until after the succeeding Congress has been elected.

The evils of this arrangement are thus described by a member of the House:

"The lower branch of Congress should at the earliest practicable time enact the principles of the majority of the people as expressed in the election of each Congress. That is why the Constitution requires the election of a new Congress every two years. If it were not to reflect the sentiments of the people then frequent elections would have no meaning or purpose. Any evasion of that rule is subversive of the fundamental principle of our

[1] The states of Maine, Oregon and Vermont still elect their representatives to Congress before the general November election. Maine holds her election on the second Monday in September, Oregon on the first Monday in June and Vermont on the first Tuesday in September next preceding the general November election.

21

government that the majority shall rule. No other government in the world has its legislative body convene so long after the expression of the people. . . .

"As an election often changes the political complexion of a Congress, under the present law, many times we have the injustice of a Congress that has been repudiated by the people enacting laws for the people diametrically opposed to the last expression of the people. Such a condition is an outrage on the rights of the majority. . . .

"Under the present law a representative in Congress who has been turned down by the people legislates for that people in the second regular session. . . .

"A man who has been defeated for re-election is not in a fit frame of mind to legislate for his people. There is a sting in defeat that tends to engender the feeling of resentment which often finds expression in the vote of such members against wholesome legislation. That same feeling often produces such a want of interest in proceedings as to cause the members to be absent nearly all the second session. . . .

"It is then that some are open to propositions which they would never think of entertaining if they were to go before the people for re-election. It is then that the attorneyship of some corporation is often tendered and a vote is afterward found in the record in favor of legislation of a

general or special character favoring the corporation."[1]

To appreciate the magnitude of the evils above
described, it is necessary to remember that upon
the average only about one-half of the members of
one Congress are elected to the succeeding Congress. This large number is, therefore, influenced
during the second regular session neither by the
hope of re-election nor the fear of defeat. Under
these circumstances it is not surprising that the
second regular session should be notoriously
favorable to corporation measures.

That Congress has not attempted to remedy this
evil is striking proof of its indifference to the
wishes of the people. Otherwise it would have
so employed the power which it possesses to perfect its organization, as to ensure the most prompt
and complete expression of public opinion in legislation possible under our constitutional arrangements. Having the power to change both the time
of electing a Congress and the beginning of its
sessions, it could easily remedy the evils described.
Both sessions of a Congress could be held before
the succeeding Congress is elected. This could
be accomplished by having Congress convene, as
advocated by the writer of the article above men-

[1] John F. Shafroth, When Congress Should Convene;
North Am. Rev., Vol.' 164. The writer of this article makes
the common but erroneous assumption that the fundamental
principle of our government is majority rule. From the
standpoint of democracy, however, his argument is un-
assailable.

tioned, for the first regular session on the Monday
following the fourth of March next after the election, and for the second regular session on the first
Monday after January first of the following year.
In this case the second regular session would
doubtless come to an end before the fall election.
Some such adjustment is required to give the people anything like adequate control over the House
of Representatives during the second regular
session.

The present arrangement which makes the
House of Representatives largely an irresponsible
body, while not provided for or perhaps even
contemplated by the framers of the Constitution,
is nevertheless the logical outcome of their plan to
throttle the power of the majority.   But although
in harmony with the general purpose and spirit of
the Constitution, it is a flagrant violation of the
basic principle of popular government.[1]

This tendency may be still more clearly seen in
the growth of the committee system by which the
division of power and its consequence, political
irresponsibility, have been carried much farther
than the Constitution contemplated, especially in
the organization of the House of Representatives.
No standing committees were provided for by the

[1] A modification of this check on public opinion has been
incorporated in the charter of one of our new Western cities.
In Spokane, Washington, one-half of the councilmen take
their seats immediately after the regular municipal election,
and the other half, though elected at the same time, do not
enter upon the discharge of their duties until one year later.

Constitution and few were established by the House during the early years of its existence. The system once introduced, however, has gradually developed until the House now has more than fifty-five of these committees.

Every legislative proposal must under the rules after its second reading be referred to the committee having jurisdiction over that particular branch of legislation. Theoretically, any member has a right to introduce any bill whatever. But as it must be referred to the proper committee and be reported by it to the House before the latter can discuss and adopt or reject it, it is evident that the right to initiate legislation has in effect been taken from the individual members and vested in the various standing committees. Under this method of procedure no proposed legislation can be enacted by the House without the consent of the committee having that particular branch of legislation in charge. The fact that a measure must be referred to a committee does not imply that that committee is obliged to report it back to the House. This the committee will, of course, do if the proposed bill is one which it wishes to have passed. But if it views the proposed legislation with disfavor, it may revise it so as to make it conform to its own wishes, or it may report it so late in the session as to prevent its consideration by the House, or it may neglect to report it altogether. This virtually gives a small body of men constituting a committee a veto on every legislative proposal. The extent to which this system diminishes the responsibility of the House can not be fully appreciated without bearing in mind the manner of appointment and composition of the committees. The Constitution provides that "the House of Representatives shall choose their speaker and other officers,"[1] but it makes no mention of the speaker's powers. The right to appoint the committees is not conferred on the speaker by the Constitution. The extent and character of the powers exercised by that official are determined very largely by the rules and usages of the House. This is the source of his power to appoint the chairman and other members of the various standing committees.

The speaker is elected at the beginning of each Congress and retains his office during the life of that body. The same is now true of the standing committees which he appoints, though previous to 1861 they were appointed for the session only.

The speaker is, of course, a member of the dominant party in the House, and is expected to use the powers and prerogatives of his office to advance in all reasonable ways the interests of the party which he represents. The selection of committees which he makes is naturally enough influenced by various considerations of a political and personal nature. It is largely determined by

[1] Art. I, Sec. 2.

the influences to which he owes his elevation to the speakership. In return for the support of influential members in his own party certain important chairmanships have been promised in advance. And even where no definite pledges have been made he must use the appointive power in a manner that will be acceptable to his party. This does not always prevent him, however, from exercising enough freedom in making up the committees to insure him a large measure of control over legislation.

All the chairmanships and a majority of the places on each committee are given to the members of his own party. As the speaker's right to appoint does not carry with it the power to remove, he has no control over a committee after it is appointed. The committees, as a matter of fact, are in no true sense responsible either to the speaker or to the House itself, since once appointed they can do as they please. They are in fact just so many small, independent, irresponsible bodies, each controlling in its own way and from motives known only to itself the particular branch of legislation assigned to it. The only semblance of responsibility attaching to the committee is found in the party affiliation of the majority of its members with the majority in the House. But ineffectual and intangible as this is, it is rendered even more so by the fact that the opposition party is also represented on each committee. This allows the dominant party to escape responsibility, since it can claim that its failure to satisfy the popular demand has been due to the opposition of the minority in the various committees, which has made concession and compromise necessary.

"The deliberations of committees," as Bryce says, "are usually secret. Evidence is frequently taken with open doors, but the newspapers do not report it, unless the matter excite public interest; and even the decisions arrived at are often noticed in the briefest way. It is out of order to canvass the proceedings of a committee in the House until they have been formally reported to it; and the report submitted does not usually state how the members have voted, or contain more than a very curt outline of what has passed. No member speaking in the House is entitled to reveal anything further."[1]

A system better adapted to the purposes of the lobbyist could not be devised. "It gives facilities for the exercise of underhand and even corrupt influence. In a small committee the voice of each member is well worth securing, and may be secured with little danger of a public scandal. The press can not, even when the doors of committee rooms stand open, report the proceedings of fifty bodies; the eye of the nation can not follow and mark what goes on within them; while the subsequent proceedings in the House are too hurried

[1] The American Commonwealth, Vol. I, Ch. 15.

to permit a ripping up there of suspicious bargains struck in the purlieus of the Capital, and fulfilled by votes given in a committee."[1]

A system which puts the power to control legislation in the hands of these small independent bodies and at the same time shields them so largely against publicity affords ample opportunity for railway and other corporate interests to exercise a controlling influence upon legislation.

This subdivision of the legislative power of the House and its distribution among many small, irresponsible bodies precludes the possibility of any effective party control over legislation. And since the majority in the House can not control its own agents there can be no effective party responsibility. To ensure responsibility the party in the majority must act as a unit and be opposed by an active and united minority. But our committee system disintegrates both the majority and the minority.

Another practice which has augmented the authority and at the same time diminished the responsibility of the committees is the hurried manner in which the House disposes of the various measures that come before it. The late Senator Hoar has estimated that the entire time which the House allows for this purpose during the two sessions which make up the life of a Congress "gives an average of no more than two hours apiece to

[1] The American Commonwealth, Vol. I, Ch. 15.

the committees of the House to report upon, debate, and dispose of all the subjects of general legislation committed to their charge. From this time is taken the time consumed in reading the bill, and in calling the yeas and nays, which may be ordered by one-fifth of the members present, and which require forty minutes for a single roll-call."[1]

Moreover, the member "who reports the bill dictates how long the debate shall last, who shall speak on each side, and whether any and what amendments shall be offered. Any member fit to be intrusted with the charge of an important measure would be deemed guilty of an inexcusable blunder if he surrendered the floor which the usages of the House assign to his control for an hour, without demanding the previous question."[2]

Nothing more would seem to be necessary to give the committee control of the situation. True the House may reject the bill which it submits, but the committee may easily prevent the House from voting upon a measure which a majority of that body desires to enact.

As there are many committees and the time which the House can give to the consideration of their reports is limited, it naturally follows that each committee is anxious to get all other business out of the way in order that it may have an oppor-

[1] The Conduct of Business in Congress, North Am. Rev., Vol. CXXVIII, p. 121.
[2] *Ibid.*, p. 122.

tunity to bring the measures which it has prepared to the attention of the House. This struggle between the various committees for an opportunity to report the bills which they have framed and have them considered by the House explains the acquiescence of that body in a system that so greatly restricts the freedom of debate. Very rarely will a committee encounter any formidable opposition in bringing the discussion of its measures to a close.

The speaker's power of recognition is another check upon the majority in the House. This power which he freely uses in an arbitrary manner enables him to prevent the introduction of an obnoxious bill by refusing to recognize a member who wishes to obtain the floor for that purpose.[1] Moreover, as chairman of the Committee on Rules he virtually has the power to determine the order in which the various measures shall be considered by the House. In this way he can secure an opportunity for those bills which he wishes the House to pass and ensure the defeat of those to which he is opposed by giving so many other matters the preference that they can not be reached before the close of the second session.

The power thus exercised by the speaker, coupled with that of the committees, imposes an effectual restraint not only on the individual

[1] For instances of the exercise of this power see Follett, The Speaker of the House of Representatives, Ch. IX.

members, but on the majority as well. A large majority of the bills introduced are vetoed by the committees or "killed" by simply not reporting them back to the House. There is no way in which the House can override the veto of a committee or that of the speaker, since even when the rules are suspended no measure can be considered that has not been previously reported by a committee, while the speaker can enforce his veto through his power of recognition. Both the committees and the speaker have what is for all practical purposes an absolute veto on legislation.

A motion to suspend the rules and pass any bill that has been reported to the House may be made on the first and third Mondays of each month or during the last six days of each session. "In this way, if two-thirds of the body agree, a bill is by a single vote, without discussion and without change, passed through all the necessary stages, and made law so far as the consent of the House can accomplish it. And in this mode hundreds of measures of vital importance receive, near the close of exhausting sessions, without being debated, amended, printed, or understood, the constitutional assent of the representatives of the American people."[1]

This system which so effectually restricts the power of the majority in the House affords no safeguard against local or class legislation. By

[1] Senator Hoar's Article.

making it difficult for any bill however worthy of consideration to receive a hearing on its own merits, it naturally leads to the practice known as log-rolling. The advocates of a particular measure may find that it can not be passed unless they agree to support various other measures of which they disapprove. It thus happens that many of the bills passed by the House are the result of this bargaining between the supporters of various measures. Certain members in order to secure the passage of a bill in which they are especially interested will support and vote for other bills which they would prefer to vote against. In this way many bills secure a favorable vote in the House when a majority of that body are really opposed to their enactment. It is entirely within the bounds of possibility that no important measure desired by the people at large and which would be supported by a majority of the House, can be passed, since any powerful private interest opposed to such legislation may be able to have the measure in question quietly killed in committee or otherwise prevented from coming to a final vote in the House. But while legislation in the interest of the people generally may be defeated through the silent but effective opposition of powerful private interests, many other measures which ought to be defeated are allowed to pass. A system which makes it possible to defeat the will of the majority in the House by preventing on the one hand the enactment of laws which that majority favors, and by permitting on the other hand the enactment of laws to which it is opposed, certainly does not allow public opinion to exercise an effective control over the proceedings of the House.

As a foreign critic observes, "the House has ceased to be a debating assembly; it is only an instrument for hasty voting on the proposals which fifty small committees have prepared behind closed doors. . . . At the present time it is very much farther from representing the people than if, instead of going as far as universal suffrage, it had kept to an infinitely narrower franchise, but had preserved at the same time the freedom, fullness, and majesty of its debates."[1]

[1] Boutmy, Studies in Constitutional Law, pp. 98-99.

CHAPTER VIII

THE PARTY SYSTEM

The political party is a voluntary association which seeks to enlist a majority of voters under its banner and thereby gain control of the government. As the means employed by the majority to make its will effective, it is irreconcilably opposed to all restraints upon its authority. Party government in this sense is the outcome of the efforts of the masses to establish their complete and untrammeled control of the state.

This is the reason why conservative statesmen of the eighteenth century regarded the tendency towards party government as the greatest political evil of the time. Far-sighted men saw clearly that its purpose was revolutionary; that if accomplished, monarchy and aristocracy would be shorn of all power; that the checks upon the masses would be swept away and the popular element made supreme. This would lead inevitably to the overthrow of the entire system of special privilege which centuries of class rule had carefully built up and protected.

When our Constitution was framed responsible party government had not been established in

England. In theory the Constitution of Great Britain recognized three coördinate powers, the King, the Lords, and the Commons. But as a matter of fact the government of England was predominantly aristocratic. The landed interests exerted a controlling influence even in the House of Commons. The rapidly growing importance of capital had not yet seriously impaired the constitutional authority of the landlord class. Land had been until recently the only important form of wealth; and the right to a voice in the management of the government was still an incident of land ownership. Men as such were not entitled to representation. The property-owning classes made the laws and administered them, officered the army and navy, and controlled the policy of the government in every direction.

"According to a table prepared about 1815, the House of Commons contained 471 members who owed their seats to the goodwill and pleasure of 144 Peers and 123 Commoners, 16 government nominees, and only 171 members elected by popular suffrages."[1]

As the real power behind the government was the aristocracy of wealth, the English system, though nominally one of checks and balances, closely resembled in its practical working an unlimited aristocracy.

[1] Ostrogorski, Democracy and the Organization of Political Parties, Vol. I, p. 20.

The framers of our Constitution, as shown in previous chapters, took the English government for their model and sought to establish the supremacy of the well-to-do classes. Like the English conservatives of that time they deplored the existence of political parties and consequently made no provision for them in the system which they established. Indeed, their chief purpose was to prevent the very thing which the responsible political party aimed to establish, viz., majority rule.

"Among the numerous advantages promised by a well-constructed union," wrote Madison in defense of the Constitution, "none deserves to be more accurately developed than its tendency to break and control the violence of faction. . . .

"By a faction, I understand a number of citizens, whether amounting to a majority or minority of the whole, who are united and actuated by some common impulse of passion, or of interest, adverse to the rights of other citizens, or to the permanent and aggregate interests of the community. . . .

" . . . But the most common and durable source of factions has been the various and unequal distribution of property. Those who hold and those who are without property have ever formed distinct interests in society. Those who are creditors, and those who are debtors, fall under a like discrimination. A landed interest, a manufacturing interest, a mercantile interest, a moneyed interest, with many lesser interests, grow up of necessity in civilized nations, and divide them into different classes actuated by different sentiments and views. . . .

"If a faction consists of less than a majority, relief is supplied by the republican principle, which enables the majority to defeat its sinister views by a regular vote. It may clog the administration, it may convulse the society; but it will be unable to execute and mask its violence under the forms of the Constitution. When a majority is included in a faction, the form of popular government, on the other hand, enables it to sacrifice to its ruling passion or interest both the public good and the rights of other citizens. To secure the public good and private rights against the danger of such a faction, and at the same time to preserve the spirit and the form of popular government, is then the great object to which our inquiries are directed."[1]

The very existence of political parties would endanger the system which they set up, since in their efforts to strengthen and perpetuate their rule they would inevitably advocate extensions of the suffrage, and thus in the end competition between parties for popular support would be destructive of all those property qualifications for voting and holding office which had up to that

[1] *Federalist*, No. 10.

time excluded the propertyless classes from any participation in public affairs. Hence Washington though a staunch Federalist himself saw nothing inconsistent in trying to blend the extremes of political opinion by giving both Hamilton and Jefferson a place in his Cabinet.

In England the party by the Reform bill of 1832 accomplished its purpose, broke through the barriers erected against it, divested the Crown of all real authority, subordinated the House of Lords, and established the undisputed rule of the majority in the House of Commons. This accomplished, it was inevitable that the rivalry between political parties should result in extensions of the suffrage until the House should come to represent, as it does in practice to-day, the sentiment of the English people.

The framers of the American Constitution, however, succeeded in erecting barriers which democracy has found it more difficult to overcome. For more than a century the constitutional bulwarks which they raised against the rule of the numerical majority have obstructed and retarded the progress of the democratic movement. The force of public sentiment soon compelled, it is true, the adoption of the Twelfth Amendment, which in effect recognized the existence of political parties and made provision for the party candidate for President and Vice-President. At most, however, it merely allowed the party to name the executive without giving it any effective control over him after he was elected, since in other respects the general plan of the Constitution remained unchanged.

The political party, it is true, has come to play an important rôle under our constitutional system; but its power and influence are of a negative rather than a positive character. It professes, of course, to stand for the principle of majority rule, but in practice it has become an additional and one of the most potent checks on the majority.

To understand the peculiar features of the American party system one must bear in mind the constitutional arrangements under which it has developed. The party is simply a voluntary political association through which the people seek to formulate the policy of the government, select the officials who are to carry it out in the actual administration of public affairs, and hold them to strict accountability for so doing. Under any government which makes full provision for the political party, as in the English system of to-day, the party has not only the power to elect but the power to remove those who are entrusted with the execution of its policies. Having this complete control of the government, it can not escape responsibility for failure to carry out the promises by which it secured a majority at the polls. This is the essential difference between the English system on the one hand and the party under the

American constitutional system on the other. The one well knows that if it carries the election it will be expected to make its promises good. The other makes certain promises with the knowledge that after the election is over it will probably have no power to carry them out.

It is this lack of power to shape the entire policy of the government which, more than anything else, has given form and character to the party system of the United States. To the extent that the Constitution has deprived the majority of the power to mold the policy of the government through voluntary political associations, it has defeated the main purpose for which the party should exist.

The fact that under the American form of government the party can not be held accountable for failure to carry out its ante-election pledges has had the natural and inevitable result. When, as in England, the party which carries the election obtains complete and undisputed control of the government, the sense of responsibility is ever present in those who direct it. If in the event of its success it is certain to be called upon to carry out its promises, it can not afford for the sake of obtaining votes to make promises which it has no intention of keeping. But when the party, even though successful at the polls may lack the power to enforce its policy, it can not be controlled by a sense of direct responsibility to the people.

Promises may be recklessly and extravagantly made merely for the sake of getting votes. The party platform from the point of view of the party managers ceases to be a serious declaration of political principles. It comes to be regarded as a means of winning elections rather than a statement of what the party is obligated to accomplish.

The influence thus exerted by the Constitution upon our party system, though generally overlooked by students and critics of American politics, has had profound and far-reaching results. That the conduct of individuals is determined largely by the conditions under which they live is as well established as any axiom of political science. This must be borne in mind if we would fully understand the prevailing apathy—the seeming indifference to corruption and ring rule which has so long characterized a large class of intelligent and well-meaning American citizens. To ascribe the evils of our party system to their lack of interest in public questions and their selfish disregard of civic duties, is to ignore an important phase of the problem—the influence of the system itself. In the long run an active general interest can be maintained only in those institutions from which the people derive some real or fancied benefit. This benefit in the case of the political party can come about only through the control which it enables those who compose it to exercise over the government. And where, as under the

American system, control of the party does not ensure control of the government, the chief motive for an alert and unflagging interest in political questions is lacking. If the majority can not make an effective use of the party system for the attainment of political ends, they can not be expected to maintain an active interest in party affairs.

But although our constitutional arrangements are such as to deprive the people of effective control over the party, it has offices at its disposal and sufficient power to grant or revoke legislative favors to make control of its organization a matter of supreme importance to office seekers and various corporate interests. Thus while the system discourages an unselfish and public-spirited interest in party politics, it does appeal directly to those interests which wish to use the party for purely selfish ends. Hence the ascendency of the professional politician who, claiming to represent the masses, really owes his preferment to those who subsidize the party machine.

The misrepresentative character of the American political party seems to be generally recognized by those who have investigated the subject. It is only when we look for an explanation of this fact that there is much difference of opinion. The chief difficulty encountered by those who have given attention to this problem has been the point of view from which they have approached it.

The unwarranted assumption almost universally made that the principle of majority rule is fundamental in our scheme of government has been a serious obstacle to any adequate investigation of the question. Blind to the most patent defects of the Constitution, they have ignored entirely its influence upon the development and character of the political party. Taking it for granted that our general scheme of government was especially designed to facilitate the rule of the majority, they have found it difficult to account for the failure of the majority to control the party machine. Why is it that under a system which recognizes the right and makes it the duty of the majority to control the policy of the government, that control has in practice passed into the hands of a small minority who exercise it often in utter disregard of and even in direct opposition to the wishes and interests of the majority? On the assumption that we have a Constitution favorable in the highest degree to democracy, how are we to explain the absence of popular control over the party itself? Ignoring the obstacles which the Constitution has placed in the way of majority rule, American political writers have almost invariably sought to lay the blame for corruption and machine methods upon the people. They would have us believe that if such evils are more pronounced here than elsewhere it is because in this country the masses control the government.

If the assumption thus made concerning the nature of our political system were true, we would be forced to accept one of two conclusions: either that popular government inevitably results in the despotism of a corrupt and selfish oligarchy, or if such is not a necessary consequence, then at any rate the standard of citizenship in this country intellectually and morally is not high enough to make democracy practicable. That the ignorance, selfishness and incapacity of the people are the real source of the evils mentioned is diligently inculcated by all those who wish to discredit the theory of popular government. No one knows better than the machine politician and his allies in the great corporate industries of the country how little control the people generally do or can exercise over the party under our present political arrangements. To disclose this fact to the people generally, however, might arouse a popular movement of such magnitude as to sweep away the constitutional checks which are the source of their power. But as this is the very thing which they wish to prevent, the democratic character of the Constitution must be taken for granted; for by so doing the people are made to assume the entire responsibility for the evils which result from the practical operation of the system. And since the alleged democratic character of our political arrangements is, it is maintained, the real source of the evils complained of, the only effective remedy would be the restriction of the power of the people. This might take the form of additional constitutional checks which would thereby diminish the influence of a general election upon the policy of the government without disturbing the present basis of the suffrage; or it might be accomplished by excluding from the suffrage those classes deemed to be least fit to exercise that right. Either method would still further diminish the influence of the majority, and instead of providing a remedy for the evils of our system, would only intensify them, since it would augment the power of the minority which is, as we have seen, the main source from which they proceed.

A government which limits the power of the majority might promote the general interests of society more effectually than one controlled by the majority, if the checks were in the hands of a class of superior wisdom and virtue. But in practice such a government, instead of being better than those for whom it exists, is almost invariably worse. The complex and confusing system of checks, with the consequent diffusion of power and absence of direct and definite responsibility, is much better adapted to the purposes of a self-seeking, corrupt minority than to the ends of good government. The evils of such a system which are mainly those of minority domination must be carefully distinguished from those which result from majority control. The critics of American political institutions have as a rule ignored the former or constitutional aspect of our political evils, and have held majority rule accountable for much that our system of checks has made the majority powerless to prevent. The evils of our party system, having their roots in the lack of popular control over the party machine, are thus largely a consequence of the checks on the power of the majority contained in the Constitution itself. In other words, they are the outcome, not of too much, but of too little democracy.

22

The advocates of political reform have directed their attention mainly to the party machine. They have assumed that control of the party organization by the people would give them control of the government. If this view were correct, the evils which exist could be attributed only to the ignorance, want of public spirit and lack of capacity for effective political co-operation on the part of the people. But as a matter of fact this method of dealing with the problem is open to the objection that it mistakes the effect for the cause. It should be clearly seen that a system of constitutional checks, which hedges about the power of the majority on every side, is incompatible with majority rule; and that even if the majority controlled the party organization, it could control the policy of the government only by breaking down and sweeping away the barriers which the Constitution has erected against it. It follows that all attempts to establish the majority in power by merely reforming the party must be futile.

Under any political system which recognizes the right of the majority to rule, responsibility of the government to the people is the end and aim of all that the party stands for. Party platforms and popular elections are not ends in themselves, but only means by which the people seek to make the government responsive to public opinion. Any arrangement of constitutional checks, then, which defeats popular control, strikes down what is most vital and fundamental in party government. And since the party under our system can not enforce public opinion, it is but natural that the people should lose interest in party affairs. This furnishes an explanation of much that is peculiar to the American party system. It accounts for that seeming indifference and inactivity on the part of the people generally, which have allowed a small selfish minority to seize the party machinery and use it for private ends.

The party, though claiming to represent the people, is not in reality a popular organ. Its chief object has come to be the perpetuation of minority control, which makes possible the protection and advancement of those powerful private interests to whose co-operation and support the party boss is indebted for his continuance in power.[1] To accomplish these ends it is necessary

[1] For a discussion of the causes of present-day corruption,

to give the party an internal organization adapted to its real, though not avowed, purpose. The people must not be allowed to use the party as a means of giving clear and definite expression to public opinion concerning the questions wherein the interests of the general public are opposed to the various private interests which support the party machine. For a strong popular sentiment well organized and unequivocally expressed could not be lightly disregarded, even though without constitutional authority to enforce its decrees. To ensure successful minority rule that minority must control those agencies to which the people in all free countries are accustomed to look for an authoritative expression of the public will. The party machine can not serve the purpose of those interests which give it financial support and at the same time allow the people to nominate its candidates and formulate its political creed. Nevertheless, the semblance of popular control must be preserved. The outward appearance of the party organization, the external forms which catch the popular eye, must not reveal too clearly the secret methods and cunningly devised arrangements by which an effective minority control is maintained over the nomination of candidates and the framing of party platforms. The test of fitness for office is not fidelity to the rank and file of the

see an article by Professor Edward A. Ross in *The Independent,* July 19, 1906, on "Political Decay: An Interpretation."

people who vote the party ticket, but subserviency to those interests which dominate the party machine. The choice of candidates is largely made in the secret councils of the ruling minority and the party conventions under color of making a popular choice of candidates merely ratify the minority choice already made. Popular elections under such a system do not necessarily mean that the people have any real power of selecting public officials. They merely have the privilege of voting for one or the other of two lists of candidates neither of which may be in any true sense representative of the people or their interests.

But in nothing is the lack of popular control over the party more clearly seen than in the party platforms. These are supposed to provide a medium for the expression of public opinion upon the important questions with which the government has to deal. Under a political system which recognized the right of the majority to rule, a party platform would be constructed with a view to ascertaining the sense of that majority. Does the platform of the American political party serve this purpose? Does it seek to crystallize and secure a definite expression of public opinion at the polls, or is it so constructed as to prevent it? This question can best be answered by an examination of our party platforms.

The Constitution, as we have seen, was a reaction against and a repudiation of the theory of government expressed in the Declaration of Independence, although this fact was persistently denied by those who framed it and urged its adoption. The high regard in which popular government was held by the masses did not permit any open and avowed attempt to discredit it. The democracy of the people, however, was a matter of faith rather than knowledge, a mere belief in the right of the masses to rule rather than an intelligent appreciation of the political agencies and constitutional forms through which the ends of popular government were to be attained. Unless this is borne in mind, it is impossible to understand how the Constitution, which was regarded at first with distrust, soon came to be reverenced by the people generally as the very embodiment of democratic doctrines. In order to bring about this change in the attitude of the people, the Constitution was represented by those who sought to advance it in popular esteem as the embodiment of those principles of popular government to which the Declaration of Independence gave expression. The diligence with which this view of the Constitution was inculcated by those who were in a position to aid in molding public opinion soon secured for it universal acceptance. Even the political parties which professed to stand for majority rule and which should therefore have sought to enlighten the people have

not only not exposed but actually aided in perpetuating this delusion.

In the Democratic platform of 1840 we find the
following:

"Resolved, That the liberal principles embodied
by Jefferson in the Declaration of Independence,
and sanctioned in the Constitution, which makes
ours a land of liberty and the asylum of the
oppressed of every nation, have ever been cardinal
principles in the Democratic faith." This was
reaffirmed in the Democratic platforms of 1844,
1848, 1852, and 1856.

Finding its advocacy of the Declaration of Independence somewhat embarrassing in view of its
attitude on the slavery question, the Democratic
party omitted from its platform all reference to
that document until 1884, when it ventured to
reaffirm its faith in the liberal principles which it
embodied. Again, in its platform of 1900, it
referred to the Declaration of Independence as
"the spirit of our government" and the Constitution as its "form and letter."

In the Republican platform of 1856 we read
"That the maintenance of the principles promulgated in the Declaration of Independence and
embodied in the Federal Constitution is essential
to the preservation of our republican institutions."
This was repeated in the Republican platform of
1860, and the principles of the Declaration of
Independence alleged to be embodied in the Con-

stitution were specified, viz., "That all men are created equal; that they are endowed by their Creator with certain inalienable rights; that among these are life, liberty, and the pursuit of happiness; that to secure these rights governments are instituted among men, deriving their just powers from the consent of the governed." The authority of the Declaration of Independence was recognized by the Republican party in its platform of 1868, and again in its platform of 1876.[1]

Both parties have during recent years expressed their disapproval of monopolies and trusts, though neither when in power has shown any disposition to enact radical anti-monopoly legislation.

The Democratic party which favored "honest money" in 1880 and 1884 and demanded the repeal of the Sherman Act in 1892 stood for free coinage of silver at 16 to 1 in 1896 and 1900. The Republican party which advocated international bimetallism in 1884, condemned the Democratic party in 1888 for trying to demonetize silver and endorsed bimetallism in 1892, favored "sound money" and international bimetallism in 1896 and renewed its "allegiance to the principle of the gold standard" in 1900.

The Republican platform of 1860 branded "the

[1] In the enabling acts for the admission of Nebraska and Nevada (1864), Colorado (1875), North Dakota, South Dakota, Montana and Washington (1889), and Utah (1896), we find the provision that the state constitution shall not be repugnant to the Constitution of the United States and the principles of the Declaration of Independence.

recent reopening of the African slave trade, under the cover of our national flag, aided by perversions of judicial power, as a crime against humanity." The Democratic party in its platform of 1896 expressed its disapproval of the Income Tax decision of the United States Supreme Court and in both 1896 and 1900 condemned "government by injunction." With these exceptions neither party has ever expressed its disapproval of any exercise of authority by the Federal judiciary.

Neither of the great parties has ever taken a stand in favor of an income tax, government ownership of the railroads or the telegraph, or, if we except the declaration in favor of direct election of United States senators in the Democratic platforms of 1900 and 1904, advocated any important change in our system of government.

Let us now inquire how far the results of a general election can be regarded as an expression of public opinion upon the questions raised in the party platforms. Does a popular majority for a party mean that the majority approve of the policies for which that party professes to stand? It is generally assumed by the unthinking that this is the case. But such a conclusion by no means follows. If there were but one question at issue between the parties and every vote was for principle, not for particular candidates, the policy of the successful party would have the approval of the majority. But when the party defines its position on a number of issues this is no longer true. Take, for instance, the Democratic and Republican platforms of 1900, the former containing twenty-five and the latter twenty-nine separate articles in its party creed. Does a majority vote for a party indicate that the majority approve of the entire platform of that party? No thoughtful person would maintain for a moment that all who support a party approve of its entire platform. In the case of the Republican party in 1900, one large class of its supporters who believed the money question to be paramount and who feared the consequences of free coinage of silver voted the Republican ticket, though opposed to the attitude of that party on expansion and also on protection. The ardent protectionist may have given the party his support on the strength of its tariff plank alone. He may even have been opposed to the party's position on the silver question and on expansion. Another class who may have disapproved of both gold monometallism and protection, but who regarded expansion as the all-important question, supported the Republican party because of its attitude in this matter. It is certain that some who voted the Republican ticket did not approve its expansion policy; some did not approve of its extreme protectionist policy; and some did not approve of its attitude on the money question. Every man who voted the Republican ticket is assumed to have endorsed the entire policy of the party, though, as a matter of fact, the party may have secured his vote by reason of its position on the one question which he deemed to be of supreme importance. It is, to say the least, extremely probable that every intelligent man who supported the party disapproved of its attitude on one or more questions. Each plank in the platform was put there for the purpose of catching votes. Some gave their vote for one reason, some for another and some for still other reasons. And when, as in our present day party platforms, many separate and distinct bids are made for votes, it is not only possible but highly probable that no single plank in that party's creed was approved by all who voted the party ticket. If the various issues could be segregated and each voted upon separately, it is conceivable that not one of them would command a majority of the entire vote; and yet, by lumping them all together and skilfully pushing to the front and emphasizing each article of its creed before the class or in the region where it would find most support, the party may secure a popular majority for its platform as a whole. Both parties in their platforms of 1900 stood for the admission as states of Arizona, New Mexico, and Oklahoma; both declared in favor of legislation against monopolies and trusts; both favored liberal pensions, the construction of an Isthmian canal, irrigation of arid lands, reduction of war taxes and protection of American workmen against cheap foreign labor. Yet it does not by any means follow that a majority of the people voting really endorsed even these planks which were common to both platforms.

Moreover the party does not always state its position in a clear and unequivocal manner. The Democratic platform while opposing Republican expansion did so with some important reservation. While denouncing the recent expansion policy of the Republican party it made a bid for the support of those who believed in a moderate and conservative expansion policy. The same is true of its attitude on protection. It did not condemn the principle of protection, but merely the abuse of the system through which monopolies and trusts had been fostered. The vague and ambiguous manner in which the party defines its attitude, together with the highly composite character of its platform, largely defeats the end for which it should be framed. As a means of arriving at a definite and authoritative expression of public opinion concerning the political questions of the day it is far from satisfactory. It is conceivable that a party may under this system carry an election and yet not a single principle for which it professes to stand would, if separately submitted, command the approval of a majority of the voters.

The threefold purpose for which the party

exists—(1) popular choice of candidates, (2) a clear and definite expression of public opinion concerning the questions with which the government must deal, and (3) the responsibility of the government to the popular majority are all largely defeated under the American system. The last named end of the party is defeated by the Constitution itself, and this, as hereinbefore shown, has operated to defeat the others as well.

We thus see that true party government is impossible under a constitutional system which has as its chief end the limitation of the power of the majority. Where the party which has carried the election is powerless to enforce its policy, as is generally the case in this country, there can be no responsible party government. The only branch of our governmental system which responds readily to changes in public opinion is the House of Representatives. But this is and was designed to be a subordinate body, having a voice in shaping only a part of the policy of the government, and even in this limited field being unable to act except with the concurrence of the President, Senate and Supreme Court. A change in public sentiment is not likely under these circumstances to be followed by a corresponding change in the policy of the state. Even when such change in sentiment is insistent and long-continued, it may be unable to overcome the resistance of the more conservative influences in the Constitution. The most superficial examination of our political history is sufficient to show that the practical working of our Constitution has in large measure defeated the end of party government. Calhoun's contention that the party had succeeded in breaking down the elaborate system of constitutional checks on the numerical majority is not borne out by the facts.

Eleven general elections since the adoption of the Constitution have resulted in a House of Representatives which had no political support in any other branch of the government. During eighty-four years of our history under the Constitution the party in the majority in the House has not had a majority in all the other branches of the general government, and consequently has not had the power to enforce its policy. From 1874 to 1896—a period of twenty-two years—there were but two years (the 51st Congress) during which the same party had a majority in all branches of the government. But even during this brief period it failed to control the treaty-making power since it lacked the two-thirds majority in the Senate which the Constitution requires. In fact, there has been no time since 1874 when any party had sufficient majority in the Senate to give it an active control over the treaty-making power.

The more important and fundamental changes in public policy which involve an exercise of the amending power are still more securely placed beyond the reach of party control. Not only the power to ratify amendments, but even the power to propose them, is effectually withheld from the party, since it can scarcely ever command the required two-thirds majority in both houses of Congress or a majority in both branches of the legislature in two-thirds of the states.

Under our constitutional system a political party may have a nominal majority in all branches of the government and yet lack the power to enforce its policy. That branch of the government over which the party has most control through frequent elections—viz., the House of Representatives—is the one which has least authority, while those which have most influence in shaping the policy of the government are less directly subject to the penalties of party disapproval, as in the case of the President and Senate, or entirely exempt from any effective party control as in the case of the Supreme Court. The division of authority under our Constitution makes it possible for either house of Congress to give the appearance of support to a measure which public opinion demands and at the same time really accomplish its defeat by simply not providing the means essential to its enforcement. The opportunity thus afforded for the exercise of a covert but effective veto on important legislation is a fruitful source of corruption. The extreme diffusion of power and responsibility is such as to make any effective party control and responsibility impossible. This would be the case even if the party were truly representative of public opinion. But when we consider that the party is organized on a plan which in some measure at least defeats both the popular choice of candidates and the expression of public opinion in party platforms, it is readily seen that the slight degree of party control permitted under our system is in no true sense a popular control.

CHAPTER IX

CHANGES IN THE STATE CONSTITUTIONS AFTER 1787

The effects of the conservative reaction were not confined to the general government. The movement to limit the power of the popular majority was felt in the domain of state as well as national politics. Even before the Constitutional Convention assembled the political reaction was modifying some of the state constitutions. This is seen especially in the tendency to enlarge the powers of the judiciary which was the only branch of the state government in which life tenure survived. This tendency received powerful encouragement and support in the adoption of the Federal Constitution which secured to the judiciary of the general government an absolute veto on both federal and state legislation. For as the state courts were not slow in following the precedent set by the Federal courts, what had been before the adoption of the Constitution a mere tendency soon became the practice in all the states. This in reality accomplished a revolution in the actual working of the state governments without any corresponding change in their outward form.

It effected a redistribution of political powers which greatly diminished the influence of the popularly elected and more responsible branches of the state government and gave a controlling influence to that branch over which the people had least control.

Not only was the state judiciary allowed to assume the veto power, but their independence of public opinion was more effectually safeguarded by depriving a mere majority of the legislature of the power to remove them. The provision of the Federal Constitution requiring a two-thirds majority in the legislative body for removal by impeachment or otherwise was quite generally copied. Without some such safeguard the party in control of the legislature could prevent the exercise of the judicial veto by removing from office any judges who dared to oppose its policy.

New York and South Carolina were the only states adopting constitutions during the Revolutionary period, which included provisions limiting the power of the majority to impeach public officials. The New York constitution of 1777 required a two-thirds majority in the lower house, and the South Carolina constitution of 1778 a two-thirds majority in both houses. Pennsylvania copied the impeachment provisions of the Federal Constitution in her constitution of 1790; Delaware went even farther, and in her constitution of 1792, required a two-thirds majority in both houses; Georgia followed the example of the Federal Constitution in 1798; Virginia, in 1830; North Carolina, in 1835; Vermont, in 1836; New Jersey, in 1844; and Maryland, in 1851.

With the progress of this movement to restore the system of checks in the state constitutions the governor regained his independence of the legislature and also many of the rights and prerogatives of which the Revolution had deprived him. He was made coördinate with the legislature, set over against it and generally clothed with the qualified veto power, which made him for all practical purposes the third house of that body. Georgia increased the governor's term of office to two years and gave him the qualified veto power in 1798. Pennsylvania made his term of office three years and gave him the veto power in 1790. New Hampshire conferred the veto power on him in 1792 and New York in 1821.

This tendency to make the public official less directly dependent upon the people or their immediate representatives is clearly seen in other important changes made in the state constitutions during this period. Popular control over the legislature was diminished by lengthening the terms of the members of both houses and by providing that the upper house should be elected for a longer term than the lower. Georgia established an upper house in 1789 and made the term of office of its members three years. In 1790 Pennsyl-

vania also added a senate whose members were to
be elected for four years, and South Carolina increased the term of its senators from one to four
years. Delaware extended the term from one to
two years for members of the lower house and
from three to four years for members of the upper
house and made the legislative sessions biennial
instead of annual in 1831. North Carolina increased the term of members of both houses from
one to two years and adopted biennial sessions in
1835. Maryland in 1837 extended the term of
senators from five to six years, and in 1846 established biennial sessions of the legislature.
The responsibility of the legislature was still
further diminished by the gradual adoption of the
plan of partial renewal of the senate, which was
incorporated in the Revolutionary constitutions of
Delaware, New York and Virginia and later
copied in the Federal Constitution. This ensured the conservative and steadying influence
exerted by a body of hold-over members in the
upper house.

With the exception of five states in which the
members of one branch of the legislature were
elected for terms varying from two to five years,
the Revolutionary state constitutions provided for
the annual election of the entire legislature. This
plan made both houses conform to the latest expression of public opinion by the majority of the
qualified voters at the polls. And since neither

the executive nor the courts possessed the veto power, the system ensured prompt compliance on the part of the law-making body with the demands of the people as expressed in the results of the legislative election.

The influence of public opinion on the state governments was greatly weakened by the constitutional changes above mentioned. The lower branch of the legislature, inasmuch as all its members were simultaneously elected, might be regarded as representative of recent, if not present, public opinion, though effective popular control of that body was made more difficult by lengthening the term of office, since this diminished the frequency with which the voters could express in an authoritative manner their disapproval of the official record of its members. Under the plan adopted present public opinion as formulated in the results of the last election was not recognized as entitled to control the state senate.

These changes in the state constitutions by which the executive and judicial branches of the government acquired the veto power amounted in practice to the creation of a four-chambered legislature. By thus increasing the number of bodies which it was necessary for the people to control in order to secure the legislation which they desired, their power to influence the policy of the state government was thereby diminished. And when we reflect that not only was legislative au-

thority more widely distributed, but each branch
of the state government exercising it was also
made less directly dependent on the qualified
voters, we can see that these constitutional provisions were in the nature of checks on the
numerical majority.

A consideration of the changes made in the
method of amending the state constitutions leads
to the same conclusion. During the Revolutionary period, as we have seen, the tendency was
strongly toward making the fundamental law the
expression of the will of the numerical majority.
Difficulties in the way of change were reduced to
a minimum. But under the influence of the
political reaction which followed, and which produced the Constitution of the United States, the
state governments were so organized as to make
it more difficult for the majority to exercise the
amending power. Georgia in 1789 changed the
method of amending the state constitution by
requiring a two-thirds majority in a constitutional convention, and made another change in
1798 by which a two-thirds majority in each
house of the legislature and a three-fourths majority in each house of the succeeding legislature
was required for the adoption of an amendment
to the constitution. South Carolina in 1790
adopted a provision guarding against mere majority amendment by making the approval of a
two-thirds majority in both branches of two suc-

cessive legislatures necessary for any changes in the constitution. Connecticut in 1818 restricted the power of amending by requiring a majority in the house of representatives, a two-thirds majority in both houses of the next legislature, and final approval by a majority of the electors. New York in 1821 adopted a plan which required that an amendment should receive a majority in each branch of the legislature, a two-thirds majority in each branch of the succeeding legislature, and be approved by a majority of the voters. North Carolina in 1835 made a three-fifths majority in each house of the legislature and a two-thirds majority of each house of the following legislature necessary for changes in the constitution.

The judicial veto served the purpose of preventing majority amendment under the guise of ordinary legislation, while a safeguard against constitutional changes favored by a mere majority was thus provided in the extraordinary majority required in both houses of the legislature to propose or adopt amendments. This, as has been shown in the case of the Federal Constitution, is a formidable check on the majority. In view of this restriction upon the proposing of amendments the provision for ratification by a popular majority, which owing to the progress of the later democratic movement has now been generally adopted, is no real concession to the principle of majority rule.

Assuming that a two-thirds majority in the legislature is required to propose an amendment, and that the principle of representation is so applied that each party is represented in the legislature in proportion to its popular vote, it would scarcely ever be possible for any party to propose an amendment to the state constitution, since it can not be expected under any ordinary conditions to control two-thirds of the popular vote. But inasmuch as the successful party often secures under our system much more than its proportional share of representation in the legislature, it is by no means unusual for a party to have a two-thirds majority in both houses of a state legislature. This would appear to give the numerical majority under such conditions the power to propose and adopt amendments. Such would be the case if the party were really responsible to those who supported it at the polls. But this would assume the existence of a purely state party, organized with reference to state issues only, and carrying the election as the advocate of a definite state policy. Moreover, it would presuppose all those means, political and constitutional, by which the majority in the legislature would be accountable to the popular majority in the state. This is rendered impossible, however, as has been shown, by our system of government.

The above-mentioned changes in the constitutions of the older states may be attributed in large measure to the reaction against democracy which brought about the adoption of the Federal Constitution. They may be regarded as an expression of that distrust and fear of democracy which filled the minds of those who framed and set up our Federal government. It is not contended, however, that they are now so regarded by the masses of the people. The work of deifying the Federal Constitution was soon accomplished. And when the people had come to venerate it as the most perfect embodiment of the doctrine of popular sovereignty that the intelligence of man could devise, it was but natural that they should acquiesce in the proposal to make the state governments conform more closely to the general plan of that instrument. In view of the widespread sentiment which amounted to a blind and unthinking worship of the Constitution, it is not surprising that the political institutions of the general government should have been largely copied by the states. The only surprising thing in this connection is the fact that they did not follow the Federal model more closely, since every feature of it was the object of the most extravagant eulogy. Here we see, however, an inconsistency between profession and practice. The people who tolerated no criticism of the Federal Constitution showed nevertheless a distrust of some of its more conservative features. Much as the indirect election of President and United States senators was favored by the framers of our Federal Constitution, there has been no tendency to apply that principle in the selection of the corresponding state officials.

In all the states framing new constitutions during the Revolutionary period, except Massachusetts, New Hampshire, and New York, the governor was elected by the legislature. Pennsylvania abandoned indirect election and adopted election by the qualified voters in 1790; Delaware, in 1792; Georgia, in 1824; North Carolina, in 1835; Maryland, in 1837; New Jersey, in 1844; Virginia, in 1850; and South Carolina, in 1865. South Carolina and Maryland are the only states which have ever had indirect election of the upper house. Both adopted it in 1776, the constitution of South Carolina providing that the members of the lower house should elect the members of the upper house, and the constitution of Maryland requiring that members of the upper house should be chosen by an electoral college. This was abandoned for direct election in South Carolina in 1778 and in Maryland in 1837.

The conservative reaction was soon followed by a new movement toward democracy. This no doubt largely explains the failure of the people to reproduce in their state constitutions all those features which they professed to admire in the Federal Constitution. Not only did they not copy all the new features of that document, but they even discarded some of the then existing provisions of the state constitutions which had been copied in the Federal Constitution. The principle of indirect election which was everywhere recognized in the choice of the state judiciary during the Revolutionary period was gradually abandoned for the more democratic method of direct popular choice which has now become the rule. The life tenure of judges which formerly existed in most of the states has almost entirely disappeared. In all but four states the judges are now chosen for terms varying from two to twenty-one years—the average length of the term being eight or ten years. The combination of direct popular choice with a fixed term of office has had the effect of making the state judiciary much more amenable to public opinion than the corresponding branch of the Federal government. By reason of the relatively long term for which the judges of the state supreme court are elected, however, and the plan of gradual renewal which prevents present public opinion from ever gaining the ascendency in that body, it is still the least responsible and most conservative branch of the state government.

We see, then, two motives exerting an influence

in the remolding of the state constitutions, one being the desire to copy the Federal Constitution and the other the belief that the state government should reflect the will of the people. That the attainment of one of these ends would inevitably defeat the other was not generally recognized. The conviction which had become thoroughly rooted in the popular mind that the system of checks and balances was the highest expression of democratic organization ensured the embodiment of the general features of that system in the constitutions of the various states. The constitutional changes having this end in view largely destroyed the responsibility of the state governments to the people and thus prevented the very thing they were designed to accomplish. But however much this system was in reality opposed to the principle of direct popular control, it was adopted by the people with the idea of making the government more readily reflect their will. They were not conscious of any inconsistency in holding tenaciously to the doctrine of checks and balances and at the same time seeking to give the people more control over the state governments. The latter purpose is clearly seen in the constitutional changes relating to the tenure and manner of election of the judiciary and in the adoption of universal suffrage. Summing up the effects of these changes in the state constitutions, we may say that the suffrage was placed upon a democratic basis, the state judiciary was organized on a less irresponsible plan and the appearance of political responsibility secured by applying the principle of direct election to every branch of the state government. The longer term of office established for the legislative and executive branches of the state government, however, together with the increase in the authority of the judiciary and the adoption of the system of checks and balances has upon the whole had the effect of making the state government less responsive to the electorate.

As seen in preceding chapters, the framers of the Federal Constitution made use of the scheme of checks and balances for the purpose of limiting the power of the people. There is little evidence that they favored diffusion of authority except in so far as that authority rested upon a popular basis. Hence they carried the plan much farther in curtailing the power of the House of Representatives than a logical application of the doctrine would have justified, while at the same time giving more authority and power of independent action to the other branches of the general government than was consistent with their avowed, if not real, purpose.

They gave to the executive and judicial branches of the general government power to control the administration of Federal laws. The enforcement of all laws and regulations of the

general government, in so far as the President
and Senate might desire to enforce them, was
guaranteed through the power to appoint and remove those who were entrusted with their execution, while the right of appeal from a state to the
Federal courts precluded the possibility of enforcing a state law deemed to exceed the proper
limits of state authority.

In the state governments on the other hand we
find a high degree of administrative decentralization. The governor, unlike the President, was
not given any adequate power to control those
entrusted with the execution of state laws. A
multitude of directly elected local officials are the
agents of the state for this purpose. And since
they reflect the sentiment of the various local
interests to which they owe their election, it may
and often does happen that a law to which those
interests are opposed is rendered practically inoperative through the efforts of those local officials
who are sworn to enforce it. The practical working of this system often gives to a local community an administrative veto on such general
laws of the state as may be opposed to local sentiment. By this means the general executive
authority of the state is weakened and its responsibility correspondingly diminished.

In still another respect the policy of dividing
authority and parcelling it out between separate
and distinct organs of government has been

carried much farther in the state than in the Federal Constitution. Unlike the Federal government in which executive power is centralized in the President, the state constitutions have created a number of separate officials, boards and commissions, some directly elected and some appointed, independent of each other and irresponsible except in so far as a fixed term of office implies responsibility. This means that instead of one executive the state has many. Only one of them—the governor—has, it is true, a veto on the enactment of laws; but this, as we have seen, is really a legislative and not an executive power. Each of these has what may be termed an administrative veto; that is, the power to negative the laws which they are expected to administer by simply not enforcing them. The impossibility of securing an honest and faithful administration of the laws where the responsibility for their enforcement is divided between a number of separate and practically independent officials, is clearly shown in the experience of the various states. The evils of this system are illustrated in the state laws enacted for the purpose of controlling the railway business. Provision is usually made for their enforcement through a railway commission either directly elected or appointed by the governor. That direct election by the people for a fixed term, thereby securing independence during that term, fails to guarantee the enforcement of such laws is strikingly shown in the experience of California, where this body has been continually under the domination of the railway interests.[1]

Under a system which thus minutely subdivides and distributes the administrative function, any effective control over the execution of state laws is made impossible. The governor, who is nominally the head of the executive agencies of the state, is not in reality responsible, since he has no adequate power to compel the enforcement of laws directly entrusted to other independent state officials. Any interest or combination of interests that may wish to prevent the enforcement of certain laws may be able to accomplish their end by merely controlling the one official or board whose duty it is to enforce the law in question. Their task would be a much more difficult one, if it were necessary to control for that purpose the entire executive arm of the state. The opportunity for the corrupt use of money and influence is thus vastly increased, since the people, though they might watch and judge fairly well the conduct of one state executive, can not exercise any effective censorship over a large number of such officials.

This irresponsibility which arises out of a wide diffusion of power is not confined to the executive

[1] See Annals of the American Academy of Political and Social Science, Vol. VI, p. 469.

branch of the state government. The legislature in the course of our political development has taken on the same elaborate committee organization which characterizes, as we have seen, our Federal Congress. The same sinister influences working through similar agencies oppose needed legislation. But although the good bills are frequently killed or mutilated in the secrecy of the committee room, the skilful use of money or other corrupt influence often secures the enactment of laws opposed to the interests of the people. Moreover, the practice known as log-rolling by which the representatives of various local interests combine and force through measures which secure to each of certain localities some advantage at the expense of the state at large are so common as to excite no surprise.

The relation existing between the executive and legislative branches under our system is another source of irresponsibility, since it does not follow simply because a law has been placed upon the statute books of a state that it can be enforced. An act may be passed in response to a strong public sentiment, it may be constitutional and the executive may be willing and may even desire to enforce it, and yet be unable to do so. The legislature may, and frequently does, enact laws under the pressure of public opinion while at the same time quietly exercising what is, in effect, a veto on their execution. In the case of much important legislation it can accomplish this by merely not appropriating the funds which are required for their enforcement. The laws against adulteration are a good illustration. An official known perhaps as a dairy and food commissioner may be provided for, whose duty it is to enforce these laws. The nature of the work entrusted to him requires that he should have a corps of assistants, inspectors who are to keep a watchful eye on the goods likely to be adulterated and collect samples of such goods from the various places in the state where they are exposed for sale, and chemists who are to analyze the samples thus procured and determine whether manufacturers and dealers are complying with the law. Unless an adequate sum is appropriated for this purpose, and for prosecuting those who are violating the law, such laws can not be enforced.

In our state governments the subdivision of authority has been carried so far that no effective control over the enactment or enforcement of state laws is possible. Under the influence of the doctrine of checks and balances the policy of widely distributing political authority has inured to the benefit of those private interests which are ever seeking to control the government for their own ends, since it has supplied the conditions under which the people find it difficult to fix the blame for official misconduct. Indeed it may be said that wherever power should be concentrated

to ensure responsibility, it has been almost invariably distributed.

CHAPTER X

MUNICIPAL GOVERNMENT

Our municipal government, like the rest of our political system, was originally an inheritance from England. The governing power in colonial times was a single body, the common council, such as exists in England to-day, composed of mayor, recorder, aldermen, and councilmen. As a rule the councilmen were elected annually by the qualified voters, while the mayor was appointed by the colonial governor. The council had authority to enact local regulations not in conflict with English or colonial legislation. The mayor had no veto and usually no appointing power.

The Revolution did not modify the general scheme of municipal government in any important respect. The mayor was still, as a rule, appointed by the governor, who now owed his office directly or indirectly to the qualified voters of the state. The power to grant municipal charters, which before the Revolution was exercised by the provincial governor, was now lodged in the state legislature.

The important changes in municipal government were made after, and may be regarded as an effect of the adoption of the Federal Constitution. As the centralization of authority in the hands of the common council could not be reconciled with the new doctrine of checks and balances, municipal government was reorganized on the plan of distributed powers. This effort to readjust the political organization of the city and make it conform to the general scheme of the Federal government is seen in the municipal charters granted after the adoption of the Constitution. The tendency toward a bicameral council, the extension of the term for which members of the council were elected and the veto power of the mayor may be attributed to the influence of the Constitution rather than to any intelligent and carefully planned effort to improve the machinery of municipal government.

As in the case of the state governments, the development of the system was influenced by the growing belief in democracy. Property qualifications for the suffrage disappeared, and the mayor became a directly elected local official. The changes made in municipal government, however, as a concession to the newer democratic thought, did not ensure any very large measure of popular control. Municipal government in its practical working remained essentially undemocratic.

It would be perfectly reasonable to expect that

popular government would reach its highest development in the cities. Here modern democracy was born; here we find the physical and social conditions which facilitate interchange of thought and concerted action on the part of the people. Moreover, the government of the city is more directly and immediately related to the citizens than is the government of state or nation. It touches them at more points, makes more demands upon them and is more vitally related to their everyday life and needs than either state or national government. For these reasons the most conspicuous successes of democracy should be the government of present-day cities. Under a truly democratic system this would doubtless be the case. But in this country the most glaring abuses and most conspicuous failures of government occur in the cities. The enemies of popular government have used this fact for the purpose of discrediting the theory of democracy. They would have us believe that this is the natural result of a system which places political authority in the hands of the masses—that it is the fruit of an extreme democracy. This conclusion rests upon the assumption that municipal government in this country is democratic—an assumption which will not bear investigation. American cities are far from being examples of extreme democracy. In some important respects they are less democratic than the government of either state or nation. A careful analysis of the situation shows clearly that the municipal evils so frequently attributed to an excess of democracy are really due to the system of checks by which all effective power to regulate municipal matters is withheld from the majority. In this country popular control is reduced to a minimum in the cities, while in Great Britain and the countries of western Europe we find in municipal government the nearest approach to democracy. This is the true explanation of the fact that municipal government is our greatest failure and their most conspicuous success.

Under any consistent application of the theory of democracy a city would be entitled to the fullest measure of local self-government. It ought to be given an absolutely free hand to initiate and carry out any policies of purely local concern. This right, however, the American city does not possess. Local self-government is recognized neither in theory nor in practice under our political scheme. The true local unit is the city, and this, according to our legal and constitutional theory, is merely the creature of the state legislature. The latter called it into being, determines what powers it may exercise, and may strip it of them at pleasure. According to the prevailing practice of our state legislatures and the almost uniform decisions of our courts the exercise of local self-government by our cities is to be regarded as a mere privilege and not a right.

The municipal charter was originally a grant of certain privileges of local government in return for money payments or other services rendered to the king. It was a mere concession of privileges based upon expediency, and not a recognition on the part of the Crown of local self-government as an admitted right. As an express and formal statement of the measure of local government which the king would bind himself to respect, it tended to limit his power of interference in matters covered by such charter, since privileges solemnly granted could not with safety be lightly and arbitrarily disregarded. Municipal charters thus have the same origin as the constitution of the state itself, in that they are the outcome of an effort to place a check upon an irresponsible central authority.

The legislature of the American commonwealth in succeeding to the power of the king over municipal charters manifested at first an inclination to concede to the city the right to a measure of local self-government. Thus "the city of New York received from the English kings during the colonial period a charter which, on the Declaration of the Independence of the colony of New York, and the establishment of the new state of New York, was confirmed by the first Constitution of the state. For a considerable period after the adoption of this constitution, changes in that charter were made upon the initiation of the people of the city, which initiation took place through the medium of charter conventions whose members were elected by the people of the city, and no statute which was passed by the legislature of the state relative to the affairs of the city of New York took effect within the city until it had been approved by the city."[1]

But as Professor Goodnow observes, American cities "have very largely lost their original powers of local self-government."[2] The original conception of the city charter as a contract which established certain rights of local self-government which the legislature was bound to respect, merely recognized municipal corporations as entitled to the same exemption from unreasonable legislative interference, as the courts have since the Dartmouth College decision enforced in favor of private corporations. If this view had prevailed cities could not have been deprived arbitrarily of rights once recognized by the legislature, but they could have enforced the recognition of no rights not thus granted. The recognition of this doctrine would have prevented many of the abuses that have characterized the relation between state and municipal government in this country, but it would have guaranteed no rights which the legis-

[1] Goodnow, Municipal Home Rule, p. 20.
[2] Municipal Problems, p. 9.

254

lature had not seen fit to confer. Any liberal interpretation of the theory of democracy must of
necessity go farther than this, and make municipal
self-government a fundamental right which the
central authority of the state can, not only neither
abridge nor destroy, but can not even withhold,
since it is a right having its source not in a legislative grant, but in the underlying principles of
popular government.

The failure to recognize the right of local self-
government as fundamental in any scheme of
democracy was unfortunate. Some of the worst
evils of municipal government would have been
avoided, however, if authority once granted to
municipalities had been treated by the courts as
a limitation of the power of the legislature to interfere in purely local matters. The refusal of
the state government to recognize an appropriate
sphere of municipal activity which it would have
no right to invade, has been the main cause of
corruption and inefficiency in municipal government.

The policy of state interference in municipal
affairs was the inevitable outgrowth of the doctrine that cities had no powers except such as had
been expressly given, or were necessarily implied
in their charters. This lack of the power of
initiative made it necessary for cities, as they increased in size and complexity, to make constant
appeals to the legislature for permission to supply

their wants. Every new problem which the city had to deal with, every new function which it had to perform, was a ground for state interference. This necessity of invoking the aid of the state legislature, constantly felt in every rapidly growing city, tended to develop a feeling of dependence upon legislative intervention as an indispensable factor in the solution of local problems. Thus the refusal of the state government to recognize the right of municipal initiative compelled the cities to welcome state interference as the only means of dealing with the new problems with which they were being continually confronted.

Another reason for the extension of state authority at the expense of the municipality is to be found in the twofold character of city government. Besides being a local government the city is also for certain purposes the administrative agent of the state, and as such is properly subject to state supervision. But, in the absence of any clear distinction between state and local interests, it was an easy matter for protection of the former to serve as a pretext for undue interference with the latter.

The city was thus placed at the mercy of the state government, since the legislature could make the needs of the municipality or the protection of the general interests of the state a pretext for any interference calculated to further the private or partisan ends of those who controlled the legislative machine. As cities increased in importance it was found that this unlimited power over them could be made a valuable asset of the party machine in control of the state legislature. The city offered a rich and tempting field for exploitation. It had offices, a large revenue, spent vast sums in public improvements, let valuable contracts of various kinds and had certain needs, as for water, light, rapid transit, etc., which could be made the pretext for granting franchises and other privileges on such terms as would ensure large profits to the grantees at the expense of the general public. That the political machine in control of the state government should have yielded to the temptation to make a selfish use of its powers in this direction, is only what might have been expected.

"The legislature has often claimed also the right to appoint municipal officers and to fix and change the details of municipal organization, has legislated municipal officers out of office, and established new offices. In certain cases it has even provided that certain specific city streets shall be paved, has imposed burdens upon cities for the purpose of constructing sewers or bringing in water; has regulated the methods of transportation to be adopted within the limits of cities; in a word, has attended to a great number of matters which are purely local in character; matters which do not affect the people of the state as a whole, and in regard to which there is little excuse for special legislative action."[1]

The extent to which state regulation of local matters has been carried in New York is indicated by the fact that in the year 1886 "280 of the 681 acts passed by the legislature . . . interfered directly with the affairs of some particular county, city, village, or town, specifically and expressly named. . . .

"The Philadelphia City Hall Building affords a good example of how far this lack of local responsibility may sometimes carry the legislature in the exercise of local powers, and in the imposition of financial burdens on cities. 'In 1870 the legislature decided that the city should have new buildings. The act [which was passed to accomplish this result] selected certain citizens by name, whom it appointed commissioners for the erection of the buildings. It made this body perpetual by authorizing it to fill vacancies. . . . This commission was imposed by the legislature upon the city, and given absolute control to create debts for the purpose named, and to require the levy of taxes for their payment.

" 'The public buildings at Broad and Market streets were,' in the words of Judge Paxson, 'projected upon a scale of magnificence better suited for the capitol of an empire than the municipal buildings of a debt-burdened city.' Yet this act was declared constitutional, the city was compelled to supply the necessary funds, and 'for nearly twenty years all the money that could be spared from immediate and pressing needs' was 'compulsorily expended upon an enormous pile which surpasses the town halls and cathedrals of the Middle Ages in extent if not in grandeur.' "[1]

The legislature is strongly tempted to abuse its power when the party machine in control of the state does not have the political support of the local authorities. One of the most notorious examples of such interference in recent years was the so-called "ripper" legislation enacted in Pennsylvania in 1901, by which the mayors of Pittsburg and Allegheny were removed from office and the governor given the power to appoint and remove their successors until the regular municipal election in the year 1903. The motive for this legislation was the desire to crush local opposition to the state machine by putting the control of municipal offices in the hands of a governor friendly to the political boss of the state. In order to provide an opportunity for the mayor appointed by the governor to use his office in building up and perpetuating a local machine that would support the clique in control of the state government, the appointee of the governor was declared eligible for re-election, although his

[1] Goodnow, Municipal Home Rule, pp. 24-26.

locally elected successors were made ineligible. A more flagrant abuse of legislative authority could hardly be imagined; yet this act was declared constitutional by the supreme court of the state.

Many such instances of partisan interference may be found in the recent legislation of some of the larger and more populous states.

The best example of the misgovernment of cities by the legislature for private or partisan ends is seen in the franchise legislation by which privileges of great value have been secured by street railway and other corporations without any compensation to the cities concerned. The power which the legislature can exercise in the interest of private corporations monopolizing for their own profit the very necessities of life in the modern city—water, light, transportation, communication, etc.—has been one of the most serious evils resulting from state domination of municipal affairs. It exposed the legislature to the temptation which individuals and corporations seeking valuable concessions readily took advantage of for their own gain. It thus brought into active operation those forces which have been the chief factor in corrupting both state and municipal government.

As soon as it came to be generally recognized that state control of local affairs not only did not prevent, but was, in fact, the chief source of the misrule of American cities, an effort was made to provide a remedy by the adoption of constitutional provisions regulating the power of the legislature to interfere in municipal affairs. These limitations relate to those matters wherein the evils of state interference have been most pronounced. Thus in some states the legislature is not allowed to grant the use of streets to railways or other private companies without the consent of the municipal authorities; to create special commissions and bestow upon them municipal functions; or to incorporate cities or regulate them by special laws.

It was not the purpose of these constitutional provisions to grant to municipalities any immunity from state control, but merely to forbid certain modes of exercising legislative supervision which, as experience had shown, were liable to serious abuses. The prohibition of special legislation, generally incorporated in recent state constitutions, has, however, largely failed to accomplish its purpose, owing to the fact that the courts have permitted the legislature to establish so many classes of cities that it has been able to pass special acts under the guise of general laws.

The state of Ohio furnishes a good example of the practical nullification of a constitutional provision by the legislature through the abuse of its power of classification. The constitution of 1851 prohibited the legislature from passing any special act conferring corporate powers and provided for the organization of cities by general laws. The legislature, however, adopted a method of classifying cities which defeated the object of this provision. In 1901 each of the eleven principal cities in the state was in a separate class. Consequently all laws enacted for each of these classes were in reality special acts, and as such were clearly an evasion of the constitutional prohibition of special legislation. Nevertheless, this method of classification had been repeatedly upheld by the courts. Its advantages to the party in control of the state government were obvious, since it gave the legislature a free hand in interfering in local affairs for partisan ends. It permitted the state machine to make concessions to a city which gave it political support and at the same time extend state control over those cities in which it encountered opposition. This was the situation down to 1902, when the supreme court rendered two decisions which overthrew the system of classification in vogue and invalidated the charter of every city in the state. It is unfortunate that this change in the attitude of the court, though much to be desired, occurred at a time when it had the appearance of serving a partisan end. One of these suits was brought by the Republican attorney-general of the state to have the charter of the city of Cleveland declared invalid on the ground that it was a special act. This charter had been in force for over ten years, having granted liberal corporate powers at a time when Cleveland was a Republican city. Later it passed into the Democratic column, and this suit was instituted as part of the plan of the Republican machine of the state to curb the power and influence of the mayor of that city. The new municipal code which was adopted at an extra session of the legislature provided a scheme of government applicable to Cleveland under which the powers of the mayor were much curtailed.

In the New York constitution of 1894 an effort was made to guard against the abuse of special legislation. The cities of the state were by the constitution itself divided into three classes according to population, and any law which did not apply to all the cities of a class was declared to be a special act. Special legislation was not prohibited; but when any act of this kind was passed by the legislature it was required to be submitted to the authorities of the city or cities in question, and if disapproved of by them after a public hearing, it could become law only by being passed again in the regular manner. This merely afforded to the cities affected by the proposed special legislation an opportunity to protest against its enactment, the legislature having full power to pass it in the face of local disapproval. That this is not an adequate remedy for the evils of special legislation is shown by the fact that the two charters of New York City enacted since this constitution went into effect, have both been framed by a state-appointed commission and passed over the veto of the mayor.

The constitutional changes which have been mentioned must not be understood as implying any repudiation of the doctrine that a municipal corporation is a creature of the general government of the state. These provisions merely secured, or rather sought to secure, to cities some benefits of a negative character—immunity from certain recognized abuses of legislative authority. They are the expression of an effort to find a remedy for the evils of municipal government by restricting the authority of the legislature rather than by giving cities the power to act independently in local matters. They have diminished somewhat the evils of state interference, but they failed to remove the cause by giving the cities the constitutional right to control their own affairs.

The failure of all these measures to accomplish what was expected of them finally brought the advocates of municipal reform to a realization of the fact that the American system made no provision for real local self-government, and that our refusal to recognize this principle was the chief cause of the prevalent corruption and misrule of our cities and the insuperable obstacle to all effective and thoroughgoing reform. As soon as attention was directed to this feature of the problem it was seen that no system could be devised that would be better adapted to the purpose of defeating the end of good city government, since those who would be directly benefited by the reforms in municipal government were powerless to bring them about except with the co-operation of the legislature. Moreover the consent of the legislature, though once given, was liable at any time to be withdrawn at the instigation of private or partisan interests, since this body was not directly interested in establishing and maintaining good municipal government nor responsible to those who were.

It was finally seen that some more effective measure than the prohibition of special legislation was required. The next step was the attempt to secure to cities the needed authority in local matters by means of a constitutional provision authorizing them to frame their own charters. In this movement the state of Missouri led the way by incorporating a home-rule provision in its constitution of 1875. California, Washington, Minnesota, and Colorado have since adopted similar provisions. In each of these states the charter is framed by a commission locally elected except in Minnesota, where it is appointed by the district judge.

In Missouri this privilege is accorded only to cities having more than 100,000 inhabitants.

The constitution of California adopted in 1879 also restricted the benefits of home rule to cities of more than 100,000 population, but it has since been extended to all cities having more than 3,500 inhabitants. Washington allows all cities having 20,000 or more population to frame their own charters. Minnesota extends the privilege to all cities and villages without respect to size, while Colorado restricts it to cities having more than 2,000 inhabitants.

The right to serve as a member of a charter commission is limited to freeholders in all these states except Colorado, where it is restricted to taxpayers. The object of these home-rule provisions was to give cities some measure of initiative in local affairs without at the same time permitting them to organize on the plan of simple majority rule. In the Missouri constitution of 1875 a four-sevenths vote was required to adopt a charter and a three-fifths vote to ratify an amendment, although the constitution itself was adopted and could be amended by mere majority vote. The constitution of California permits ratification by a majority of the qualified voters, but every charter thus ratified must be submitted to the legislature for its approval or rejection as a whole. No charter amendment can be adopted except by a three-fifths majority of the popular vote and subsequent legislative approval, although, as in the case of Missouri, a majority vote is sufficient to approve an amendment to the state constitution. In Washington the constitution provides for the ratification of charters and charter amendments by a majority of the qualified electors. The constitutional amendment adopted in Minnesota in 1896, with its subsequent modifications, provides for the ratification of charters and charter amendments by a four-sevenths vote except in the case of certain cities where a three-fourths majority is required. A three-fifths vote in favor of a charter amendment is necessary for its ratification. Colorado, by a constitutional amendment adopted in 1902, permits the ratification and amendment of charters by a majority vote. A constitutional amendment adopted in Missouri in 1902 provides for the ratification of charters by majority vote.

With the exception of California, where the constitutional amendment of 1902 allows 15 per cent. of the qualified voters to require the submission of a charter amendment, and Colorado, where 25 per cent. of the voters have that right, the states above mentioned make no provision in their constitutions for the popular initiative. Both Washington and Minnesota, however, have permitted it by statute, the former on the application of 15 per cent., and the latter when 5 per cent. of the qualified voters demand it.

The chief defect of these constitutional provisions relating to home rule is that they do not really grant it. There are too many restrictions imposed upon cities availing themselves of this privilege, and in two of the states in question, notably in Missouri, they are for the benefit of the larger cities only. The restriction of the charter-framing right to freeholders, the withholding from the majority of the power to amend in California and Minnesota, and the failure to provide in the constitution for the popular initiative in Missouri, Washington, and Minnesota indicate a willingness to grant the right of home rule only under such conditions as are calculated to ensure adequate limitation of the power of the majority.

These constitutional provisions certainly point in the direction which we must follow if we would find any satisfactory solution of our municipal problem. They would, if liberally interpreted by the courts, secure to cities immunity from interference in local matters. But the courts are naturally opposed to innovations in our constitutional system, and have consequently been disposed to give provisions of this character such an interpretation as will minimize their effect. The requirement that the charters framed under these provisions must be in harmony with the constitution and laws of the state has been declared by the courts to mean that they must not only conform to the laws in force at the time the charters are adopted, but also that they must conform to all legislation subsequently enacted. Had the courts been thoroughly imbued with the principle of local self-government, they could easily have given these constitutional provisions an interpretation which would have effectually deprived the legislature of the power to interfere in purely local affairs. They could have declared all acts by which the state government sought to invade the sphere of local affairs null and void, just as they have all acts of the municipal government which have encroached upon the powers reserved exclusively to the state. What the courts have done, however, is to hold that these constitutional provisions merely authorize cities to govern themselves in accordance with the constitution and in harmony with such laws as the legislature has or may hereafter enact. The city may adopt a charter which is in harmony with the constitution and the laws of the state, but the charter thus adopted may be freely modified by general laws relating to cities. The unfriendly attitude of the courts has thus largely defeated the object of these home-rule provisions. The state legislature is still free to encroach upon or abridge the sphere of municipal self-government.

The constitutional provisions above mentioned may be regarded as having a twofold purpose. They were designed to limit, if not destroy, the power of the legislature to invade the sphere of municipal affairs, and also to confer upon cities the general power to act for themselves, by virtue of which they could on their own initiative, subject to certain restrictions contained in the constitution, set up their own government, formulate and carry out a municipal policy and manage their own affairs to suit themselves. This would seem to be implied necessarily in the grant of constitutional power to frame a charter for their own government. A liberal interpretation of this feature of the constitutions in question would have held that all cities to which it applied were thereby authorized to exercise all powers not expressly withheld by the constitution or the statutes of the state. This, however, has not been the attitude of the courts. Their reluctance to give home-rule provisions a liberal interpretation may be illustrated by a decision of the supreme court of Washington. In addition to the power granted to cities of the first class to frame their own charters the constitution of this state provides that "any county, city, town, or township, may make and enforce within its limits all such local, police, sanitary and other regulations as are not in conflict with general laws." In view of the attitude that courts have generally taken in this matter it is not surprising that the supreme court of Washington has intimated that the above-mentioned constitutional provisions are not self-executing. Moreover, it does not seem disposed to concede even to cities of the first class any important powers except such as have been expressly conferred by statute. For example, the statutes of Washington authorize cities of the first class "to regulate and control the use" of gas supplied by a private corporation, and the charter of Tacoma expressly gave to the city council the power to fix the price of gas so supplied. Suit was brought to enjoin the city from exercising this power which was claimed under the constitutional and statutory authority given to cities of the first class. The supreme court held that while Tacoma had the power to regulate and control, expressly given it by statute, it did not have the power to fix the price.[1] This decision evinces a singular lack of sympathy on the part of the court with the home-rule provisions of the constitution of Washington.

But although the effort to confer upon cities by constitutional enactment the power to manage their own affairs has thus far largely failed, it indicates a growing appreciation of the nature of the problem and the character of the remedy that must be applied. A more clearly defined and effective public opinion in favor of municipal self-government must in the end overcome judicial opposition.

The most liberal interpretation of which these constitutional provisions are susceptible, however, would not have ensured complete municipal self-government. Unless a city is given adequate

[1] Tacoma Gas and Electric Light Co. v. Tacoma, 14 Wash.

financial powers, a constitutional grant of the right of local self-government does not enable it to exercise much choice in relation to the more important matters of municipal policy. By narrowly limiting the powers of cities in this direction, they have been largely deprived of the advantages which they would have enjoyed under a consistent application of the home-rule principle. A certain amount of freedom in the use of the taxing power would seem to be no less essential to the city than to the state itself. Within reasonable limits it ought to be conceded the right to formulate its own scheme of taxation. In every important American city the taxes collected for municipal purposes greatly exceed those imposed for the support of the county and state government. In a matter which so vitally concerns the city it ought to have some right to pursue a policy of its own. This right has not been recognized, however, even in the constitutions which have made most concessions to the principle of municipal home rule. By this means all innovations or reforms in municipal taxation except such as may be authorized by the state itself are effectually prevented. It could not, for instance, exempt personal property from taxation, or make a tax on ground rent the main source of its revenue.

The power to incur debt for municipal purposes is no less essential than the power to tax. The present-day city must spend large sums in making public improvements the cost of which it is necessary to distribute over a period of years. To limit too narrowly the borrowing power of cities for these purposes would prevent them from realizing the full benefits of unhampered self-government. This does not imply that a city should own and operate all industries of a quasi-public character, but it does imply that it should have the unquestioned right and the power to do so. Unless this is the case it is not in a position to secure the most favorable terms from such private corporations as may be allowed to occupy this field. Unreasonable restrictions upon the borrowing power of cities by placing obstacles in the way of municipal ownership of public utilities tend to deprive the people of the most effective safeguard against the extortion of private monopolies.

The limitation placed upon the amount of municipal indebtedness has not had altogether the effect intended. This is mainly due to the fact that the debt limit fixed in the state constitutions was in many cases so low that it did not permit cities to make absolutely necessary public improvements, such as the paving of streets and construction of sewers. To make these improvements without resorting to credit would require the owners of the property affected to advance the full amount of their cost. This would in many instances be extremely inconvenient. Accordingly, an effort was made to find some method of evading these restrictions which would be upheld by the courts. This was accomplished by issuing bonds to be paid out of a special fund which was to be created by taxes assessed against the property of the district charged with the cost of the improvements. The courts held that this was merely a lien upon the property of the district in question, and not a municipal debt within the meaning of the above-mentioned constitutional limitations. These decisions by the courts may not appear to be in harmony with the letter of the constitutional provisions relating to municipal indebtedness, but they are hardly at variance with their spirit. The object of these restrictions was not so much to limit the rights of the property-owning classes as to protect them against the extravagance of the propertyless voters. To make an exception in favor of municipal indebtedness incurred in this way and for these purposes was not calculated to work any hardship upon property owners, but rather to give them the power to authorize the employment of credit for their own advantage. They were protected against the abuse of this particular kind of indebtedness inasmuch as the consent of the owners of a majority of the property affected was quite generally required.

One influence which helped to mold a public

sentiment in favor of constitutional provisions limiting the amount of municipal indebtedness was the rapid increase in the debts of American cities during the period that immediately followed the Civil war. For this condition of affairs the state government itself was largely to blame. It had prescribed a form of municipal organization which was scarcely compatible with an efficient and responsible management of financial matters. Moreover, the state government, as we have seen, could empower its own agents to borrow money for a purpose which it had authorized and obligate the city to pay it. The effort to correct these evils, first noticeable about the year 1870, took the form of constitutional provisions limiting the amount of indebtedness which could be incurred by or on behalf of cities. The main object of these provisions was to protect municipal tax-payers against an extravagant use of the borrowing power for local purposes, whether exercised by state or municipal authorities.

Another advantage which these provisions seemed likely to secure to the capital-owning class deserves at least a passing mention. This policy of limiting the amount of municipal indebtedness was adopted at a time when, owing to the rapid growth of urban population, the local monopolies of water, light, transportation, etc., were becoming an important and extremely profitable field for the investment of private capital. The restrictions imposed upon the power of cities to borrow money would retard, if not preclude, the adoption of a policy of municipal ownership and thus enable the private capitalist to retain exclusive possession of this important class of industries.

That the constitutional restrictions upon the general indebtedness of cities have retarded the movement toward municipal ownership is beyond question. It is not likely, however, that they will much longer block the way to municipal acquisition of those industries in which private management has proven unsatisfactory, since it may be possible to evade them by resorting to the device of a *special fund*. The same line of argument which has been accepted by the courts as supporting the constitutionality of the special fund for local improvement purposes is no less applicable to special debts incurred for the purchase of revenue-producing public utilities, such as water works, lighting plants and street railways. Under this arrangement, however, the city must not assume any responsibility for the payment of the capital borrowed, the creditors advancing the purchase price or cost of construction, looking solely to the earnings under municipal operation for the payment of both principal and interest. It may be doubted whether the courts in permitting cities to employ the special fund in relation to local improvements realized its possibilities in the direction of municipal ownership.[1]

These restrictions upon the powers of cities indicate a fear that too much local self-government might jeopardize the interests of the propertied classes. This attitude on the part of those who have framed and interpreted our state constitutions is merely an expression of that distrust of majority rule which is, as we have seen, the distinguishing feature of the American system of government. It is in the cities that the non-possessing classes are numerically strongest and the inequality in the distribution of wealth most pronounced. This largely explains the reluctance of the state to allow cities a free hand in the management of local affairs. A municipal government responsive to public opinion might be too much inclined to make the public interests a pretext for disregarding property rights. State control of cities, then, may be regarded as a means of protecting the local minority against the local majority. Every attempt to reform this system must encounter the opposition of the property-owning class, which is one of the chief reasons why all efforts to establish municipal self-government have thus far largely failed.

We thus see that while property qualifications

[1] The employment of the special fund device for municipal ownership purposes has been upheld by the Supreme Court of Washington. See Winston v. Spokane, 12 Wash. 524, and Faulkner v. Seattle, 19 Wash. 320.

for the suffrage have disappeared, the influence of property still survives. In many ways and for many purposes property is directly or indirectly recognized in the organization and administration of municipal government. The movement toward democracy has had less influence upon property qualifications for the suffrage and for office-holding in its relation to municipal than in its relation to state and national affairs. When the Federal Constitution was adopted the property qualifications for voting and office-holding in force in the various states were not disturbed. The Constitution did not recognize the principle of universal suffrage. It not only allowed the states to retain the power to prescribe the qualifications of voters in state and municipal elections, but also limited the suffrage for Federal purposes to those who were qualified to vote at state elections.[1] The removal, during the first half of the nineteenth century, of property qualifications for voting at state elections and holding state offices had the effect of placing the Federal suffrage upon a popular basis.

The influence of the democratic movement was less marked, however, in the domain of municipal affairs. Here the old system under which voting and office-holding were regarded as the exclusive right of the property-owning class has not entirely disappeared. In this as in other respects

[1] Const., Art. I, sec. 2 and Art. II, sec. 1.

the American state has evinced a fear of municipal democracy. It is true that in the choice of public officials the principle of manhood suffrage prevails. But the suffrage may be exercised either with reference to candidates or measures; and in voting upon questions of municipal policy, which is far more important than the right to select administrative officers, the suffrage is often restricted to taxpayers or the owners of real estate. Thus in Colorado, which has gone as far as any state in the Union in the direction of municipal democracy, no franchise can be granted to a private corporation or debt incurred by a city for the purpose of municipal ownership without the approval of the taxpaying electors. When we consider that 72 per cent. of the families living in Denver in the year 1900 occupied rented houses,[1] and that the household goods of a head of a family to the value of two hundred dollars are exempt from taxation,[2] the effect of this restriction is obvious. In thus limiting the right to vote, the framers of the state constitution evidently proceeded upon the theory that the policy of a city with reference to its public utilities should be controlled by its taxpayers. The justification for this constitutional provision is not apparent, however, inasmuch as the burden of supporting the public service industries of a city is not borne by

[1] Abstract of the Twelfth Census, p. 133.
[2] Constitution of Colorado, Art. X, Sec. 3.

the taxpayers as such, but by the people generally. Such a system makes it possible for the taxpaying class to control public utilities in their own interest and to the disadvantage of the general public. The part of the community who are taxpayers, if given the exclusive right to control these industries, would be tempted to make them an important source of municipal revenue. They would be likely to favor high rather than low or reasonable charges for these necessary public services, since their taxes would be diminished by the amount thus taken from the non-taxpayers through excessive charges. Where the majority of the citizens are property owners and taxpayers there is but little danger that public ownership will be subject to this abuse. But where there is great inequality in the distribution of wealth and a large propertyless class, democracy is the only guarantee that the benefits of municipal ownership will not be monopolized by the property-owning class.

An investigation of the practical working of municipal ownership in American cities will show that this danger is not purely imaginary. In the year 1899 53.73 per cent. of the waterworks in this country were owned and operated by municipalities, public ownership being the rule in the larger cities. Taking the thirteen largest plants in the United States, all of which were municipally owned, the income from private users was

$20,545,409, while the total cost of production, including estimated depreciation, aggregated only $11,469,732. If to this amount be added the estimated taxes, interest on total investment and rental value of the municipally owned quarters occupied for this purpose, the total cost of production would be $22,827,825. Private consumers, however, used only 80.2 per cent. of the water supplied. If the 19.8 per cent. supplied free for public purposes had been paid for at the same rate charged to private users, the total income from these 13 municipally owned plants would have been $25,817,720. This would have been $2,-989,895 in excess of a fair return upon the total investment. No one would claim that the price of water has been increased under municipal ownership. As a matter of fact, it has been substantially reduced and the quality of the water at the same time improved. The reduction in price, however, has been less than it would have been, had the interests of the consumers alone been considered. If the object of municipal ownership is to supply pure water at the lowest possible price to the general public, there is no good reason why the city should demand a profit on the capital it has invested in the business. This would certainly be true where the earnings under municipal ownership have been sufficient to pay for the plant. In this case it would be an injustice to consumers to make them contribute, over and above the cost of operating the plant, an additional amount sufficient to pay interest on the investment, inasmuch as they have supplied the capital with which the business is carried on. Any attempt to make municipal ownership a source of revenue would mean the taxation of water consumers for the benefit of property owners. Nor is there any reason why the private consumers of water should be made to pay for the water used for public purposes. The water needed for public buildings, for cleaning streets and for extinguishing fires ought to be paid for by those chiefly benefited—the property-owning class.

If instead of considering these thirteen waterworks together, we take a single example—the third largest plant—the tendency to make public ownership a source of revenue is more clearly seen. The income from private users in the case of this plant was $4,459,404. The city used for public purposes 29.5 per cent of the total amount supplied, which if paid for at the rate charged private consumers would have made the total income from operation $6,325,395. This would have been $2,929,232 more than was required to pay all expenses, including interest on the total investment.[1]

---

[1] These figures concerning municipally owned water-works as well as those in the following paragraph relating to electric light plants, are based on the data contained in the Fourteenth Annual Report of the U. S. Commissioner of Labor on Water, Gas and Electric Light Plants.

In the case of electric-light plants private ownership is the rule, only 460 of the 3,032 plants being under municipal ownership. The Report of the United States Commissioner of Labor[1] gives the data for 952 of these plants, 320 of which are municipally owned and operated. Municipal ownership, however, is mainly confined to the smaller cities and towns. This is shown by the fact that although more than one-third of the 952 plants above mentioned are under municipal control, only 30 out of 277, or less than one-ninth of the largest plants, are municipally owned. This is to be accounted for by the more determined opposition to the policy of municipal ownership by the capitalist class in the larger cities, where private management is most remunerative. Municipal plants, too, are often restricted to public lighting, not being allowed to furnish light or power for commercial purposes. This restricted form of municipal ownership is merely a slight concession on the part of the private monopolist to the taxpaying class. The general public, as consumers of light and power, derive no benefit from such a policy.

These and other facts which might be mentioned illustrate the natural tendency of a system under which the power of the masses is limited in the interest of the property-owning class. The chief evils of municipal government in this coun-

[1] Water, Gas and Electric Light Plants, 1899,

try have their source not in majority but in minority rule. It is in the city where we find a numerically small but very wealthy class and a large class owning little or no property that the general political movement toward democracy has encountered the most obstinate resistance. Only a small part of our urban population own land or capital. The overwhelming majority of those who live in cities are employees and tenants. In the year 1900 74.3 per cent. of the families in the 160 cities of the United States having 25,000 or more population lived in rented houses and only 14.5 per cent in unmortgaged homes.[1] In the smaller towns the proportion of property owners was larger, while in the country the majority of the population belonged to the land-holding class, 64.4 per cent. of the "farm" families owning their homes, 44.4 per cent. of such families owning homes that were unencumbered.[2]

"Much has been said concerning the necessity of legislative interference in some cases where bad men were coming into power through universal suffrage in cities, but the recent experience of the country shows that this has oftener been said to pave the way for bad men to obtain office or grants of unusual powers from the legislature than with any purpose to effect local reforms. And the great municipal scandals and frauds that

[1] Abstract of the Twelfth Census, p. 133.
[2] Ibid, p. 28.

have prevailed, like those which were so notorious in New York City, have been made possible and then nursed and fostered by illegitimate interference at the seat of State government."[1]

The numerical preponderance of the property-owning class in the country and of the property-less class in the cities must be taken into account in any attempt to find an explanation of the reluctance on the part of the state to recognize the principle of municipal self-government. When we consider that the state government, even under universal suffrage, is largely government by taxpaying property owners, we can understand why the progress toward municipal democracy has been so slow. Under universal suffrage municipal self-government would mean the ascendency of the propertyless class, and this, from the standpoint of those who control the state government, would jeopardize the interests of the property-holding minority.

This is doubtless one of the chief reasons why the state government has not been willing to relinquish its control over municipal affairs. This fact is not recognized, however, by present-day writers on American politics. It is generally assumed that the corruption in state and municipal government is largely due to the ascendency of the masses. This view of the matter may be acceptable to those who from principle or interest

[1] Cooley, Constitutional Limitations, 6th ed., p. 282, n.

285

are opposed to democracy, but it ignores the facts which a careful analysis of the system discloses. Even in our state governments the changes that have been made as a concession to the newer democratic thought are less important than is generally supposed. The removal of property qualifications for voting and office-holding was a concession in form rather than in substance. It occurred at a time when there was an apparently inexhaustible supply of free land which made it possible for every one to become a landowner. Under such circumstances universal suffrage was not a radical or dangerous innovation. In fact, property qualifications for voting and office-holding were not necessary to the political ascendency of property owners in a community where the great majority of the citizens were or could become members of the property-owning class. It is not likely that property qualifications would have been removed for state purposes without a more serious struggle, if the wide diffusion of property in the state at large had not appeared to be an ample guarantee that the interests of property owners would not be endangered by universal suffrage. It was probably not intended that the abolition of property qualifications should overthrow the influence of property owners, or make any radical change in the policy of the state government.

It is easily seen that the removal of property

qualifications for voting and office-holding has had the effect of retarding the movement toward municipal home rule. Before universal suffrage was established the property-owning class was in control of both state and city government. This made state interference in local affairs unnecessary for the protection of property. But with the introduction of universal suffrage the conservative element which dominated the state government naturally favored a policy of state interference as the only means of protecting the property-owning class in the cities. In this they were actively supported by the corrupt politicians and selfish business interests that sought to exploit the cities for private ends. Our municipal conditions are thus the natural result of this alliance between conservatism and corruption.

We can understand now why the state has been unwilling to permit the same measure of democracy in municipal affairs that it has seen fit to employ for its own purposes. This is why our limited majority rule, which may be safe enough in the state government, is often deemed inexpedient for the city. It is also the reason for keeping the more important municipal powers under the control of the state government, as well as the ground for continuing property qualifications in the city after their disappearance from the government of the state.

The checks above mentioned are not the only

ones to be found, however, in our municipal government. The city is organized, like the state government, on the plan of distributed powers and diffused responsibility. It contains, as a rule, an elaborate system of checks which affords little opportunity for the prompt and effective expression of local public opinion in the administration of municipal affairs. At the same time, it gives the municipal authorities power to inaugurate and carry out policies to which local public sentiment may be strongly opposed. This is seen in the control which the mayor and council quite generally exercise over the matter of municipal franchises. Probably not a city of any importance could be mentioned in which the council has not granted privileges which have enriched individuals and private corporations at the expense of the public. This power has been the chief source of municipal corruption, since it has made the misgovernment of cities a source of great profit to a wealthy and influential class. Those who imagine that the ignorant and vicious part of our urban population is the main obstacle to reform take but a superficial view of the matter. The real source of misgovernment—the active cause of corruption—is to be found, not in the slums, not in the population ordinarily regarded as ignorant and vicious, but in the selfishness and greed of those who are the recognized leaders in commercial and industrial affairs. It is this class that, as Lincoln Steffens says, may be found "buying boodlers in St. Louis, defending grafters in Minneapolis, originating corruption in Pittsburg, sharing with bosses in Philadelphia, deploring reform in Chicago, and beating good government with corruption funds in New York."[1] This is the natural fruit of our system of municipal government. The powerful corporate interests engaged in the exploitation of municipal franchises are securely entrenched behind a series of constitutional and legal checks on the majority which makes it extremely difficult for public opinion to exercise any effective control over them. The effort to provide a remedy for this condition of affairs took the form of a movement to limit the powers of the council. Boards and commissions have been created in whose hands have been placed much of the business formerly controlled by this body. The policy of subdividing the legislative authority of the city and distributing it among a number of independent boards has been carried so far, notably in New York, that, as Seth Low observes, the council has been largely deprived of all its legislative functions with the single exception of the power to grant public franchises.[2] It must not be inferred, however, that public opinion has favored the retention of this power by the council. The attempt on the

---

[1] The Shame of the Cities, p. 5.
[2] Bryce, Vol. I, p. 663.

part of the people to control the franchise-grant-ing power has thus far largely failed, not because of any lack of popular support, but because our constitutional and political arrangements have made it almost impossible for any reasonable ma-jority to overcome the opposition of organized wealth.

Our efforts to bring about reforms in municipal government have thus far largely failed to ac-complish what was expected of them because we have persistently refused to recognize the prin-ciple of majority rule. We have clung tenaciously to the system of checks and balances with all its restraints on popular control. The evils of municipal government are not the evils of democ-racy, but the evils of a system which limits the power of the majority in the interest of the minority.

CHAPTER XI

INDIVIDUAL LIBERTY AND THE CONSTITUTION

The eighteenth-century conception of liberty was the outgrowth of the political conditions of that time. Government was largely in the hands of a ruling class who were able to further their own interests at the expense of the many who were unrepresented. It was but natural under these circumstances that the people should seek to limit the exercise of political authority, since every check imposed upon the government lessened the dangers of class rule. The problem which the advocates of political reform had to solve was how to secure the largest measure of individual liberty compatible with an irresponsible government. They were right in believing that this could be accomplished only by building up an elaborate system of constitutional restraints which would narrowly limit the exercise of irresponsible authority. Individual liberty as they understood the term was immunity from unjust interference at the hands of a minority.

This was a purely negative conception. It involved nothing more than the idea of protection against the evils of irresponsible government. It was a view of liberty adapted, however, to the needs of the time and served a useful purpose in aiding the movement to curb without destroying the power of the ruling class. Any attempt to push the doctrine of liberty farther than this and make it include more than mere immunity from governmental interference would have been revolutionary. The seventeenth and eighteenth century demand was not for the abolition, but for the limitation of irresponsible authority. It was not for popular government based upon universal suffrage, but for such modifications of the system as would give to the commercial and industrial classes the power to resist all encroachments upon their rights at the hands of the hereditary branches of the government. The basis and guarantee of individual liberty, as the term was then understood, was the popular veto such as was exercised through the House of Commons. This conception of liberty was realized for those represented in any coördinate branch of the government wherever the check and balance stage of political development had been reached.

The American revolution, which supplanted hereditary by popular rule, worked a fundamental change in the relation of the individual to the government. So far at least as the voters were concerned the government was no longer an alien institution—an authority imposed upon them from above, but an organization emanating from them—one in which they had and felt a direct proprietary interest. It was no longer a government in which the active principle was irresponsible authority, but one which rested upon the safe and trustworthy basis of popular control.

The overthrow of monarchy and aristocracy necessitated a corresponding change in the idea of liberty to make it fit the new political conditions which had emerged. In so far as government had now passed into the hands of the people there was no longer any reason to fear that it would encroach upon what they regarded as their rights. With the transition, then, from class to popular sovereignty there was a corresponding change in the attitude of the people toward the government. They naturally desired to limit the authority and restrict the activity of the government as long as they felt that it was irresponsible; but as soon as they acquired an active control over it, the reason which formerly actuated them in desiring to limit its powers was no longer operative. Their ends could now be accomplished and their interests best furthered by unhampered political activity. They would now desire to remove the checks upon the government for the same reason that they formerly sought to impose them—viz., to promote their own welfare.

This tendency is seen in the changes made in the state constitutions at the beginning of the American revolution. As shown in a previous chapter, they established the supremacy of the legislative body and through this branch of the government, the supremacy of the majority of the qualified voters. We have here a new conception of liberty. We see a tendency in these constitutional changes to reject the old passive view of state interference as limited by the consent of the governed and take the view that real liberty implies much more than the mere power of constitutional resistance—that it is something positive, that its essence is the power to actively control and direct the policy of the state. The early state constitutions thus represent a long step in the direction of unlimited responsible government.

This, as we have seen, was the chief danger which the conservative classes saw in the form of government established at the outbreak of the Revolution. They were afraid that the power of the numerical majority would be employed to further the interests of the many at the expense of the few, and to guard against such a use of the government they sought to re-establish the system of checks. The Constitution which restored the old scheme of government in a new garb also revived the old conception of individual liberty. There is, however, one important difference between the eighteenth-century conception of liberty and that which finds expression in our constitutional literature. Formerly it was because of the lack of popular control that the people generally desired to limit the authority of the government, but the framers of the ˙Constitution wished to bring about the limitation of governmental functions because they feared the consequences of majority rule. Formerly the many advocated the limitation of the power of king and aristocracy in the interest of liberty; now the few advocate the limitation of the power of the many for their own protection. With the abolition of monarchy and aristocracy the attitude of the few and the many has been reversed. The aristocratic and special interests that formerly opposed the limitation of political activity when they were predominant in the government, now favor it as a protection against the growing power of the masses, while the latter, who formerly favored, now oppose it. The conservative classes now regard the popular majority with the same distrust which the liberals formerly felt toward the king and aristocracy. In fact, the present-day conservative goes even farther than this and would have us believe that the popular majority is a much greater menace to liberty than king or aristocracy has ever been in the past.

"There can be no tyranny of a monarch so intolerable," says a recent American writer, "as that of the multitude, for it has the power behind it that no king can sway."[1] This is and has all along been the attitude of the conservative classes

[1] Willoughby, The Nature of the State, p. 416.

who never lose an opportunity to bring the theory of democracy into disrepute. The defenders of the American Constitution clearly see that unless the fundamental principle of popular government is discredited the system of checks can not survive.

There is no liberty, we are told by the present-day followers of Alexander Hamilton, where the majority is supreme. The American political system realizes this conception of liberty mainly through the Supreme Court—an organ of government which interprets the Constitution and laws of Congress and which may forbid the carrying out of the expressed will of the popular majority. It necessarily follows that the authority which can thus overrule the majority and enforce its own views of the system is an authority greater than the majority. All governments must belong to one or the other of two classes according as the ultimate basis of political power is the many or the few. There is, in fact, no middle ground. We must either recognize the many as supreme, with no checks upon their authority except such as are implied in their own intelligence, sense of justice and spirit of fair play, or we must accept the view that the ultimate authority is in the hands of the few. Every scheme under which the power of the majority is limited means in its practical operation the subordination of the majority to the minority. This inevitable consequence of the limitation of popular rule is not alluded to by the advocates of checks and balances, though it is obvious to any careful student of the system.

It would, however, do injustice to the intelligence of those who champion the scheme of checks and balances to give them credit for any real sympathy with the aims and purposes of democracy. Individual liberty as guaranteed by majority rule was not the end which the framers of the Constitution had in view, nor is it the reason why the present-day conservative defends their work. The Constitution as originally adopted did not contain that highly prized guarantee of personal liberty which democracy everywhere insists upon. The failure to make any provision for freedom of the press should be regarded as a significant omission. This, however, was not an essential part of the Federalists' scheme of government, which aimed rather to protect the property and privileges of the few than to guarantee personal liberty to the masses. This omission is the more noteworthy in view of the fact that this guarantee was at that time expressly included in a majority of the state constitutions, and that the temper of the people was such as to compel its speedy adoption as an amendment to the Federal Constitution itself.

Liberty, as the framers of the Constitution understood the term, had to do primarily with property and property rights. The chief danger which they saw in the Revolutionary state governments was the opportunity afforded to the majority to legislate upon matters which the well-to-do classes wished to place beyond the reach of popular interference. The unlimited authority which the state government had over taxation and its power to restrict or abridge property rights were viewed with alarm by the wealthy classes, who felt that any considerable measure of democracy would be likely to deprive them of their time-honored prerogatives. To guard against this danger the Constitution sought, in the interest of the classes which dominated the Federal Convention, to give the widest possible scope to private property. It prohibited private property in nothing—permitting it, as originally adopted, even in human beings. It may be said without exaggeration that the American scheme of government was planned and set up to perpetuate the ascendency of the property-holding class in a society leavened with democratic ideas. Those who framed it were fully alive to the fact that their economic advantages could be retained only by maintaining their class ascendency in the government. They understood the economic significance of democracy. They realized that if the supremacy of the majority were once fully established the entire policy of the government would be profoundly changed. They foresaw that it would mean the abolition of all private monopoly and the abridgment and regulation of property rights in the interest of the general public.

The Constitution was in form a political document, but its significance was mainly economic. It was the outcome of an organized movement on the part of a class to surround themselves with legal and constitutional guarantees which would check the tendency toward democratic legislation. These were made effective through the attitude of the United States courts which, as Professor Burgess says, "have never declined jurisdiction where private property was immediately affected on the ground that the question was political."[1]

"There can be no question that the national government has given to the minority a greater protection than it has enjoyed anywhere else in the world, save in those countries where the minority is a specially privileged aristocracy and the right of suffrage is limited. So absolute have property rights been held by the Supreme Court, that it even, by the Dred Scott decision, in effect made the whole country a land of slavery, because the slave was property, and the rights of property were sacred."[2]

In carrying out the original intent of the Constitution with reference to property the courts have developed and applied the doctrine of vested rights—a doctrine which has been used with tell-

[1] Pol. Sci. and Const. Law, Vol. I, p. 197.
[2] Ford's ed. of *The Federalist,* Introduction, p. xiii.

ing effect for the purpose of defeating democratic reforms. This doctrine briefly stated is that property rights once granted are sacred and inviolable. A rigid adherence to this policy would effectually deprive the government of the power to make the laws governing private property conform to social and economic changes. It would disregard the fact that vested rights are often vested wrongs, and that one important, if not indeed the most important, task which a government by and for the people has to perform is to rectify past mistakes and correct the evils growing out of corruption and class rule. A government without authority to interfere with vested rights would have little power to promote the general welfare through legislation.

The adoption of the Constitution brought this doctrine from the realm of political speculation into the arena of practical politics. The men who framed and set up our Federal government were shrewd enough to see that if the interests of the property-holding classes were to be given effective protection, it was necessary that political power should rest ultimately upon a class basis. This they expected to accomplish largely through the judicial veto and the power and influence of the Supreme Court. The effect of establishing the supremacy of this branch of the government was to make the legal profession virtually a ruling class. To their charge was committed under our system of government the final authority in all matters of legislation. They largely represent by virtue of their training and by reason of the interests with which they are affiliated, the conservative as opposed to the democratic influences. The power and influence exerted by lawyers in this country are the natural outgrowth of the constitutional position of our Supreme Court. Its supremacy is in the last analysis the supremacy of lawyers as a class and through them of the various interests which they represent and from which they derive their support. This explains the fact so often commented on by foreign critics, that in this country lawyers exert a predominant influence in political matters.

We are still keeping alive in our legal and constitutional literature the eighteenth-century notion of liberty. Our future lawyers and judges are still trained in the old conception of government —that the chief purpose of a constitution is to limit the power of the majority. In the meantime all other democratic countries have outgrown this early conception which characterized the infancy of democracy. They have in theory at least repudiated the eighteenth-century doctrine that the few have a right to thwart the will of the many. The majority has in such countries become the only recognized source of legitimate authority. "There is no fulcrum *outside* of the majority, and therefore there is nothing on which, as *against* the majority resistance or lengthened opposition can lean."[1]   This statement was made with reference to France, but it would apply as well to England, Switzerland, and all other countries in which the principle of majority rule has received full recognition.

On the other hand American constitutional and legal literature still inculcates and keeps alive fear and distrust of majority rule.   The official and ruling class in this country has been profoundly influenced by political ideas which have long been discarded in the countries which have made the most rapid strides in the direction of popular government.   The influence which our constitutional and legal literature, based as it is upon a profound distrust of majority rule, has had upon the lawyers, politicians, and public men of this country can hardly be overestimated.   It is true that many who have been most influenced by this spirit of distrust toward popular government would be unwilling to admit that they are opposed to majority rule—in fact, they may regard themselves as sincere believers in democracy.   This is not to be wondered at when we consider that throughout our history under the Constitution the old and the new have been systematically jumbled in our political literature.   In fact, the main effort of our constitutional writers would appear to be to give to the undemocratic eighteenth-cen-

[1] Boutmy, Studies in Constitutional Law, p. 155.

tury political ideas a garb and setting that would in a measure reconcile them with the democratic point of view. The natural and inevitable result has followed. The students of American political literature have imbibed the fundamental idea of the old system—its distrust of majority rule—along with a certain sentimental attachment to and acceptance of the outward forms of democracy. This irreconcilable contradiction between the form and the substance, the body and the spirit of our political institutions is not generally recognized even by the American students of government. Constitutional writers have been too much preoccupied with the thought of defending and glorifying the work of the fathers and not enough interested in disclosing its true relation to present-day thought and tendencies. As a consequence of this, the political ideas of our educated classes represent a curious admixture of democratic beliefs superimposed upon a hardly conscious substratum of eighteenth-century doctrines. It is this contradiction in our thinking that has been one of our chief sources of difficulty in dealing with political problems. While honestly believing that we have been endeavoring to make democracy a success, we have at the same time tenaciously held on to the essential features of a political system designed for the purpose of defeating the ends of popular government.

CHAPTER XII

INDIVIDUAL LIBERTY AND THE ECONOMIC SYSTEM

The American doctrine of individual liberty had its origin in economic conditions widely different from those which prevail to-day. The tools of production were simple and inexpensive and their ownership widely diffused. There was no capital-owning class in the modern sense. Business was carried on upon a small scale. The individual was his own employer, or, if working for another, could look forward to the time when, by the exercise of ordinary ability and thrift, he might become an independent producer. The way was open by which every intelligent and industrious wage-earner could become his own master. Industrially society was democratic to a degree which it is difficult for us to realize at the present day. This economic independence which the industrial classes enjoyed ensured a large measure of individual liberty in spite of the fact that political control was in the hands of a class.

The degree of individual freedom and initiative which a community may enjoy is not wholly, or even mainly, a matter of constitutional forms.

The actual liberty of the individual may vary greatly without any change in the legal or constitutional organization of society. A political system essentially undemocratic would be much less destructive of individual liberty in a society where the economic life was simple and ownership widely diffused than in a community possessing a wealthy capitalist class on the one hand and an army of wage-earners on the other. The political system reacts, it is true, upon the economic organization, but the influence of the latter upon the individual is more direct and immediate than that of the former. The control exerted over the individual directly by the government may, as a matter of fact, be slight in comparison with that which is exercised through the various agencies which control the economic system. But the close interdependence between the political and the business organization of society can not be overlooked. Each is limited and conditioned by the other, though constitutional forms are always largely the product and expression of economic conditions.

Individual liberty in any real sense implies much more than the restriction of governmental authority. In fact, true liberty consists, as we have seen, not in divesting the government of effective power, but in making it an instrument for the unhampered expression and prompt enforcement of public opinion. The old negative conception of liberty would in practice merely result in limiting the power of the government to control social conditions. This would not necessarily mean, however, the immunity of the individual from external control. To limit the power of the government may permit the extension over the individual of some other form of control even more irresponsible than that of the government itself—the control which inevitably results from the economic supremacy of a class who own the land and the capital.

The introduction of the factory system forced the great majority of small independent producers down into the ranks of mere wage-earners, and subjected them in their daily work to a class rule under which everything was subordinated to the controlling purpose of the employers—the desire for profits.

The significance of this change from the old handicraft system of industry to present-day capitalistic production is fully understood by all students of modern industry. Even Herbert Spencer, the great expounder of individualism, admitted that the so-called liberty of the laborer "amounts in practice to little more than the ability to exchange one slavery for another" and that "the coercion of circumstances often bears more hardly on him than the coercion of a master does on one in bondage."[1] This dependence of the

[1] Principles of Sociology, Vol. III, p. 525.

laborer, however, he regarded as unfortunate, and looked forward to the gradual amelioration of present conditions through the growth of co-operation in production.

Individualism as an economic doctrine was advocated in the eighteenth century by those who believed in a larger measure of freedom for the industrial classes. The small business which was then the rule meant the wide diffusion of economic power. A *laissez faire* policy would have furthered the interests of that large body of small independent producers who had but little representation in and but little influence upon the government. It would have contributed materially to the progress of the democratic movement by enlarging the sphere of industrial freedom for all independent producers. It does not follow, however, that this doctrine which served a useful purpose in connection with the eighteenth-century movement to limit the power of the ruling class is sound in view of the political and economic conditions which exist to-day. The so-called industrial revolution has accomplished sweeping and far-reaching changes in economic organization. It has resulted in a transfer of industrial power from the many to the few, who now exercise in all matters relating to production an authority as absolute and irresponsible as that which the ruling class exercised in the middle of the eighteenth century over the state itself. The simple decentralized and more democratic system of production which formerly prevailed has thus been supplanted by a highly centralized and thoroughly oligarchic form of industrial organization. At the same time political development has been tending strongly in the direction of democracy. The few have been losing their hold upon the state, which has come to rest, in theory at least, upon the will of the many. A political transformation amounting to a revolution has placed the many in the same position in relation to the government which was formerly held by the favored few.

As a result of these political and economic changes the policy of government regulation of industry is likely to be regarded by the masses with increasing favor. A society organized as a political democracy can not be expected to tolerate an industrial aristocracy. As soon, then, as the masses come to feel that they really control the political machinery, the irresponsible power which the few now exercise in the management of industry will be limited or destroyed as it has already been largely overthrown in the state itself. In fact the doctrine of *laissez faire* no longer expresses the generally accepted view of state functions, but merely the selfish view of that relatively small class which, though it controls the industrial system, feels the reins of political control slipping out of its hands. The limitation of governmental functions which was the rallying-cry of the liberals a century ago has thus become the motto of the present-day conservative.

The opponents of government regulation of industry claim that it will retard or arrest progress by restricting the right of individual initiative. They profess to believe that the best results for society as a whole are obtained when every corporation or industrial combination is allowed to manage its business with a free hand. It is assumed by those who advocate this policy that there is no real conflict of interests between the capitalists who control the present-day aggregations of corporate wealth and the general public. No argument is needed, however, to convince any one familiar with the facts of recent industrial development that this assumption is not true.

The change in the attitude of the people toward the let-alone theory of government is, as a matter of fact, the outcome of an intelligently directed effort to enlarge and democratize—not abridge— the right of initiative in its relation to the management of industry. The right of individual initiative in the sense of the right to exercise a real control over production was lost by the masses when the substitution of machinery for tools made them directly dependent upon a class of capital-owning employers. The subsequent growth of large scale production has centralized the actual control of industry in the hands of a small class of large capitalists. The small capitalists as separate and independent producers are being rapidly crushed or absorbed by the great corporation. They may still belong to the capitalist class in that they live upon an income derived from the ownership of stock or bonds. But they have no real control over the business in which their capital is invested. They no longer have the power to organize and direct any part of the industrial process. They enjoy the benefits which accrue from the ownership of wealth, but they can no longer take an active part in the management of industry. For them individual initiative in the sense of an effective control over the industrial process has disappeared almost as completely as it has in the case of the mere wage-earner. Individual initiative even for the capital-owning class has thus largely disappeared. It has been superseded by corporate initiative which means the extinguishment of individual initiative except in those cases where it is secured to the large capitalist through the ownership of a controlling interest in the business.

The abandonment of the *laissez faire* policy, then, in favor of the principle of government regulation of industry is the outgrowth, not of any hostility to individual initiative, but of the conviction that the monopoly of industrial power by the few is a serious evil. It is manifestly impossible to restore to the masses the right of individual initiative. Industry is too complex and too highly organized to permit a return to the old system of decentralized control. And since the only substitute for the old system of individual control is collective control, it appears to be inevitable that government regulation of business will become a fixed policy in all democratic states.

The *laissez faire* policy is supposed to favor progress by allowing producers to make such changes in business methods as may be prompted by the desire for larger profits. The doctrine as ordinarily accepted contains at least two erroneous assumptions, viz., (1) that any innovation in production which makes it possible for the capitalist to secure a larger return is necessarily an improvement in the sense of augmenting the average efficiency of labor, and (2) that policies are to be judged solely by their economic effects. Even if non-interference resulted in industrial changes which in all cases increase the efficiency of labor, it would not follow that such changes are, broadly considered, always beneficial. Before drawing any sweeping conclusion we must consider all the consequences direct and indirect, immediate and remote, political and social as well as economic. Hence the ordinary test—the direct and immediate effect upon productive efficiency—is not a satisfactory one. Moreover, many changes in the methods or organization of business are designed primarily to alter distribution in the interest of the capitalist by decreasing wages or by raising prices. In so far as a policy of non-interference permits changes of this sort, it is clearly harmful to the community at large, though advantageous to a small class.

In all democratic countries the conservative classes are beginning to realize that their ascendency in production is imperiled by the ascendency of the masses in the state. It thus happens that in the hope of checking or retarding the movement toward regulation of business in the interest of the people generally, they have taken refuge behind that abandoned tenet of democracy, the doctrine of non-interference.

At the same time they strongly favor any deviation from this policy which will benefit themselves. This is exemplified in their attitude in this country toward our protective tariff system, which, as originally adopted, was designed to encourage the development of our national resources by offering the prospect of larger profit to those who would invest their capital in the protected industries. Under a capitalistic system development naturally follows the line of greatest profit, and for this reason any protective tariff legislation which did not augment the profits of the capitalist would fail to accomplish its purpose. This was recognized and frankly admitted when the policy was first adopted. Later, however, when the suffrage was extended and the laboring class became an important factor in national elections the champions of protection saw that the system would have to be given a more democratic interpretation. Thus the Whig platform of 1844 favored a tariff "discriminating with special reference to the protection of the domestic labor of the country." This was, however, the only political platform in which the labor argument was used until 1872, when the Republican party demanded that "duties upon importations . . . should be so adjusted as to aid in securing remunerative wages to labor, and promote the industries, prosperity, and growth of the whole country." Protection, since that time, has been defended, not as a means of augmenting profits, but as a means of ensuring high wages to American workers. The interests of the wage-receiving class, however, were far from being the chief concern of those who were seeking to maintain and develop the policy of protection. It was to the capitalist rather than the wage-earner that the system of protection as originally established made a direct appeal, and it was primarily in the interest of this class that it was maintained even after the labor argument came to be generally used in its defense. The capitalist naturally favored a policy that would discourage the importation of foreign goods and at the same time encourage the importation of foreign labor. It was to his advantage to keep the labor market open to all who might wish to compete for employment, since this would tend to force wages down and thus give him the benefit of high prices.

Any system of protection established in the interest of labor would have excluded all immigrants accustomed to a low standard of living. But as a matter of fact the immigration of cheap foreign labor was actively encouraged by the employers in whose interest the high tariff on foreign goods was maintained. The efforts of the wage-earning class to secure for themselves some of the benefits of protection by organizing to obtain an advance or prevent a reduction in wages was largely defeated through the wholesale importation of cheap foreign labor by the large manufacturing, mining and transportation companies. The agitation against this evil carried on by the labor unions finally resulted in the enactment by Congress of legislation forbidding the importation of labor under contract of employment. This, however, did not, and even if it had been efficiently enforced, would not have given the American workingman any real protection against cheap foreign labor. The incoming tide of foreign immigration has been rising and the civic quality of the immigrant has visibly declined. The free lands which formerly attracted the best class of European immigrants are now practically a thing of the past, and with the disappearance of this opportunity for remunerative self-employment the last support of high wages has been removed. With unrestricted immigration the American laboring man must soon be deprived of any economic advantage which he has heretofore enjoyed over the laboring classes of other countries.

There has been one notable exception to this immigration policy. The invasion of cheap Asiatic labor upon the Pacific coast aroused a storm of protest from the laboring population, which compelled Congress to pass the Chinese Exclusion Act. But this legislation, while shutting out Chinese laborers, has not checked the immigration from other countries where a low standard of living prevails. In fact the most noticeable feature of the labor conditions in this country has been the continual displacement of the earlier and better class of immigrants and native workers by recent immigrants who have a lower standard of living and are willing to work for lower wages. This has occurred, too, in some of the industries in which the employer has been most effectually protected against the competition of foreign goods.[1]

[1] In the year 1857 over 37 per cent. of the immigrants arriving in the United States were from Germany, and over 39 per cent. were from Great Britain and Ireland. The bulk of our foreign immigration continued to come from these two countries until about 1886 or 1887. In 1890 these countries together contributed but little more than 47 per cent. of our foreign immigrants, and in 1904 but 17 per cent. Italy, including Sicily and Sardinia, supplied but 6 per cent. of the total number of immigrants in 1886 and 23 per cent. in 1904.

The time has certainly arrived when the policy of protection ought to be more broadly considered and dealt with in a public-spirited and statesman-like manner. If it is to be continued as a national policy, the interests of employees as well as employers must be taken into account. The chief evils of the protective system have been due to the fact that it has been too largely a class policy, and while maintained in the interest of a class, it has been adroitly defended as a means of benefiting the classes who derived little or no benefit—who were, indeed, often injured by our tariff legislation.

The large capitalist may grow eloquent in defense of that broad humanitarian policy under which the weak, the oppressed, and the ignorant of all nations are invited to come among us and share in the economic and political opportunities and privileges of American citizens. Such high-sounding and professedly disinterested cosmopolitanism appeals to a certain class of sentimental believers in democracy. It does not appeal, however, to any one who fully understands present-day industrial and political conditions. This capitalistic sympathy for the weak and the oppressed of other nations may be regarded by some

The Russian Empire and Finland furnished only 5 per cent. of the total number in 1886 and about 18 per cent. in 1904. In 1886 the immigration from Asiatic countries was insignificant, but in 1904 it had increased to 26,186. See Report of the Commissioner-General of Immigration, 1904.

as the expression of a broader patriotism, but its tap-root is class selfishness—the desire to secure high profits through maintaining active competition among laborers. As a matter of fact, all legislation does, and always must, appeal to the interest of those without whose influence and support it could not be enacted, and nothing is ever gained for true progress by making the pretence of disinterested love for humanity the cloak for class greed.

The desire of the employing class for cheap labor has been responsible for the greatest dangers which menace this country to-day. It was the demand for cheap labor which led to the importation of the African slave and perpetuated the institution of slavery until, with the voluntary immigration of foreign labor, it was no longer an economic necessity from the standpoint of the employing class. Indeed the very existence of slavery, by discouraging immigration, tended to limit the supply of labor, and by so doing, to cripple all enterprises in which free labor was employed. In this sense the abolition of slavery was the result of an economic movement. It was to the advantage of the employing class as a whole who found in the free labor hired under competitive conditions a more efficient and cheaper instrument of production than the slave whom they had to buy and for whose support they were responsible.

Had it not been for this eagerness on the part of the employing class to secure cheap labor at first through the importation of the African slave and later through the active encouragement of indiscriminate foreign immigration, we would not now have the serious political, social and economic problems which owe their existence to the presence among us of vast numbers of alien races who have little in common with the better class of American citizens. This element of our population, while benefiting the employing class by keeping wages down, has at the same time made it more difficult to bring about that intelligent political co-operation so much needed to check the greed of organized wealth.

The limitation of governmental powers in the Constitution of the United States was not designed to prevent all interference in business, but only such as was conceived to be harmful to the dominant class. The nature of these limitations as well as the means of enforcing them indicate their purpose. The provision relating to direct taxes is a good example. The framers of the Constitution were desirous of preventing any use of the taxing power by the general government that would be prejudicial to the interests of the well-to-do classes. This is the significance of the provision that no direct taxes shall be laid unless in proportion to population.[1] The

[1] Art. I, sec. 9.

only kind of a direct tax which the framers intended that the general government should have power to levy was the poll tax which would demand as much from the poor man as from the rich. This was indeed one of the reasons for opposing the ratification of the Constitution.

"Many specters," said Hamilton, "have been raised out of this power of internal taxation to excite the apprehensions of the people: double sets of revenue officers, a duplication of their burdens by double taxations, and the frightful forms of odious and oppressive poll-taxes, have been played off with all the ingenious dexterity of political legerdemain. . . .

"As little friendly as I am to the species of imposition [poll-taxes], I still feel a thorough conviction that the power of having recourse to it ought to exist in the Federal government. There are certain emergencies of nations, in which expedients, that in the ordinary state of things ought to be forborne, become essential to the public weal. And the government, from the possibility of such emergencies, ought ever to have the option of making use of them."[1]

It is interesting to observe that Hamilton's argument in defense of the power to levy poll-taxes would have been much more effective if it had been urged in support of the power to levy a direct tax laid in proportion to wealth. But this

[1] *Federalist*, No. 36.

kind of a tax would, in the opinion of the framers, have placed too heavy a burden upon the well-to-do. Hence they were willing to deprive the general government of the power to levy it even at the risk of crippling it in some great emergency when there might be urgent need of a large revenue.

This is not strange, however, when we remember that it was the property-owning class that framed and secured the adoption of the Constitution. That they had their own interests in view when they confined the general government practically to indirect taxes levied upon articles of general consumption, and forbade direct taxes levied in proportion to wealth, seems highly probable. It appears, then, that the recent decision of the United States Supreme Court declaring the Federal Income Tax unconstitutional merely gave effect to the original spirit and purpose of this provision.

The disposition to guard the interests of the property-holding class rather than to prevent legislation for their advantage is also seen in the interpretation which has been given to the provision forbidding the states to pass any laws impairing the obligation of contracts. The framers of the Constitution probably did not have in mind the extended application which the courts have since made of this limitation on the power of the states. Perhaps they intended nothing more than that the states should be prevented from repudiating their just debts. But whatever may have been the intention of the framers themselves, the reactionary movement in which they were the recognized leaders, finally brought about a much broader and, from the point of view of the capitalist class, more desirable interpretation of this provision.

There is evidence of a desire to limit the power of the states in this direction even before the Constitutional Convention of 1787 assembled. The legislature of Pennsylvania in 1785 passed a bill repealing an act of 1782 which granted a charter to the Bank of North America. James Wilson, who is said to have suggested the above-mentioned clause of the Federal Constitution, made an argument against the repeal of the charter, in which he claimed that the power, or at least the right of the legislature, to modify or repeal did not apply to all kinds of legislation. It could safely be exercised, he thought, in the case of "a law respecting the rights and properties of all the citizens of the state."

"Very different," he says, "is the case with regard to a law, by which the state grants privileges to a congregation or other society. . . . Still more different is the case with regard to a law by which an estate is vested or confirmed in an individual: if, in this case, the legislature may, at discretion, and without any reason assigned, divest or destroy his estate, then a person seized of an estate in fee-simple, under legislative sanction, is, in truth, nothing more than a solemn tenant at will. . . .

"To receive the legislative stamp of stability and permanency, acts of incorporation are applied for from the legislature. If these acts may be repealed without notice, without accusation, without hearing, without proof, without forfeiture, where is the stamp of their stability? . . . If the act for incorporating the subscribers to the Bank of North America shall be repealed in this manner, a precedent will be established for repealing, in the same manner, every other legislative charter in Pennsylvania. . . . Those acts of the state, which have hitherto been considered as the sure anchors of privilege and of property, will become the sport of every varying gust of politics, and will float wildly backwards and forwards on the irregular and impetuous tides of party and faction."[1]

In 1810 the case of Fletcher v. Peck[2] was decided in the Supreme Court of the United States. Chief Justice Marshall, in delivering the opinion of the court, said:

"The principle asserted is that one legislature is competent to repeal any act which a former legislature was competent to pass; and that one

[1] Considerations, on the Power to Incorporate the Bank of North America, Works, Vol. I.
[2] 6 Cranch, 87.

legislature can not abridge the powers of a succeeding legislature. The correctness of this principle, so far as respects general legislation, can never be controverted. But if an act be done under a law, a succeeding legislature can not undo it. . . .

"When then a law is in the nature of a contract, when absolute rights have vested under that contract, a repeal of the law can not devest those rights; . . .

"It may well be doubted whether the nature of society and of government does not prescribe some limits to the legislative power; . . .

"It is, then, the unanimous opinion of the court, that, in this case, the estate having passed into the hands of a purchaser for a valuable consideration, without notice, the state of Georgia was restrained, either by general principles, which are common to our free institutions, or by the particular provisions of the Constitution of the United States, from passing a law whereby the estate of the plaintiff in the premises so purchased could be constitutionally and legally impaired and rendered null and void."

It is evident from this opinion that the court would have been disposed at that time to declare state laws impairing property rights null and void, even if there had been nothing in the Constitution of the United States to justify the exercise of such a power. Justice Johnson, in a separate opinion, said:

"I do not hesitate to declare that a state does not possess the power of revoking its own grants. But I do it on a general principle, on the reason and nature of things: a principle which will impose laws even on the Deity. . . .

"I have thrown out these ideas that I may have it distinctly understood that my opinion on this point is not founded on the provision in the Constitution of the United States, relative to laws impairing the obligation of contracts."

It was contended in this case that the state of Georgia had the right to revoke the grant on the ground that it was secured by corrupt means. This argument evidently failed to appeal to the court. It was referred to by Justice Johnson who said "as to the idea that the grants of a legislature may be void because the legislature are corrupt, it appears to me to be subject to insuperable difficulties. . . . The acts of the supreme power of a country must be considered pure. . . ."

It is interesting to observe that the Federalist judges in the early years of our history under the Constitution did not deem it necessary to find a constitutional ground for decisions of this sort. But with the overthrow of the Federalist party and the progress of belief in popular government, there is an evident disposition on the part of the court to extend the protection of the Federal Constitution to all the powers which it claimed the right to exercise. Thus in the Dartmouth College case, decided in 1819, the United States Supreme Court appears to have abandoned its earlier position and to have recognized the Constitution as the source of its power to annul state laws.

"It is under the protection of the decision in the Dartmouth College case," says Judge Cooley, "that the most enormous and threatening powers in our country have been created; some of the great and wealthy corporations actually having greater influence in the country at large, and upon the legislation of the country than the states to which they owe their corporate existence. Every privilege granted or right conferred—no matter by what means or on what pretence—being made inviolable by the Constitution, the government is frequently found stripped of its authority in very important particulars, by unwise, careless, or corrupt legislation; and a clause of the Federal Constitution, whose purpose was to preclude the repudiation of debts and just contracts, protects and perpetuates the evil."[1]

Any government framed and set up to guard and promote the interests of the people generally ought to have full power to modify or revoke all rights or privileges granted in disregard of the public welfare. But the Supreme Court, while permitting the creation or extension of property

[1] Constitutional Limitations, 6th ed., pp. 335-336, n.

rights, has prevented the subsequent abridgment of such rights, even when the interests of the general public demanded it. The effect of this has been to make the corporations take an active part in corrupting state politics. Special legislation was not prohibited. In fact, it was a common way of creating property rights. If a bank, an insurance company, or a railway corporation was organized, it was necessary to obtain a charter from the legislature which defined its powers and privileges. The corporation came into existence by virtue of a special act of the legislature and could exercise only such powers and enjoy only such rights and privileges as that body saw fit to confer upon it. The legislature might refuse to grant a charter, but having granted it, it became a vested right which could not be revoked. The charter thus granted by the legislature was a special privilege. In many instances it was secured as a reward for political services by favorites of the party machine, or through the corrupt expenditure of money or the equally corrupt distribution of stock in the proposed corporation among those who controlled legislation. Not only did this system invite corruption in the granting of such charters, but it also created a motive for the further use of corrupt means to keep possible competitors from securing like privileges. It was worth the while to spend money to secure a valuable privilege if when once obtained the legislature could not revoke it. And it was also worth the while to spend more money to keep dangerous competitors out of the field if by so doing it could enjoy some of the benefits of monopoly. By thus holding that a privilege granted to an individual or a private corporation by special act of the legislature was a contract which could not be revoked by that body, the courts in their effort to protect property rights opened the door which allowed corporation funds to be brought into our state legislatures early in our history for purposes of corruption.

But little attention has been given as yet to this early species of corruption which in some of the states at least assumed the proportions of a serious political evil.

"During the first half century banking in New York," says Horace White, "was an integral part of the spoils of politics. Federalists would grant no charters to Republicans, and Republicans none to Federalists. After a few banks had been established they united, regardless of politics, to create a monopoly by preventing other persons from getting charters. When charters were applied for and refused, the applicants began business on the common-law plan. Then, at the instigation of the favored ones, the politicians passed a law to suppress all unchartered banks. The latter went to Albany and bribed the legislature. In short, politics, monopoly, and bribery constitute the key to banking in the early history of the state."[1]

The intervention of the courts which made the conditions above described possible, while ostensibly limiting the power of the state legislature, in reality enlarged and extended it in the interest of the capital-owning class. It gave to the state legislature a power which up to that time it had not possessed—the power to grant rights and privileges of which the grantees could not be deprived by subsequent legislation. Before the adoption of the Federal Constitution no act of the legislature could permanently override the will of the qualified voters. It was subject to modification or repeal at the hands of any succeeding legislature. The voters of the state thus had what was in effect an indirect veto on all legislative acts—a power which they might exercise through a subsequent legislature or constitutional convention. But with the adoption of the Constitution of the United States the Federal courts were able to deprive them of this power where it was most needed. This removed the only effective check on corruption and class legislation, thus placing the people at the mercy of their state legislatures and any private interests that might temporarily control them.

The power which the legislatures thus acquired

[1] Money and Banking, p. 327. See also Myers, The History of Tammany Hall, pp. 113-116.

to grant charters which could not be amended or repealed made it necessary for the people to devise some new method of protecting themselves against this abuse of legislative authority. The outcome of this movement to re-establish some effective popular check on the legislature has taken the form in a majority of the states of a constitutional amendment by which the right is reserved to amend or repeal all laws conferring corporate powers. Such constitutional changes provide no remedy, however, for the evils resulting from legislative grants made previous to their adoption. The granting of special charters is now also prohibited in many states, the constitution requiring that all corporations shall be formed under general laws. These constitutional changes may be regarded as in the interest of the capitalist class as a whole, whose demand was for a broader and more liberal policy—one which would extend the advantages of the corporate form of organization to all capitalists in every line of business. But even our general corporation laws have been enacted too largely in the interest of those who control our business undertakings and without due regard to the rights of the general public.

A study of our political history shows that the attitude of the courts has been responsible for much of our political immorality. By protecting the capitalist in the possession and enjoyment of privileges unwisely and even corruptly granted, they have greatly strengthened the motive for employing bribery and other corrupt means in securing the grant of special privileges. If the courts had all along held that any proof of fraud or corruption in obtaining a franchise or other legislative grant was sufficient to justify its revocation, the lobbyist, the bribe-giver, and the "innocent purchaser" of rights and privileges stolen from the people, would have found the traffic in legislative favors a precarious and much less profitable mode of acquiring wealth.

CHAPTER XIII

THE INFLUENCE OF DEMOCRACY UPON THE CONSTITUTION

The distinguishing feature of the Constitution, as shown in the preceding chapters of this book, was the elaborate provisions which it contained for limiting the power of the majority. The direction of its development, however, has in many respects been quite different from that for which the more conservative of its framers hoped.[1] The checks upon democracy which it contained were nevertheless so skilfully contrived and so effective that the progress of the popular movement has been more seriously hampered and retarded here than in any other country where the belief in majority rule has come to be widely accepted. In some important respects the system as originally set up has yielded to the pressure of present-day tendencies in political thought; but many of its features are at variance with what has come to be regarded as essential in any well-organized democracy.

[1] "Over and over again our government has been saved from complete breakdown only by an absolute disregard of the Constitution, and most of the very men who framed the compact would have refused to sign it, could they have foreseen its eventual development." Ford's Federalist, Introduction, p. vii.

It is not so much in formal changes made in the Constitution as in the changes introduced through interpretation and usage that we must look for the influence of nineteenth-century democracy. In fact, the formal amendment of the Constitution, as shown in Chapter IV, is practically impossible. But no scheme of government set up for eighteenth-century society could have survived throughout the nineteenth and into the twentieth century without undergoing important modifications. No century of which we have any knowledge has witnessed so much progress along nearly every line of thought and activity. An industrial and social revolution has brought a new type of society into existence and changed our point of view with reference to nearly every important economic and political question. Our constitutional and legal system, however, has stubbornly resisted the influence of this newer thought, although enough has been conceded to the believers in majority rule from time to time to keep the system of checks from breaking down.

Some of the checks which the founders of our government established no longer exist except in form. This is true of the electoral college through which the framers of the Constitution hoped and expected to prevent the majority of the qualified voters from choosing the President. In this case democracy has largely defeated the end of the framers, though the small states, through their disproportionately large representation in the electoral college, exert an influence in Presidential elections out of proportion to their population.

The most important change in the practical operation of the system has been accomplished indirectly through the extension of the suffrage in the various states. Fortunately, the qualifications of electors were not fixed by the Federal Constitution. If they had been, it is altogether probable that the suffrage would have been much restricted, since the right to vote was at that time limited to the minority. The state constitutions responded in time to the influence of the democratic movement and manhood suffrage became general. This placed not only the various state governments but also the President and the House of Representatives upon a basis which was popular in theory if not in fact. Much remained and still remains to be done in the matter of perfecting the party system and the various organs for formulating and expressing public opinion with reference to political questions, before there will be any assurance that even these branches of the general government will always represent public sentiment.

There is one serious defect in the method of choosing the President. The system makes possible the election of an executive to whom a majority and even a large majority of the voters might be bitterly opposed. From the point of view of the framers of the Constitution the choice of a mere popular favorite was undesirable and even dangerous; but according to the view now generally accepted the chief executive of the nation should represent those policies which have the support of a majority of the people.

It is possible that the candidate receiving a majority of all the votes cast may be defeated,[1] while it often happens that the successful candidate receives less than a majority of the popular vote.[2] When three or more tickets are placed in the field, the candidate having a majority in the electoral college may fall far short of a majority of the popular vote. This was the case when Lincoln was elected President in 1860. There were four candidates for the Presidency, and while Lincoln received a larger popular vote than any other one candidate, he received less than the combined vote for either Douglas and Breckenridge, or Douglas and Bell. In fact, he received less than two-fifths of the total popular vote.

It is easily seen that a system is fraught with grave danger, especially in times of bitter sectional and party strife, which makes possible the election of a minority President. At such times opposition to governmental policies is most likely to assume the form of active resistance when a minority secures control of the government. In

[1] This was true of Samuel J. Tilden, the Democratic candidate in 1876.

[2] Supra p. 56.

other words, a majority is more likely to resist a minority than a minority is to resist a majority. This would be true especially in a country where the people generally accept the principle of majority rule.

It can not be claimed that Lincoln was, or that the South regarded him as, the choice of a majority of the people. A different system which would have precluded the election of a President who did not have a clear majority of the popular vote might have done much toward discouraging active resistance on the part of the Southern States.

No one, in fact, has stated the case against minority rule more clearly or forcefully than Lincoln himself. In a speech made in the House of Representatives January 12, 1848, on "The War with Mexico," he said:

"Any people anywhere, being inclined and having the power, have the *right* to rise up and shake off the existing government, and form a new one that suits them better. This is a most valuable, a most sacred right—a right which, we hope and believe, is to liberate the world. Nor is this right confined to cases in which the whole people of an existing government may choose to exercise it. Any portion of such people that *can may* revolutionize, and make their *own* of so much of the territory as they inhabit. More than this, a *majority* of any portion of such people may revolutionize, putting down a *minority*, intermingled with, or near about them, who may oppose their movements. Such minority was precisely the case of the Tories of our own Revolution."[1]

This was quoted in defense of the right of secession by Alexander H. Stephens in his "Constitutional View of the Late War between the States."[2]

The chief remaining obstacles to popular legislation are the Senate and the Supreme Court. Some means must be found to make these two branches of the government responsible to the majority before the government as a whole can be depended upon to give prompt and effective expression to public opinion. The Senate presents the most difficult problem for democracy to solve. The present method of choosing senators is altogether unsatisfactory. It has resulted in making the upper house of our Federal legislature representative of those special interests over which there is urgent need of effective public control. It has also had the effect of subordinating the making of laws in our state legislatures to that purely extraneous function—the election of United States senators. The exercise of the latter function has done more than anything else to confuse state politics by making it necessary for those interests that would control the United

[1] Appendix to the Congressional Globe, 1st sess., 30th Cong., p. 94.
[2] Vol. I, p. 520.

States Senate to secure the nomination and election of such men to the state legislatures as can be relied upon to choose senators who will not be too much in sympathy with anti-corporation sentiments.

The Senate has fulfilled in larger measure than any other branch of the government the expectation of the founders. It was intended to be representative of conservatism and wealth and a solid and enduring bulwark against democracy. That it has accomplished this purpose of the framers can scarcely be denied. But the political beliefs of the framers are not the generally accepted political beliefs of to-day. It is immaterial to the people generally that the attitude of the Senate on public questions is in line with the purpose for which that body was originally established. The criticism of the Senate's policy expressed in the phrase "all brakes and no steam"[1] indicates not so much a change in the character and influence of that body as in the attitude of the people toward the checks which the Constitution imposed upon democracy. Conservatism has always been characteristic of the United States Senate, which, as Sir Henry Maine says, is "the one thoroughly successful institution [upper house] which has been established since the tide of modern democracy began to run."[2] Measuring success by the

---

[1] *Outlook,* Vol. 79, p. 163.
[2] Popular Government, p. 181.

degree of resistance offered to the will of the majority, as this writer does, the conclusion is correct. This is the standard of judgment which the framers of the Constitution would have applied, but it is not the generally accepted standard according to which the success of that body would be judged to-day. We have now come to accept the view that every organ of government must be approved or condemned according as it furthers or thwarts the ends of democracy. Applying this test, the conclusion is inevitable that the Senate as now constituted is out of harmony with present-day political thought.

What, then, can be done to make that body an organ of democracy? There are three distinct evils in the Senate as it is now organized. The first pertains to the irresponsibility of its members due to their method of election and long term of office. But inasmuch as this could be remedied only by a constitutional amendment, it is not likely that anything short of a revolutionary public sentiment in favor of such change could compel the preliminary two-thirds majority in that body which the Constitution makes necessary. A body made up of men who for the most part realize that they owe their political advancement to a minority would naturally be loth to support a change in the system which would place the election to membership in that body directly in the hands of the people. It is improbable that any such reform can be accomplished at present. Any such direct attack upon the system would under present conditions be almost certain to fail. Some method of accomplishing this object must be employed which does not require the co-operation of the Senate, and which, without any constitutional amendment, really deprives the legislature of the power to select United States Senators as the electoral college has been deprived of all power in the choice of President.

The second defect in the Senate is the equal representation of the states in that body. It is not only absurd but manifestly unjust that a small state like Nevada should have as much representation in the controlling branch of Congress as New York with more than one hundred and seventy-one times as much population. A more inequitable distribution of representation it would be difficult to imagine; yet this evil could not be removed even by constitutional amendment, since this matter does not come within the scope of the amending power, unless the state or states affected by such proposed change should all give their assent.

The third defect in the Senate is the extraordinary power which the Constitution has conferred upon it. If it were a directly elected body whose members were apportioned among the states according to population, the overshadowing influence of the Senate would not be a serious matter. But, as shown in Chapter VI, that body controls jointly with the President the appointing and the treaty-making power. Moreover, the latter power may be exercised with reference to many things concerning which Congress has or could legislate. The Senate and the President may thus repeal what Congress has enacted. We thus have the peculiar situation that a law enacted with the concurrence of the House may be repealed without its consent, while a law which takes the form of a treaty can not be repealed without the consent of the Senate.

Theoretically, the Constitution could be amended so as to diminish the power of the Senate, but as a matter of fact no change in the Constitution would be more difficult to bring about. Any proposal to reduce the power of the Senate would jeopardize the prestige and influence of the smaller states no less than the proposal to deprive them of equal representation in that body. The small states approach political equality with the large, just in proportion as the influence of the Senate is a dominating factor in the policy of the government. Any attack on this equality of representation would ally the small states together in defense of this privilege, and make it impossible to obtain the assent of three-fourths of the states to any such change.

There is still another respect in which this equality of representation in the Senate is unfortunate. It tends to make it easier for corporation influences to dominate that body. This arises out of the fact that it is more difficult and more expensive to control the election of senators in a large than in a small state. This tends to make the small states a favorite field for political activity on the part of those corporations which wish to secure or prevent Federal legislation.

The Supreme Court is generally regarded as the most effective of all our constitutional checks upon democracy. Still, if the Senate were once democratized, it would not be a difficult matter to bring the Federal judiciary into line with the popular movement. In fact, the means employed in England to subordinate the House of Lords to the Commons indicates the method which might be employed here to subordinate the Supreme Court to Congress. The Ministry in England, virtually appointed by and responsible to the majority in the House of Commons, secured control of the prerogatives of the Crown, one of which was the right to appoint peers. No sooner did the House of Commons come into possession of this power through a responsible Ministry than it realized the possibility of making use of it to overcome opposition to their policies on the part of the Lords. If the House of Lords did not yield to the House of Commons, the latter, through its Cabinet, could create new peers in sufficient number to break down all resistance in that body.

The possession of that power by the Commons and the warning that it would be used if necessary has been sufficient to ensure compliance on the part of the Lords. In a similar manner Congress and the President could control the Supreme Court. The Constitution does not fix the number of Supreme judges. This is a matter of detail which was left to Congress, which may at any time provide for the addition of as many new judges to the Supreme Court as it may see fit. Thus Congress, with the co-operation of the President, could control the policy of the Supreme Court in exactly the same way and to the same extent that the House of Commons controls the House of Lords.

That the Federalists who were in possession of our general government during the early years of its history appreciated the advantage of controlling the policy of the Supreme Court was pointed out in the chapter on the Federal judiciary. They accomplished their purpose, however, by selecting for membership in that body, men whose political record was satisfactory and whose views concerning judicial functions were in harmony with the general plan and purpose of the Federalist party. In fact, the scheme of government which they set up contemplated no such possibility as the democratization of the Executive or the Senate. If their expectation in this regard had been fully realized, a judicious use of the appointing power would have been all that was necessary to ensure a conservative court. Perhaps the framers of the Constitution did not imagine that the power to increase the number of judges would ever be needed to enable the President and Senate to secure the co-operation of the Supreme Court. At any rate, the power given to Congress and the President to enlarge the membership of that body was not, in the opinion of the framers, a power that could ever be employed against the conservative class, since the radical element, it was believed, would never be able to control more than one branch of the government, the House of Representatives. But, although it can not be determined whether the Federalists had in mind the possibility of using this power to control the policy of the court, it should be noted that, according to their view of the government, it might be used by, but not against, the conservative class. Nor is it likely that they would have hesitated to use this power had it been necessary to the success of their plan.

The failure of the Federalists to check the growth of democratic ideas and the success of the more liberal party in bringing about the election of Jefferson alarmed the conservative class. It was seen that if all other branches of the government should come under the influence of the liberal movement, the judicial check could be broken down. To guard against this danger, an effort was made by the conservative interests to mold a public sentiment that would protect the Supreme Court against political interference at the hands of those who might wish to override judicial opposition to radical measures. This took the form of what might be called the doctrine of judicial infallibility. The judiciary in general and the Supreme Court in particular were held up as the guardian and protector of American liberty. The security of the people was represented as bound up with the freedom of the courts from political interference. At the same time it was proclaimed that the Supreme Court exercised only judicial functions and that any attempt on the part of the President or Congress to interfere with them would make that body the organ of faction or class. But, as a matter of fact, the danger which they foresaw to the Supreme Court was not a danger growing out of its judicial, but out of its legislative functions. It was not because the Supreme Court was a purely judicial body, but because it exercised a supremely important legislative function, that they were so solicitous to guard it against anything approaching popular control. The threefold division of governmental powers into legislative, executive, and judicial, as shown in a preceding chapter, has no logical basis. There are, as Professor Goodnow has said,[1] but two functions of government,

---

[1] Politics and Administration, p. 9.

that of expressing and that of executing the will of the state. The Supreme Court, in so far as it is a purely judicial body—that is, a body for hearing and deciding cases—is simply a means of executing the will of the state. With the performance of this function there was little danger that any democratic movement would interfere. Nor was this the danger which the conservative classes really feared, or which they wished to guard against. What they desired above all else was to give the Supreme Court a final voice in expressing the will of the state, and by so doing to make it operate as an effective check upon democratic legislation. It is this power of expressing the will of the state which our conservative writers defend as the pre-eminently meritorious feature of our judicial system. Indeed, this is, in the opinion of the conservative class, the most important of all the checks on democracy. Any suggestion of using the power vested in Congress and the President to reorganize the Supreme Court is naturally enough denounced as the most dangerous and revolutionary of political heresies. It is not probable, however, that the Supreme Court would much longer be permitted to thwart the will of the majority if the other branches of the Federal government were thoroughly imbued with the belief in democracy. As explained in Chapter V, the Constitution contains no hint of this power to declare acts of Congress null and void. It was injected into the Constitution, as the framers intended, by judicial interpretation, and under the influence of a thoroughly democratic President, and Congress might be eliminated in the same way.

The most important feature of the Constitution from the standpoint of democracy is the provision contained in article V, requiring Congress "on the application of the legislatures of two-thirds of the several states" to "call a convention for proposing amendments." The progress of democracy in the various state governments is likely to compel resort to this method of changing the Federal Constitution if the Senate much longer persists in disregarding the will of the people. In fact, this is, in the opinion of the conservative class, the one fatal defect in the scheme of constitutional checks established by our forefathers. It in reality opens the door to the most revolutionary changes in our political arrangements. Congress can not refuse to call a general constitutional convention when two-thirds of the states demand it, and this convention might propose an entirely new constitution framed in accord with the most advanced ideas of democracy. It might also follow the precedent set by the framers of our present Constitution and prescribe an entirely new method of ratification, as our more conservative forefathers did when they disregarded the then existing provision governing the amendment of the Articles of Confederation. It is true that they ignored the established method of amending as well as the instructions from the states by which they were appointed, in order to bring about the adoption of a political system more acceptable to the conservative classes. But what has been done in the interest of the minority may also be done in the interest of the majority. A new Federal constitution might be framed which would eliminate the whole system of checks on the people and provide for direct ratification by a majority of the voters, as has already been done in the case of most of our state constitutions. If the Constitution does not yield sufficiently to satisfy the popular demand for reform, it is possible that the reactionary forces will, in their anxiety to defeat moderate democratic measures, arouse sufficient opposition on the part of the people to compel sweeping constitutional changes.

The fact that two-thirds of the states can require Congress to call a convention of all the states to propose changes in the Constitution is a matter of no small importance. True, even this method of initiating changes in the system would be very difficult, since the smaller states would naturally fear an attempt to establish a more equitable plan of representation, and the special and privileged interests of all sorts which have found the present system satisfactory would use every means at their command to prevent the states from resorting to this power. It is possible, if not indeed probable, that a serious and concerted attempt by the people to force changes in the Constitution by this method would sufficiently alarm the opponents of democracy to convince them of the wisdom and expediency of such amendments as would appease the popular clamor for reform without going too far in the direction of majority rule. To prevent the complete overthrow of the system, which might be the outcome if the states were compelled to assume the initiative in amending the Constitution, the minority may accept the inevitable, and, choosing what appears to them to be the lesser of two evils, allow Congress to propose such amendments as the people are determined to bring about.

It is in the state and in the municipal governments, however, that the influence of democracy has been greatest. Yet even here much still remains to be done before the practical operation of the system will be in accord with the principle of majority rule. Direct election and universal suffrage have not under our scheme of checks and balances secured any large measure of political responsibility. The logical result of this system has been the growing distrust of public officials and especially of such representative bodies as state legislatures and city councils. This lack of confidence in the local governmental machinery, due to the irresponsibility of public officials, is certain to lead to the adoption of radical changes in the organization of our state and municipal governments. Either the tenure of public officials will be made to depend in some more effective way upon the will of the majority, or the power which they now have and which they often use to further private interests at the expense of the people will be taken from them and conferred directly upon the majority of the voters.

The movement to give the people greater control over the officials whom they have elected is really just beginning. Heretofore the effort to make the government truly representative of the people has been mainly along the line of broadening the suffrage and perfecting the method of voting. This, the people are just beginning to realize, does not guarantee political responsibility. The secret ballot under present conditions is important, but it is by no means adequate. The right of the majority to elect one or the other of two men, both of whom may have been nominated through the machinations of a corrupt and selfish minority, does not give the people any real control over the officials whom they vote into office. What they need, to ensure responsibility, is the power to make a real, not a merely nominal choice, coupled with the power to remove in case the person selected should lose the confidence of the majority.

The plan for depriving the minority of the power to control the selection of public officials, which is now rapidly gaining adherents among the advocates of political reform, is the direct primary. That some such change in our method of nominating candidates is necessary to make the so-called popular election of public officials anything more than an empty form is apparent to any intelligent student of American politics. But any proposal to deprive the minority of this power must encounter the determined opposition of the party machine and the various private interests which now prosper at the expense of the people. These opponents of political reform are continually declaiming against the corruption and incapacity of the people and trying to make it appear that a government can be no better than its source—those who elect the public officials. That a government is not likely to be better than the people whom it represents may be admitted. But this is aside from the question. Our present system in its practical operation is not a democracy. It is not truly representative, but misrepresentative To prevent this evil—this betrayal of public trust in the interest of the minority— is the aim of the direct primary. That it will go far toward breaking the power of the machine may be safely predicted, and that it will be generally adopted as soon as the people realize its significance there is scarcely room for doubt.

But while the direct nomination of candidates would doubtless go far toward making public officials respect the wishes of the people, it would not provide adequate protection against misconduct in office under our plan of election for a definite term without any effective power of removal. A corrupt official may often find that by favoring private interests at the expense of the people who have elected him, he can afford to forfeit all chance of re-election. The independence of public officials which our forefathers were so anxious to secure has been found to be a fruitful source of corruption. A realization of this fact has been responsible for the introduction of the recall system under which the people enforce official responsibility through their power to remove by a vote of lack of confidence in the form of a petition signed by a certain percentage of the voters. Such an expression of popular disapproval has the effect of suspending from office the offending official who can regain the office only by offering himself again as a candidate at an election called for that purpose. This is as yet merely an innovation in municipal government, but if it proves to be satisfactory, the principle will doubtless be incorporated, not only in municipal charters generally, but in our state constitutions as well.

Simultaneous with this movement to make government really representative by enforcing official responsibility is another movement which also

aims to make the will of the majority supreme,
but by a totally different method of procedure.
This is the movement looking toward the establishment of the initiative and the referendum.
Instead of leaving power in the hands of representative bodies and seeking to make them
responsible as the first plan of reform contem-
plates, the second plan would guard representative
bodies against temptation by divesting them of all
powers which they are liable to misuse and conferring them directly upon the people. This is
merely an attempt to get back to the basic idea of
the old town meeting, where local measures were
directly proposed and adopted or rejected by the
people. It is, moreover, the logical outcome of
the struggle which the advocates of majority rule
have been and are now making to secure control
of our state and municipal governments. The
constitutional checks on democracy have greatly
obstructed and delayed the progress of political
reform. Some of them have been removed, it is
true, but enough still remain to make it possible
for the minority to defeat the will of the majority
with reference to many questions of vital importance.

It must be admitted, when we review the course
of our political development, that much progress
has been made. But the evolution has been toward a direct rather than toward a representative
democracy. The reason for this is not far to

seek. The system of checks which limited the power of the majority made the legislature largely an irresponsible body; and since it could not be trusted, it was necessary to take out of its hands the powers it was most likely to abuse.

The legislature was first deprived of its power to enact constitutional legislation, though it was allowed to retain an effective veto on such changes through its refusal to take the initiative. With the progress of the democratic movement some of the legislative powers most frequently abused were, like the state constitution itself, made subject to popular ratification. This submission of constitutional and certain kinds of statutory legislation to the people before it could go into effect merely gave them to this extent a veto on the recommendations of their legislatures and constitutional conventions. There was still no way to prevent the legislature from misrepresenting the people with respect to those measures which did not require popular ratification. The tendency was to diminish the power of the legislature by including in the constitution itself much that might have taken the form of ordinary statutory legislation, as well as by requiring that some of the more important acts passed by the legislature should receive the direct assent of the voters. This merely gave to the people a partial negative. It enabled them to reject some measures which they did not approve of, but not all, since in those cases where popular ratification was not required, public sentiment could be disregarded by the law-making body. Moreover, the people did not have the right to initiate measures—a right which is indispensable if the people are to have any real power to mold the policy of the state. The logical outcome of this line of development is easily seen. As pointed out in an earlier part of this volume, constitutional development first limits and eventually destroys irresponsible power, and in the end makes the responsible power in the state supreme. The prevalent lack of confidence in our state legislatures is no indication of hostility to the principle of representative government; for representative government in the true sense means government that is responsible to the people. The popular movement has in modifying our state and municipal governments merely taken the line of least resistance, and that has involved the transfer of legislative powers to the people themselves.

Just how far this movement will go it is impossible to foresee. A government of the representative type, if responsive to public sentiment, would answer all the requirements of a democratic state. It would at the same time be merely carrying out in practice what has long been the generally accepted, if mistaken, view of our political system. The adoption of some effective plan of direct nomination and recall of officials would accomplish much in the way of restoring confidence in legislative bodies. To this extent it would check the tendency to place the law-making power directly in the hands of the people. Popular ratification of all important laws would be unnecessary, if our legislative bodies were really responsible to the people. Nevertheless, the popular veto is a power which the people should have the right to use whenever occasion demands. This would prevent the possibility of legislation in the interest of the minority as now often happens. The popular veto through the referendum is not, however, of itself sufficient. The people need the power to initiate legislation as well as the power to defeat it. The initiative combined with the referendum would make the majority in fact, as it now is in name only, the final authority in all matters of legislation.

It is in our state and municipal governments that democracy is likely to win its first victories. The minority, however, will make a desperate struggle to prevent the overthrow of the system which has been and still is the source of its power. The political machine supported by every privileged interest will oppose by every means in its power the efforts of the people to break down the checks upon the majority. To this end we must expect them to make large use in the near future, as they have in the past, of the extraordinary powers exercised by our courts. In fact the courts as the least responsible and most conservative of our organs of government have been the last refuge of the minority when defeated in the other branches of the government. The disposition so generally seen among the opponents of democracy to regard all measures designed to break down the checks upon the majority as unconstitutional points to the judiciary as the chief reliance of the conservative classes. Indeed, the people are beginning to see that the courts are in possession of political powers of supreme importance —that they can, and often do, defeat the will of the majority after it has successfully overcome opposition in all other branches of the government. If the will of the majority is to prevail, the courts must be deprived of the power which they now have to declare laws null and void. Popular government can not really exist so long as judges who are politically irresponsible have power to override the will of the majority. The democratic movement will either deprive the judicial branch of the government of its political powers or subject it to the same degree of popular control applied to other political organs. The extension of direct nomination and recall to the members of our state judiciary would deprive the special interests of the power to use the courts as the means of blocking the way to popular reforms. In any democratic community the final interpreter of the constitution must be the majority. With the evolution of complete popular government, then, the judicial veto must disappear, or the court must become a democratic body.

It is through our state governments that we must approach the problem of reforming the national government. Complete control of the former will open the door that leads to eventual control of the latter. Democratize the state governments, and it will be possible even to change the character of the United States Senate. With a state legislature directly nominated and subject to removal through the use of the recall, it will be possible to deprive that body of any real power in the selection of United States senators. Under these conditions the legislature would merely ratify the candidate receiving a majority of the popular vote just as the electoral college has come to ratify the popular choice of the President. In this way direct nomination and direct election of United States senators could be made really effective, while at the same time preserving the form but not the substance of election by the state legislatures.[1]

[1] This was one of the objects of the Oregon Direct Primary Law, which was enacted by the people of that state upon initiative petition at the general election held June 6, 1904. Under this law the elector seeking nomination for the office of senator or representative in the legislative assembly is expected to sign and file, as part of his petition for nomination, one of the two following statements:

No. 1. "I further state to the people of Oregon as well as to the people of my legislative district, that during my term of office, I will always vote for that candidate for United States Senator in Congress who has received the highest number of the people's votes for that position at the

This would make possible that much needed separation of state and municipal from national politics. Candidates for the state legislature are now nominated and elected largely with reference to the influence of that body upon the composition of the United States Senate. This has a tendency to, and in fact does, make state legislation in no small degree a by-product of senatorial elections. By divesting the legislature of this function, it would cease to be, as it is now, one of the organs of the Federal government, and in assuming its proper rôle of a local legislative body, it would become in fact what it has hardly been even in theory—a body mainly interested in formulating and carrying out purely local policies. Experience has shown beyond question that its function as an electoral college for the choice of United States senators is incompatible with the satisfactory exercise of local legislative functions. The latter will be sacrificed in the interest of the former. This of itself is no small evil. For if there is any advantage in our Federal form of government, it is in the opportunity thus provided for the faithful expression of local public opinion in local legislation. But in addition to

general election next preceding the election of a Senator in Congress, without regard to my individual preference."

No. 2. "During my term of office I shall consider the vote of the people for United States Senator in Congress as nothing more than a recommendation, which I shall be at liberty to wholly disregard if the reason for doing so seems to me to be sufficient."

this subordination of state to national politics, which might be justified under existing conditions on the ground that local measures and local interests should be sacrificed whenever by so doing it would contribute to the success of the larger and more important matters of national policy, it has become a prolific source of corruption.

It is not a mere accident that the United States Senate is to-day the stronghold of railway and other corporate interests. Possessing as it does more extended powers than the House of Representatives, it is for that very reason the body in which every privileged interest will make the greatest effort to obtain representation. Moreover, the indirect method of election is one that readily lends itself to purposes of corruption. It is a notorious fact that it is much easier to buy the representatives of the people than to buy the people themselves. Money expended in influencing elections always has in view certain benefits direct or indirect which those who contribute the funds for that purpose expect to receive. Such funds invariably come in the main from special interests which expect to get back from the people more than the amount of their political investments. If they had to deal with the people directly, the latter would demand an equivalent for any concession granted, since it would not be to their advantage to enrich special interests at their own expense. But where the concession can be granted by a small body such as a state legislature, the latter may find that it is to its advantage to co-operate with a selfish and unscrupulous class in furthering purely private interests at the expense of the public. The opportunity for the successful employment of corrupt means is greatly augmented, too, through the confusion of state and national issues under the present system. Many measures may be sacrificed by the party in control of the state legislature under the plea that it is necessary in order to advance the general interests of the party by the election of a United States senator. This possibility of evading responsibility for the nonfulfillment of its duty as a local legislative body would disappear as soon as it is deprived of the part which it now plays in the choice of United States senators.

CHAPTER XIV

EFFECT OF THE TRANSITION FROM MINORITY TO MAJORITY RULE UPON MORALITY

In tracing the influence which the growth of democracy has had upon morality, we should be careful to look below the surface of present-day affairs. The deeper and more enduring social movements and tendencies are not always obvious to the superficial observer. For this reason much that has been written in recent years concerning our alleged decline in public morality is far from convincing. Facts tending to show the prevalence of fraud and corruption in politics and business are not in themselves sufficient to warrant any sweeping conclusions as to present tendencies. Paradoxical as it may seem, an increase in crime and other surface manifestations of immorality, is no proof of a decline, but may as a matter of fact be merely a transient effect of substantial and permanent advance toward higher standards of morality.

Before making any comparison between the morality of two different periods, we should first find out whether, in passing from the one period to the other, there has been any change in the accepted ideas of right and wrong. Now, if such is the case, it is manifestly an important factor in the problem—one that should not be ignored; and yet this is just what many writers are doing who imagine that they are proving by statistics a decline in morality. Their error consists in overlooking the one fact of paramount importance, viz., that the accepted standard of morality has itself been raised. We are not judging conduct to-day according to the ideas of civic duty in vogue a century, or even a generation ago. We are insisting upon higher standards of conduct both in politics and in business. Our ideas of right and wrong in their manifold applications to social life have been profoundly changed, and in many respects for the better. We are trying to realize a new conception of justice. Many things which a century ago were sanctioned by law, or at least not forbidden, are no longer tolerated. Moreover, enlightened public opinion now condemns many things which have not yet been brought under the ban of the law.

During any period, such as that in which we are now living, when society is rapidly assuming a higher ethical type, it is inevitable that much resistance should be made to the enforcement of the new standard of justice. Old methods of business and old political practices are not easily repressed, even when the public opinion of the community has come to regard them as socially injurious. Forms of conduct once permitted, but now regarded as anti-social, tend to persist in spite of the effort of law and public opinion to dislodge them. The more rapid the ethical progress of society, the more frequent and the more pronounced will be the failure of the morally backward individuals to meet the requirements of the new social standard. At such a time we always see an increase in crimes, misdemeanors and acts which enlightened public opinion condemns. This is due, however, not to any decline in public morality, but to the fact that the ethical progress of society as a whole has been more rapid than that of the offending class.

There is another source of error which we must guard against. Social immorality is not always detected even when it exists. Much that is socially immoral both in politics and in business escapes observation. Nevertheless, the agencies for ferreting out and holding up to public condemnation offences against society, are far more efficient and active to-day than they have ever been in the past. Both the corrupt public official and the unscrupulous business man dread the searchlight of public opinion, which is becoming more and more effective as a regulator of conduct with the growth of intelligence among the masses. Nor is it surprising that when the hitherto dark recesses of politics and business are exposed to view, an alarming amount of fraud and corruption should be revealed. We are too prone to forget, however, that publicity is something new—that in our day the seen may bear a much larger proportion to the unseen than it has in the past. What appears, then, to be an increase in business and political immorality may, after all, be largely accounted for as the result of more publicity. Here, again, we see that the facts usually taken to indicate a decline in public morality are susceptible of a very different interpretation.

Another feature of present-day society which deserves careful consideration by reason of its far-reaching effect upon public morality is the change now taking place in theological beliefs. Heretofore the church has been by far the most important agency for enforcing conformity to the accepted moral standard. The hope of reward or fear of punishment in the world to come has been the chief support upon which the church has in the past rested its system of social control. But this other-world sanction is now losing its compelling force in consequence of the growing disbelief in the old doctrine of rewards and punishments. The fear of the supernatural, which has its highest development in the savage, steadily declines with the progress of the race. When the general level of intelligence is low, the supernatural sanction is a far more potent means of regulating conduct than any purely temporal authority. But, just in proportion as society advances, the other-world sanction loses its potency and increasing reliance must, therefore, be placed upon purely human agencies.

The immediate effect of this change in our attitude toward the hereafter and the supernatural has been to remove or at least to weaken an important restraint upon anti-social tendencies. There is no reason, however, for apprehension as to the final outcome. Society always experiences some difficulty, it is true, in making the transition from the old to the new. In every period of social readjustment old institutions and beliefs lose their efficacy before the new social agencies have been perfected. But if the new is higher and better than the old, the good that will accrue to society will in the long run greatly outweigh any temporary evil.

But great as has been the change in our point of view with reference to the church, our attitude toward the state has been even more profoundly changed. We do not have to go very far back into the past to find government everywhere controlled by a king and privileged class. The ascendency of the few was everywhere established by the sword, but it could not be long maintained by force alone. The ignorance of the masses was in the past, as it is now, the main reliance of those who wished to perpetuate minority rule. Fraud and deception have always been an indispensable means of maintaining class ascendency in government. The primitive politician no less than his present-day successor saw the possibility of utilizing the credulity of the masses for the purpose of furthering his own selfish ends. This explains the long-continued survival of that interesting political superstition which for so many centuries protected class rule under the pretended sanction of a God-given right.

The growth of intelligence among the masses by discrediting the doctrine of divine right made it necessary to abandon the old defense of class rule. From that time down to the present the disintegration of the old political order has been rapid. Every effort has been made by the defenders of the old system to find some means of justifying and maintaining class rule—a task which is becoming more and more difficult with the growing belief in democracy. At the present time we are in a transition stage. The divine theory of the state, which was the foundation and support of the old system of class rule, is no longer accepted by intelligent people in any civilized country. But class rule still has its advocates, even in the countries that have advanced farthest in the direction of popular government. The opponents of democracy, however, comprise but a small part of the population numerically, yet, owing to their great wealth and effective organization, their influence as a class is every-

where very great. Over against these is arrayed
the bulk of the population, who are struggling,
though not very intelligently always, to overcome
the opposition of the few and make the political
organization and the policy of the state a complete
and faithful expression of the popular will. No
modern state has yet passed entirely through this
transition stage. Everywhere the movement toward democracy has been and is now being
energetically resisted by those who fear that
thoroughgoing popular government would deprive
them of economic or political privileges which
they now enjoy. Let us not deceive ourselves by
thinking that the old system of class rule has been
entirely overthrown. No fundamental change in
government or any other social institution ever
comes about suddenly. Time, often much time,
is required for those intellectual and moral readjustments without which no great change in
social institutions can be made. And when we
remember that only a century ago every government in the Western world was avowedly organized on the basis of minority rule, we can
readily understand that society has not yet had
sufficient time to outgrow the influence of the old
political order.

No one can discuss intelligently the question of
political morality if he ignores the effect of this
struggle between the old system of minority
domination and the new system of majority rule.

And yet scarcely ever do our text-books or maga-
zine articles dealing with present political evils
even so much as allude to this most important fact
—the one, indeed, on which hinges our whole
system of business fraud and political corruption.
We often hear the opinion expressed by people of
more than ordinary intelligence that the public
immorality so much in evidence in this country is
the natural and inevitable result of popular government. This view is industriously encouraged
by the conservative and even accepted by not a
few of those whose sympathies are with democracy. Yet no conclusion could be more erroneous. It would be just as logical to attribute the
religious persecutions of the Middle Ages to the
growth of religious dissent. If there had been
no dissenters, there would have been no persecution; neither would there have been any reforma-
tion or any progress toward a system of religious
liberty. Persecution was the means employed to
repress dissent and defeat the end which the
dissenters had in view. Corruption sustains
exactly the same relation to the democratic movement of modern times. It has been employed,
not to promote, but to defeat the ends of popular
government. No intelligent person should any
longer be in doubt as to the real source of corruption. It is to be eradicated, not by placing
additional restrictions on the power of the people,
but by removing those political restraints upon

the majority which now preclude any effective popular control of public officials. We forget that when our government was established the principle of majority rule was nowhere recognized— that until well along into the nineteenth century the majority of our forefathers did not even have the right to vote. The minority governed under the sanction of the Constitution and the law of the land. Then a great popular movement swept over the country, and in the political upheaval which followed, the masses secured the right of suffrage. But universal suffrage, though essential to, does not ensure popular government. The right to vote for some, or even all, public officials, does not necessarily involve any effective control over such officials by, or any real responsibility to, the majority of the voters. Nor is any constitutional system set up to achieve the purpose of minority rule likely to contain those provisions which are necessary for the enforcement of public opinion in the management of political affairs. It was thought by the masses, of course, when they acquired the suffrage that they acquired the substance of political power. Their expectation, however, was but partially realized. Indirect election, official independence, and the rigidity of the constitutional system as a whole, with its lack of responsiveness to popular demands, largely counteracted the results expected from universal suffrage. But the extension of the suffrage to the masses, though having much less direct and immediate influence upon the policy of the state than is generally supposed, was in one respect supremely important. In popular thought it worked a transformation in the form of the government. The old view which recognized the political supremacy of the minority was now largely superseded by the new view that the will of the majority ought to be the supreme law of the land.

The minority, however, still continue to exert a controlling influence in most matters of public policy directly affecting their interests as a class, although the extension of the suffrage made the exercise of that control a much more difficult matter and left little room for doubt that actual majority rule would ultimately prevail. A large measure of protection was afforded them through the checks which the Constitution imposed upon the power of the majority. There was no certainty, however, that these checks could be permanently maintained. A political party organized in the interest of majority rule, and supported by a strong public sentiment, might find some way of breaking through or evading the constitutional provisions designed to limit its power. Certain features of the Constitution, however, afforded excellent opportunities for offering effective resistance to the progress of democratic legislation. Entrenched behind these constitutional bulwarks, an active, intelligent and wealthy minority might hope to defeat many measures earnestly desired by the majority and even secure the adoption of some policies that would directly benefit themselves. Here we find the cause that has been mainly responsible for the growth of that distinctively American product, the party machine, with its political bosses, its army of paid workers and its funds for promoting or opposing legislation, supplied by various special interests which expect to profit thereby. With the practical operation of this system we are all familiar. We see the results of its work in every phase of our political life—in municipal, state and national affairs. We encounter its malign influence every time an effort is made to secure any adequate regulation of railways, to protect the people against the extortion of the trusts, or to make the great privileged industries of the country bear their just share of taxation. But the chief concern of those in whose interest the party machine is run is to defeat any popular attack on those features of the system which are the real source of the great power which the minority is able to exert. Try, for example, to secure a constitutional amendment providing for the direct election of United States senators, the adoption of the initiative and the referendum, a direct primary scheme, a measure depriving a city council of the power to enrich private corporations by giving away valuable franchises, or any provision intended to give the people an effective control over their so-called public servants, and we find that nothing less than an overwhelming public sentiment and sustained social effort is able to make any headway against the small but powerfully entrenched minority.

Many changes will be required before efficient democratic government can exist. The greatest and most pressing need at the present time, however, is for real publicity, which is the only means of making public opinion effective as an instrument of social control. The movement toward publicity has been in direct proportion to the growth of democracy. Formerly the masses were not regarded by the ruling class as having any capacity for political affairs, or right to criticise governmental policies and methods. With the acceptance of the idea of popular sovereignty, however, the right of the people to be kept informed concerning the management of governmental business received recognition; but practice has lagged far behind theory.

Much would be gained for good government by extending publicity to the relations existing between public officials and private business interests. This would discourage the corrupt alliance which now too often exists between unscrupulous politicians and corporate wealth. The public have a right and ought to know to what extent individuals and corporations have contributed money for the purpose of carrying elections. The time has come when the political party should be generally recognized and dealt with as a public agency—as an essential part or indispensable organ of the government itself. The amount of its revenue, the sources from which it is obtained, the purposes for which it is expended, vitally concern the people and should be exposed to a publicity as thorough and searching as that which extends to the financial transactions of the government itself. The enforcement of publicity in this direction would not be open to the objection that the government was invading the field of legitimate private activity, though it would bring to light the relations which now exist between the party machine and private business, and in so doing would expose the true source of much political corruption.

But this is not all that the people need to know concerning party management. They can not be expected to make an intelligent choice of public officials, unless they are supplied with all the facts which have a direct bearing upon the fitness of the various candidates. Popular elections will not be entirely successful until some plan is devised under which no man can become a candidate for office without expecting to have all the facts bearing upon his fitness, whether relating to his private life or official conduct, made public.

Publicity of this sort would do much toward securing a better class of public officials.

Publicity concerning that which directly pertains to the management of the government is not all that will be required. The old idea that all business is private must give way to the new and sounder view that no business is entirely private. It is true that the business world is not yet ready for the application of this doctrine, since deception is a feature of present-day business methods. It is employed with reference to business rivals on the one hand and consumers on the other. This policy of deception often degenerates into downright fraud, as in the case of secret rebates and other forms of discrimination through which one competitor obtains an undue and perhaps crushing advantage over others; or it may take the form of adulteration or other trade frauds by which the business man may rob the general public.

"Deception," says Lester F. Ward, "may almost be called the foundation of business. It is true that if all business men would altogether discard it, matters would probably be far better even for them than they are; but, taking the human character as it is, it is frankly avowed by business men themselves that no business could succeed for a single year if it were to attempt single-handed and alone to adopt such an innovation. The particular form of deception characteristic of business is called *shrewdness,* and it is universally considered proper and upright. There is a sort of code that fixes the limit beyond which this form of deception must not be carried, and those who exceed that limit are looked upon somewhat as a pugilist who 'hits below the belt.' But within these limits every one expects every other to suggest the false and suppress the true, while *caveat emptor* is lord of all, and 'the devil take the hindmost.' "[1]

Under this system the strong, the unscrupulous and the cunning may pursue business tactics which enable them to accumulate wealth at the expense of consumers or business rivals, but which, if generally known, would not be tolerated. The great profits which fraudulent manufacturers and merchants have made out of adulterated goods would have been impossible under a system which required that all goods should be properly labeled and sold for what they really were. Such abuses as now exist in the management of railroads and other corporations could not, or at least would not long be permitted to exist, if the general public saw the true source, character, extent and full effects of these evils.

The greatest obstacle to publicity at the present time is the control which corporate wealth is able to, and as a matter of fact does, exercise over those agencies upon which the people must largely depend for information and guidance regarding

[1] Pure Sociology, p. 487.

contemporary movements and events. The telegraph and the newspaper are indispensable in any present-day democratic society. The ownership and unregulated control of the former by the large corporate interests of the country, and the influence which they can bring to bear upon the press by this means, as well as the direct control which they have over a large part of the daily press by actual ownership, does much to hinder the progress of the democratic movement. This hold which organized wealth has upon the agencies through which public opinion is formed, is an important check on democracy. It does much to secure a real, though not generally recognized, class ascendency under the form and appearance of government by public opinion.

This great struggle now going on between the progressive and the reactionary forces, between the many and the' few, has had a profound influence upon public morality. We have here a conflict between two political systems—between two sets of ethical standards. The supporters of minority rule no doubt often feel that the whole plan and purpose of the democratic movement is revolutionary—that its ultimate aim is the complete overthrow of all those checks designed for the protection of the minority. The only effective means which they could employ to retard the progress of the popular movement involved the use of money or its equivalent in ways that have had a corrupting influence upon our national life. Of course this need not, and as a rule does not, take the coarse, crude form of a direct purchase of public officials. The methods used may in the main conform to all our accepted criteria of business honesty, but their influence is none the less insidious and deadly. It is felt in many private institutions of learning; it is clearly seen in the attitude of a large part of our daily press, and even in the church itself. This subtle influence which a wealthy class is able to exert by owning or controlling the agencies for molding public opinion is doing far more to poison the sources of our national life than all the more direct and obvious forms of corruption combined. The general public may not see all this or understand its full significance, but the conviction is gaining ground that it is difficult to enact and still more difficult to enforce any legislation contemplating just and reasonable regulation of corporate wealth. The conservative classes themselves are not sat-- isfied with the political system as it now is, believing that the majority, by breaking through restraints imposed by the Constitution, have acquired more power than they should be permitted to exercise under any well-regulated government. It is but a step, and a short one at that, from this belief that the organization of the government is wrong and its policy unjust, to the conclusion that one is justified in using every available means of defeating the enactment or preventing the enforcement of pernicious legislation. On the other hand, the supporters of majority rule believe that the government is too considerate of the few and not sufficiently responsive to the wishes of the many. As a result of this situation neither the advocates nor the opponents of majority rule have that entire faith in the reasonableness and justice of present political arrangements, which is necessary to ensure real respect for, or even ready compliance with the laws.

Here we find the real explanation of that widespread disregard of law which characterizes American society to-day. We are witnessing and taking part in the final struggle between the old and the new—a struggle which will not end until one or the other of these irreconcilable theories of government is completely overthrown, and a new and harmonious political structure evolved. Every age of epoch-making change is a time of social turmoil. To the superficial onlooker this temporary relaxation of social restraints may seem to indicate a period of decline, but as a matter of fact the loss of faith in and respect for the old social agencies is a necessary part of that process of growth through which society reaches a higher plane of existence.

CHAPTER XV

DEMOCRACY OF THE FUTURE

The growth of the democratic spirit is one of the most important facts in the political life of the nineteenth century. All countries under the influence of Western civilization show the same tendency. New political ideas irreconcilably opposed to the view of government generally accepted in the past are everywhere gaining recognition. Under the influence of this new conception of the state the monarchies and aristocracies of the past are being transformed into the democracies of the future. We of the present day, however, are still largely in the trammels of the old, though our goal is the freedom of the new. We have not yet reached, but are merely traveling toward democracy. The progress which we have made is largely a progress in thought and ideals. We have imbibed more of the spirit of popular government. In our way of thinking, our point of view, our accepted political philosophy, there has been a marked change. Everywhere, too, with the progress of scientific knowledge and the spread of popular education, the masses are coming to a consciousness of their strength. They are circumscribing the power of ruling classes and abolishing their exclusive privileges which control of the state has made it possible for them to defend in the past. From present indications we are at the threshold of a new social order under which the few will no longer rule the many.

Democracy may be regarded, according to the standpoint from which we view it, either as an intellectual or as a moral movement. It is intellectual in that it presupposes a more or less general diffusion of intelligence, and moral in that its aim is justice. It could not have appeared or become a social force until man became a thinker and critic of existing social arrangements. It was first necessary that he should acquire a point of view and a habit of thought that give him a measure of intellectual independence and enable him to regard social institutions and arrangements as human devices more or less imperfect and unjust. This thought can not be grasped without its correlative—the possibility of improvement. Hence democracy everywhere stands for political and social reform.

Democracy is modern, since it is only within recent times that the general diffusion of knowledge has been possible. The invention of printing, by making possible a cheap popular literature, contributed more than any other one fact to the intellectual and moral awakening which marks the beginning of modern times. The introduction of printing, however, did not find a democratic literature ready for general distribution, or the people ready for its appearance. A long period of slow preparation followed, during which the masses were being educated. Moreover, it is only within recent times that governments would have permitted the creation and diffusion of a democratic literature. For a long time after printing was invented the ruling classes carefully guarded against any use of the newly discovered art that might be calculated to undermine their authority. Books containing new and dangerous doctrines were rigorously proscribed and the people carefully protected from the disturbing influence of such views as might shake their faith in the wisdom and justice of the existing social order.[1]

[1] "The art of printing, in the hands of private persons, has, until within a comparatively recent period, been regarded rather as an instrument of mischief, which required the restraining hand of the government, than as a power for good, to be fostered and encouraged.....The government assumed to itself the right to determine what might or might not be published; and censors were appointed without whose permission it was criminal to publish a book or paper upon any subject. Through all the changes of government, this censorship was continued until after the Revolution of 1688, and there are no instances in English history of more cruel and relentless persecution than for the publication of books which now would pass unnoticed by the authorities ....

"So late as 1671, Governor Berkeley, of Virginia, expressed his thankfulness that neither free schools nor printing were introduced in the Colony, and his trust that these breeders of disobedience, heresy, and sects, would long be unknown...

"For publishing the laws of one session in Virginia, in 1682, the printer was arrested and put under bonds until the King's pleasure could be known, and the King's pleasure was declared that no printing should be allowed in the Colony.

It is perhaps fortunate for the world that the political and social results of printing were not comprehended at the time of its introduction. Had the ruling classes foreseen that it would lead to the gradual shifting of political power from themselves to the masses, it is not unlikely that they would have regarded it as a pernicious innovation.

But, as is the case with all great inventions, its full significance was not at first understood. Silently and almost imperceptibly it paved the way for a social and political revolution. The gradual diffusion of knowledge among the people prepared them for the contemplation of a new social order. They began to think, to question and to doubt, and thenceforth the power and prestige of the ruling classes began to decline. From that time on there has been an unceasing struggle between the privileged few and the unprivileged many. We see it in the peaceful process of legislation as well as in the more violent contest of war. After each success the masses have demanded still greater concessions, until now, with a broader outlook and a larger conception of human destiny, they demand the complete and untrammeled control of the state.

There were not wanting instances of the public burning of books as offenders against good order. Such was the fate of Elliot's book in defense of unmixed principles of popular freedom, and Calef's book against Cotton Mather, which was given to the flames at Cambridge." Cooley, Constitutional Limitations, 6th ed., pp. 513-515.

To the student of political science, then, the spirit and temper, the aims and ideals of the new social order now coming into existence, are a matter of supreme importance. That our industrial system will be profoundly modified may be conceded. Other consequences more difficult to foresee because less direct and immediate, but not necessarily less important, may be regarded as not unlikely. That our ideas of right and wrong, our conception of civic duty, and human character itself will be modified as a result of such far-reaching changes in social relations, may be expected. But while the more remote and indirect consequences of democracy may not be foreseen, some of its immediate results are reasonably certain.

The immediate aim of democracy is political. It seeks to overthrow every form of class rule and bring about such changes in existing governments as will make the will of the people supreme. But political reform is regarded not as an end in itself. It is simply a means. Government is a complex and supremely important piece of social machinery. Through it the manifold activities of society are organized, directed and controlled. In a very real sense it is the most important of all social institutions, since from its very nature it is the embodiment of social force, asserting and maintaining a recognized supremacy over all other social institutions and agencies whatever, modifying and adapting them to suit the purposes and achieve the ends of those who control the state.

The form or type of government is all-important, since it involves the question as to the proper end of government as well as the proper means of attaining it. Our notion of what constitutes the best political system depends on our general theory of society—our conception of justice, progress and social well-being. As government by the few inevitably results in the welfare of the few being regarded as the chief concern of the state, the widest possible diffusion of political power is the only guarantee that government will seek the welfare of the many.

The advocate of democracy does not think that it will be a perfect government, but he does believe that it will in the long run be the best, most equitable and most progressive which it is possible to establish. Government by the few and government by the many stand for widely divergent and irreconcilable theories of progress and social well-being. As the methods, aims, and social ideals of an aristocracy are not those of which a democratic society would approve, it necessarily follows that the purposes of democracy can be accomplished only through a government which the people control.

Modern science has given a decided impetus to the democratic movement by making a comfortable existence possible for the many. It has explored the depths of the earth and revealed hidden treasures of which previous ages did not even dream. Inventions and discoveries far-reaching in influence and revolutionary in character have followed each other in rapid succession. With the progress of the sciences and mechanical arts, man's power to control and utilize the forces and materials which nature has so bountifully provided has been enormously increased; and yet, much as has been accomplished in this field of human endeavor, there is reason to believe that the conquest of the material world has but just begun. The future may hold in store for us far greater achievements along this line than any the world has yet seen.

It is not surprising, then, that the masses should feel that they have received too little benefit from this marvelous material progress. For just in proportion as the old political system has survived, with its privileged classes, its checks on the people and its class ascendency in government, the benefits of material progress have been monopolized by the few. Against this intrusion of the old order into modern society the spirit of democracy revolts. It demands control of the state to the end that the product of industry may be equitably distributed. As the uncompromising enemy of monopoly in every form, it demands first of all equality of opportunity.

Democracy, however, is not a mere scheme for the redistribution of wealth. It is fundamentally a theory of social progress. In so far as it involves the distribution of wealth, it does so as a necessary condition or means of progress, and not as an end in itself.

Democracy would raise government to the rank and dignity of a science by making it appeal to the reason instead of the fear and superstition of the people. The governments of the past, basing their claims upon divine right, bear about the same relation to democracy that astrology and alchemy do to the modern sciences of astronomy and chemistry. The old political order everywhere represented itself as superimposed on man from above, and, thus clothed with a sort of divine sanction, it was exalted above the reach of criticism. The growth of intelligence has dispelled one by one the crude political superstitions upon which the old governmental arrangements rested. More and more man is coming to look upon government as a purely human agency which he may freely modify and adapt to his purposes. The blind unthinking reverence with which he regarded it in the past is giving way to a critical scientific spirit. Nor has this change in our point of view in any way degraded government. In stripping it of the pretence of divine authority, it has in reality been placed upon a more enduring basis. In so far as it can no longer claim respect to which it is not entitled we have a guarantee that it can not persistently disregard the welfare of the people.

Democracy owes much to modern scientific research. With the advance of knowledge we have gained a new view of the world. Physics, astronomy, and geology have shown us that the physical universe is undergoing a process of continual change. Biology, too, has revolutionized our notion of life. Nothing is fixed and immutable as was once supposed, but change is universal. The contraction of the earth's crust with its resultant changes in the distribution of land and water, and the continual modification of climate and physical conditions generally have throughout the past wrought changes in the form and character of all animal and vegetable life. Every individual organism and every species must change as the world around it changes, or death is the penalty. No form of life can long survive which does not possess in a considerable degree the power of adaptation. Innumerable species have disappeared because of their inability to adjust themselves to a constantly changing environment. It is from this point of view of continuous adjustment that modern science regards the whole problem of life individual and collective.

We must not, however, assume that what is true of the lower forms of life is equally true of the higher. In carrying the conceptions of biology over into the domain of social science we must be careful to observe that here the process of adapting life to its environment assumes a new and higher phase. In the lower animal world the life-sustaining activities are individual. Division of labor is either entirely absent or plays a part so unimportant that we may for purposes of comparison assume its absence. The individual animal has free access to surrounding nature, unrestrained by social institutions or private property in the environment. For the members of a given group there is what may be described as equality of opportunity. Hence it follows that the individuals which are best suited to the environment will thrive best and will tend to crowd out the others.

But when we come to human society this is not necessarily true. Here a social environment has been created—a complex fabric of laws, usages, and institutions which envelopes completely the life of the individual and intervenes everywhere between him and physical nature. To this all his industrial activities must conform. The material environment is no longer the common possession of the group. It has become private property and has passed under the control of individuals in whose interests the laws and customs of every community ancient and modern have been largely molded. This is a fact which all history attests. Wherever the few acquire a monopoly of political power it always tends to develop into a monopoly of the means and agents of production. Not content with making the physical environment their own exclusive property, the few have often gone farther and by reducing the many to slavery have established and legalized property in human beings themselves. But even when all men are nominally free and legalized coercion does not exist, the fact nevertheless remains that those who control the means of production in reality control the rest. As Mr. W. H. Mallock, the uncompromising opponent of democracy and staunch defender of aristocracy, puts it: "The larger part of the progressive activities of peace, and the arts and products of civilization, result from and imply the influence of kings and leaders in essentially the same sense as do the successes of primitive war, the only difference being that the kings are here more numerous, and though they do not wear any arms or uniforms, are incomparably more autocratic than the kings and czars who do."[1] "Slavery, feudalism, and capitalism," he tells us, "agree with one another in being systems under which the few"[2] control the actions of the many.

This feature of modern capitalism—the control

---

[1] Aristocracy and Evolution, p. 58.
[2] Ibid p. 377.

of the many by the few—which constitutes its chief merit in the eyes of writers like Mr. Mallock is what all democratic thinkers consider its chief vice. Under such a system success or failure is no longer proof of natural fitness or unfitness. Where every advantage that wealth and influence afford is enjoyed by the few and denied to the many an essential condition of progress is lacking. Many of the ablest, best, and socially fittest are hopelessly handicapped by lack of opportunity, while their inferiors equipped with every artificial advantage easily defeat them in the competitive struggle.

This lack of a just distribution of opportunity under existing industrial arrangements, the defenders of the established social order persistently ignore. Taking no account of the unequal conditions under which the competitive struggle is carried on in human society, they would make success proof of fitness to survive and failure evidence of unfitness. This is treating the complex problem of social adjustment as if it were simply a question of mere animal struggle for existence. Writers of this class naturally accept the Malthusian doctrine of population, and ascribe misery and want to purely natural causes, viz., the pressure of population on the means of subsistence. Not only is this pressure with its attendant evils unavoidable, they tell us, but, regarded from the standpoint of the highest interests of the race it is desirable and beneficent in that it is the method of evolution—the means which nature makes use of to produce, through the continual elimination of the weak, a higher human type. To relieve this pressure through social arrangements would arrest by artificial contrivances the progress which ˙the free play of natural forces tends to bring about. If progress is made only through the selection of the fit and the rejection of the unfit, it would follow that the keener the struggle for existence and the more rapid and relentless the elimination of the weak, the greater would be the progress made. This is exactly the contention of Kidd in his Social Evolution. He claims that if the pressure of population on the means of subsistence were arrested, and all individuals were allowed equally to propagate their kind, the human race would not only not progress, but actually retrograde.[1] If we accept this as true, it would follow that a high birth rate and a high death rate are necessary in order that the process of selection and rejection may go on. This is indeed a pleasant prospect for all except the fortunate few. But the question, of course, is not whether this is pleasant to contemplate or unpleasant, but whether it is true. Is the evolution of a higher human type the same kind of a process as that of a higher animal or vegetable type? Is progress achieved only

[1] Social Evolution, p. 39.

through the preservation of the fit and the elimination of the unfit? If it could be shown that this is the case, then certainly the conditions under which this struggle to the death is carried on would be a matter of supreme importance. Are our social adjustments such as to facilitate, or at least not interfere with it? Do they make the question of success or failure, survival or elimination, depend upon individual fitness or unfitness? This, as we have seen, is not the case, though the partisans of the biological theory of human progress have constantly assumed it. Mr. Mallock takes even a more extreme position than most writers of this class, and actually says "that the social conditions of a time are the same for all, but that it is only exceptional men who can make exceptional use of them."[1] The unequal distribution of wealth he seeks to justify on the ground that "the ordinary man's talents as a producer . . . have not appreciably increased in the course of two thousand years and have certainly not increased within the past three generations."[2]

"In the domain of modern industrial activity the many" . . . he tells us, "produce only an insignificant portion of the total, . . . and in the domain of intellectual and speculative progress the many produce or achieve nothing."[3] If we

[1] Aristocracy and Evolution, p. 105.
[2] Ibid p. 218.
[3] Ibid p. 219.

accept his premises, we must agree with his conclusion that democracy's indictment of our modern industrial system falls to the ground. This view of the matter is acceptable, of course, to those who are satisfied with present social arrangements. It furnishes a justification for the system under which they have prospered while others have failed. It relieves their conscience of any misgiving and soothes them with the assurance that only through the poverty and misery of the unfit can a higher civilization be evolved. This largely explains the popularity among the well-to-do classes of such books as Malthus' Principle of Population and Kidd's Social Evolution.

Such a treatment of the social problem, however, will not bear the test of analysis, since it assumes that the present distribution of opportunity is just. To ignore or treat as unimportant the influence of social arrangements upon the struggle for existence between individuals, as apologists for the existing social order are too much inclined to do, is like ignoring the modern battle-ship as a factor in the efficiency of the modern navy.

But while this biological theory of evolution has been made to serve the purpose of defending existing social arrangements, it is in reality no adequate explanation of human progress. Selection and rejection do not, as a matter of fact, play any important part in the progress of civilized

communities. Here the struggle for existence
has assumed the form of a struggle for domination. The vanquished are no longer eliminated
as a result of the competitive struggle; for, as
Mr. Spencer says, social institutions preserve the
incapables.[1] Not only are the unsuccessful not
eliminated but, as sociological students well know,
they increase more rapidly than the successful
few. If, then, we accept the biological theory of
social evolution, we are forced to the conclusion
that the human race, instead of advancing, is
really retrograding. Seeing that this is not a
satisfactory explanation of human progress, Mr.
Mallock supplements it with a new factor which
he describes as "the unintended results of the
intentions of great men."[2] But, like all of these
writers, he makes progress depend entirely on the
biological struggle for existence or the industrial
struggle for supremacy, not recognizing the all-
important part which social ideals and conscious
social choice play in human evolution.

There is, then, as we have seen, ample justification for the hostility to privilege which the
democratic movement everywhere exhibits. In
making equality of opportunity a feature of the
new social order, the advocates of reform are
proceeding in harmony with the teaching of
modern science. Such changes must be brought

[1] Principles of Biology, Vol. I, p. 469.
[2] Aristocracy and Evolution, p. 105.

about in the organization of industry, the laws of property, the scope and character of public and private activities, as will sweep away entirely the whole ancient system of special privileges, and by placing all individuals upon the same footing, make success the unfailing reward of merit. To accomplish this is to solve the monopoly problem. Some progress has been made in this direction, but it consists for the most part in discovering that such a problem exists. Just how posterity will deal with it, it is impossible to foresee; but of one thing we may be sure—this new conception of justice will exert a profound influence upon the legislation of the future.

The attention of the democratic movement has up to the present time been occupied almost exclusively with the question of a just distribution of opportunity; yet this is not the only problem which democracy will have to solve. Indeed, it is but the first step in a continuous process of conscious social readjustment. This fact many writers on social science have not fully grasped. There is still a tendency to regard society as a sort of divinely ordered mechanism, which, if properly started, will automatically work out the process of social evolution. For an explanation of this popular misconception we must go back to the theological speculations of the past, which represented a divine intelligence as everywhere present and a divine purpose as running through every fact and detail of nature. From this belief in direct and immediate supervision by an all-wise being it was an easy step to the conclusion that whatever is, is right. Thus the old social order was securely entrenched behind the ramparts of mediaeval theology. From this once impregnable position it has been dislodgd by modern science, which has thoroughly discredited the notion of direct supernatural intervention and given us instead the conception of a universe which illustrates in its every process the working of natural law. Nevertheless, in accepting this newer view, we have not entirely discarded the old, which has more largely stamped itself upon modern thought than we are willing to allow. This accounts for our deification of the natural—our conception of evolution as having behind all its phases a divine purpose which is everywhere working toward the realization of a higher type. The general acceptance of this optimistic view by both liberal and conservative is striking proof that mediaeval theology has largely influenced our interpretation of modern science. In fact, optimism belongs not to the age of science, but to the age of faith. It confuses the natural with the morally right in that it would make all nature the direct expression of a divine purpose. If we accept this belief in the beneficent and progressive character of all natural processes, the conclusion is irresistible that nature's methods should not be interfered with.

This is largely the point of view of the earlier English political economists, and it partly explains their belief in the policy of non-interference. The best and most comprehensive statement of this view of social progress is found in Adam Smith's Wealth of Nations. In this work he attempted to show that legislative interference with industry is unnecessary. Therefore he advocated the repeal of all laws which interfered with or in any way restricted the liberty of the individual. He believed that the natural principle of competition would of itself effectually regulate industrial life. The desire of each individual to pursue his own interests made state interference, in his opinion, unnecessary. In the absence of legal restraints industrial matters would spontaneously regulate themselves. The varied economic activities of individuals in society would be adequately controlled and harmonized with the general interests of society, if statute or human law did not interfere with natural or divine law. Reliance on competition would ensure order, harmony and continuous progress in society, just as in the realm of matter the influence of gravitation has transformed by a long-continued development the original chaos into an orderly universe. Each individual acting in obedience to this law would be "led by an invisible hand to promote"[1] the well-being of society, even though he was conscious only of a selfish desire to further his own ends.

Such was the industrial philosophy of Adam Smith. It was in harmony with and the natural outcome of the movement which had already revolutionized religious and philosophic thought. In every department of human activity emphasis was being put on the individual. Liberty was the watchword of society—the panacea for all social ills. The Western world was breaking through the old system of restraints under which the individual had been fettered in religion, politics and business. A new conception of the state, its duties and its functions, had been evolved. Mere human law was being discredited. Philosophers, distrusting the coercive arrangements of society, were looking into the nature of man and the character of the environment for the principles of social organization and order. Belief in the curative power of legislation was being supplanted by a growing faith in the sufficiency of natural law.

The underlying motives for advocating the *laissez faire* policy were, however, mainly political and economic.[2] The ready acceptance of this doctrine must be attributed largely to the fact that it offered a plausible ground for opposing the

[1] Adam Smith, Wealth of Nations, Book I, Ch. 2.
[2] Supra, chapters XI and XII.

burdensome restraints of the old system of class rule.

This is the origin of our modern doctrine of *laissez faire* which has so profoundly influenced our political and economic life. But as movements of this character are likely to do, it carried society too far in the opposite direction. This is recognized by that most eminent expounder of the let-alone theory of government, Mr. Herbert Spencer, who, in the third volume of his Principles of Sociology, admits that "there has been a change from excess of restriction to deficiency of restriction."[1] This means that in our accepted political and economic philosophy we have overvalued the organizing power of unregulated natural law, and have consequently undervalued the state as an agency for controlling and organizing industrial forces.

All new ideas have to be harmonized with much that is old. As at first accepted they are only partially true. A new philosophy requires time before its benefits can be fully realized. It must pass through a process of adaptation by which it is gradually modified, broadened and brought into orderly relations with life in general.

The theory of industrial freedom has during the nineteenth century been passing through just such a stage of development. The contention of Adam Smith and his followers that the mere de-

[1] P. 534.

sire for gain would of itself ensure adequate regulation of industry is certainly not true under existing conditions. Natural law is not, as he assumed, always beneficent in its operation. It is just as liable to produce harm as benefit unless it is regulated, controlled and directed by appropriate human agencies. It needs no argument to convince one that this is true so far as the forces of the physical world are concerned. Gravitation, steam and electricity contributed nothing to human progress until man discovered the means whereby they could be harnessed and controlled. Material civilization means nothing else but the development of control over and the consequent utilization of the materials and forces of the physical world. The important part played by mere human agencies is the only feature that distinguishes civilization from barbarism. Everything which in any way contributes to material progress augments the power of man to control, modify and adapt his environment.

And though it may not be so obvious, this general principle is just as true in the moral and spiritual world as in the physical. All progress, material and moral, consists in the due subordination of natural to human agencies. Laws, institutions and systems of government are in a sense artificial creations, and must be judged in relation to the ends which they have in view. They are good or bad according as they are well or poorly adapted to social needs. Civilization in its highest sense means much more than the mere mastery of mind over inanimate nature; it implies a more or less effective social control over individual conduct. Certain impulses, instincts and tendencies must be repressed; others must be encouraged, strengthened, and developed.

It is a mistake to suppose that the unrestrained play of mere natural forces ensures progress. Occasional advance is the outcome, but so also is frequent retrogression. There is no scientific basis for the belief in a natural order that everywhere and always makes for progress. Competition or the struggle for existence ensures at most merely the survival of the fittest; but survival of the fittest does not always mean survival of the best. Competition is nature's means of adapting life to its environment. If the environment is such as to give the more highly organized individuals the advantage, progress is the result. But if it is such as to place them at a disadvantage, retrogression, not progress, is the outcome. The higher types of character, no less than the higher organic forms, presuppose external conditions favorable to their development. Competition is merely the means through which conformity to these external conditions is enforced. It eliminates alike that which is better than the environment and that which is worse. It is indifferent to good or bad, to high or low. It simply picks out, preserves and perpetuates those types best suited to environing conditions. Both progress and retrogression are a process of adaptation, and their cause must be sought, not in the principle of competition itself, but in the general external conditions to which it enforces conformity. Success, then, is a matter of adaptation to the environment, or the power to use it for individual ends—not the power to improve and enrich it. The power to take from, is nature's sole test of fitness to live; but the power to enrich is a higher test, and one which society must enforce through appropriate legislation.

Laws, institutions and methods of trade which make it possible for the individual to take from more than he adds to the general resources of society tend inevitably toward general social deterioration. Competition is wholesome only when all our social arrangements are such as to discourage and repress all individual activities not in harmony with the general interests of society. This is the point of view from which all social and industrial questions must be studied. The problem which democracy has to solve is the problem of so organizing the environment as to assure progress through the success and survival of the best.

WORKS CITED BY J. ALLEN SMITH

Ames, H. V. "Proposed Amendments to the Constitution of the United States," American Historical Association, *Report* 2 (1896).

Ashley, Sir William J. *Introduction to English Economic History and Theory*. New York, 1894.

Baldwin, Simeon E. *Modern Political Institutions*. Boston, 1898.

Boutmy, Emile G. *Studies in Constitutional Law*. Eng. trans. New York, 1891.

Bryce, James. *The American Commonwealth*. New York, 1888. 2d ed. New York, 1889.

Burgess, John W. *Political Science and Comparative Constitutional Law*. Boston, 1890.

Butler, C. H. *Treaty-Making Power of the United States*. New York, 1902.

Calhoun, John C. *Works*. Ed. R. K. Crallé. New York, 1854.

Channing, Edward. *The Jeffersonian System*. New York, 1906.

Cooley, T. M. *A Treatise on the Constitutional Limitations . . . of the States of the American Union*. 6th ed. Boston, 1890.

——, et al. *Constitutional History of the United States as Seen in the Development of the American Law*. New York, 1889.

Coxe, Brinton. *An Essay on Judicial Power and Unconstitutional Legislation*. Philadelphia, 1893.

Dunbar, W. H. "Government by Injunction," *Economic Studies*, 3 (1898).

Elliot, Jonathan, ed. *Debates in the Several State Conventions on the Adoption of the Federal Constitution . . . Together with the Journal of the Federal Convention and Other Papers*. 2d ed. Philadelphia, 1876.

Fiske, John. *The Critical Period of American History*. Boston, 1888.

Follett, M. P. *The Speaker of the House of Representatives*. New York, 1896.

Ford, Henry J. *The Rise and Growth of American Politics*. New York, 1898.

Ford, P. L., ed. *The Federalist*. New York, 1898.

Goodnow, Frank J. *Municipal Home Rule*. New York, 1906.

——. *Municipal Problems*. New York, 1897.

——. *Politics and Administration*. New York, 1900.

Gordy, J. P. *History of Political Parties in the United States*. Athens, Ohio, 1895.

Greene, Evarts B. *The Provincial Governor in the English Colonies of North America*. New York, 1898.

Hoar, George F. "The Conduct of Business in Congress," *North American Review*, 128 (1879), 113–134.

Holst, Hermann E. von. *Constitutional and Political History of the United States*. Tr. Alfred B. Mason. Chicago, 1887.

James, E. J. "The Legal Tender Decisions," *Publications of the American Economic Association*, 3 (1888), 49–80.

Jefferson, Thomas. *Writings of Thomas Jefferson*. Ed. P. L. Ford. New York, 1892–1898.

Kidd, Benjamin. *Social Evolution*. New York and London, 1902.

Lalor, John. *Cyclopaedia of Political Science, Political Economics, and United States History*. New York, 1890.

Lecky, William E. H. *Democracy and Liberty*. London and New York, 1899.

Lee, Guy C. *Source Book of English History*. New York, 1900.

Lincoln, Abraham. "The War with Mexico," *Congressional Globe* (30th Cong. 1st sess.), appendix, pp. 93–95.

Lowell, A. Lawrence. *Essays on Government*. Boston, 1889.

——. *Governments and Parties in Continental Europe*. Boston and New York, 1897.

MacDonald, William. *Select Charters.* New York, 1899.

McMaster, John B. *With the Fathers.* New York, 1896.

Maine, Sir Henry. *Popular Government.* New York, 1886.

Mallock, W. H. *Aristocracy and Evolution.* New York, 1898.

Mason, E. C. *The Veto Power.* Boston, 1890.

Medley, D. J. *Original Illustrations of English Constitutional History.* London, 1910.

Miller, S. F. *Lectures on the Constitution of the United States.* New York, 1891.

Moffett, S. E. "The Railroad Commission of California," *Annals of the American Academy of Political and Social Sciences,* 6 (1895), 469–477.

Myers, Gustavus. *The History of Tammany Hall.* New York, 1901.

Ostrogorski, M. I. *Democracy and the Organization of Political Parties.* New York, 1902.

Outlook (editorials), 74 (1903), 871; 79 (1905), 161–163.

Poore, B. P. *Constitutions and Charters.* Washington, D.C., 1877.

——, ed. *Federal and State Constitutions, Colonial Charters . . . of the United States.* Washington, D.C., 1877.

Porritt, Edward. *The Unreformed House of Commons.* Cambridge, 1903.

Report of the Commissioner-General of Immigration (House Doc. 404, 58th Cong. 3d sess.). Washington, D.C., 1904.

Report (14th Annual) *of the United States Commissioner of Labor on Water, Gas, and Electric Light Plants.* Washington, D.C., 1900.

"Reporting," *Encyclopaedia Britannica,* 20 (9th ed., 1886), 404–407.

Rogers, James E. T. *Six Centuries of Work and Wages.* New York, 1884.

Ross, Edward A. "Political Decay: An Interpretation," *The Independent,* 61 (July 19, 1906), 123–125.

Schouler, James. *Constitutional Studies*. New York, 1897.

Seebohm, Frederic. *English Village Community*. London, 1883.

Shafroth, John F. "When Congress Should Convene," *North American Review,* 164 (1897), 374–376.

Smith, Adam. *Wealth of Nations*. Dublin, 1776.

Spencer, Herbert. *The Principles of Biology*. New York, 1866.

———. *The Principles of Sociology*. New York, 1896.

Steffens, Lincoln. *The Shame of the Cities*. New York, 1904.

Stephens, Alexander H. *Constitutional View of the Late War between the States*. Chicago, 1868.

Stimson, F. J. *Handbook to the Labor Law of the United States*. New York, 1896.

Story, Joseph. *Commentaries on the Constitution*. Boston, 1873.

Taft, William Howard, "Recent Criticisms of the Federal Judiciary," American Bar Association, *Report* (1895), pp. 237–273.

Thorpe, F. N. *A Short Constitutional History of the United States*. Boston, 1904.

Traill, Henry D. *Social England*. 2d ed. New York and London, 1894.

Tyler, Moses C. *The Literary History of the American Revolution*. New York, 1897.

United States Supreme Court Reports. Banks and Brothers ed. Vol. 131, appendix ccxxxv.

Ward, Lester F. *Pure Sociology*. New York, 1903.

White, Horace. *Money and Banking*. Boston, 1895.

Willoughby, W. W. *An Examination of the Nature of the State*. New York, 1896.

Wilson, James. *Works*. Ed. J. D. Andrews. Chicago, 1896.

Wilson, Woodrow. *Congressional Government*. Boston, 1885.

———. *Division and Reunion*. New York, 1893.

1 (p. 33). There were eight signers of the Declaration in the Convention itself.

2 (p. 34). Neither Gerry nor Randolph, however, signed the Constitution.

3 (p. 37). Hamilton's plan was rejected; hence it is not evidence for the framers' views.

4 (p. 37). Madison was defending, according to Yates's minutes, the need of landholders for protection against the future day when they would be overbalanced by the growth of trade and manufactures, as in England. Madison's own notes refer to the *future* danger of indigents with "a levelling spirit" and the need for a remedy based "on Republican principles." (Tuesday, June 26. In Convention.)

5 (pp. 41–42). See p. 37 and editorial note 4.

6 (p. 43). Madison himself, however, found the source of the distress not in the governments as such but in the "factious spirit" which had "tainted" their administrations. See *The Federalist,* No. 10.

7 (p. 43). These conclusions are shown to be false, at least for Massachusetts, in Robert E. Brown, *Middle-Class Democracy and the Revolution in Massachusetts, 1691–1780* (Ithaca, N.Y., 1955).

8 (p. 47). As of 1960 out of 5170 proposals for amendment 28 had been submitted and 23 ratified. In 1964 the 24th Amendment, eliminating the poll tax, was ratified. See editorial note 19 for p. 176, below.

9 (p. 52). It should be noted that Wilson criticized the system for its lack of strength, promptness, and efficiency, rather than for its being "undemocratic." See his *Congressional Government* (Boston, 1885).

10 (p. 56). Only John Quincy Adams in 1824, Hayes in 1876, and Harrison in 1888, however, were elected without either a popular majority or popular plurality.

11 (p. 114). It is not, in fact, clear who did shift his opinion.

For analysis of the controversy see Arnold M. Paul, *Conservative Crisis and the Rule of Law: Attitudes of Bar and Bench, 1887–1895* (Ithaca, N.Y., 1960), pp. 214–218.

12 (p. 115). These cases dealt with the problem of the relationship of Puerto Rico, Hawaii, the Philippines, and Alaska to the federal union and the question of whether they could claim the right to uniform tariffs and trial by jury.

13 (p. 130). The context of this question is, in fact, fatal to Smith's point. Monroe complained, contrary to Smith's argument, that the Constitution *lacked* the mixture of orders found in the English government.

14 (p. 136). On this point of Madison's fear of the majority see editorial note 4 for p. 37.

15 (p. 146). Smith ignored the fact that Art. II, Sec. 3 requires the President to "take care that the laws be faithfully executed."

16 (p. 160). According to Madison, "federal" meant *confederated,* like the Articles of Confederation, while the Union was "a compound republic" of both "federal" and "national" principles. Smith obscured this distinction by using "federal" as a synonym for divided sovereignty.

17 (p. 164). Art. VI, however, does make the Constitution, laws made under it, and treaties "supreme law of the land," binding the judges *in every state.* This provision is incompatible with the idea of states having equal rank with the national government, even though it does not explicitly make the Supreme Court a final interpreter of what the Constitution means.

18 (p. 166). As Smith later notes, Madison opposed the Alien and Sedition Laws. But, if Smith's argument were correct, Madison should have favored them.

19 (p. 176). Martin Diamond suggests that "the real aim and practical effect of the complicated amending procedure was not at all to give power to minorities, but to ensure that passage of an amendment would require a *nationally* distributed majority, though one that legally could consist of a bare numerical majority." See "Democracy and *The Federalist:* A Reconsideration of the Framers' Intent," *American Political Science Review,* 53 (March 1959), 57.

20 (p. 188). The 20th Amendment (1933) dated the beginning

of the Presidential and Congressional terms in January, correcting the lag of which Smith complains.

21 (p. 189). This is no longer true.

22 (p. 215). Modern political scientists would stress the relevance of a "federal" system on a continental scale to the diffused make-up of American parties. (This use of "federal" differs, of course, from Madison's meaning.)

23 (p. 218). Since 1928 presidential nominating conventions have been largely determined by popular verdicts of the primaries, opinion polls, mass media, and nationally organized interest groups. See William G. Carleton, "How Free Are the Nominating Conventions?" *Virginia Quarterly Review,* 40 (Spring 1964), 205–223.

24 (p. 320). In fact, the decision reversed a precedent as old as 1796 when Hamilton argued for the government in *Hylton v. United States* that direct taxes, undefined in the Constitution, ought only to include capitation taxes, land taxes, and general assessments on the whole property of individuals. The Court, including two former members of the Convention, accepted his argument.

25 (p. 339). The 17th Amendment, requiring popular election of Senators, was ratified in 1913.

INDEX

THE INDEX IS FROM THE ORIGINAL EDITION.

INDEX

INDEX

James I, on the divine right of kings, 104.

Jefferson, Thomas, on the independence of Federal judges, 68, 73 note, 100 note; on the right of a state to nullify a federal law, 173.

Johnson, Alexander, on the conservatism of the Federal Convention, 33 note.

Judges, reason for advocating the independence of, 67; removal of, under the early state constitutions, 71. See Impeachment, Judicial Veto, Supreme Court.

Judicial infallibility, 115, 344.

Judicial veto, effort to revive, 87; how conferred, 92; in England, 85; relation of, to the executive veto, 85; relation of, to popular government, 99, 356; significance of, 97.

Judiciary Act of 1789, 182; why not incorporated in the Constitution, 183.

Kentucky resolutions, 172.

Kidd, Benjamin, on social progress, 391.

Labor, free trade in, 314.

Laissez faire, opposition of the masses to, 308; relation of, to progress, 309, 311, 398.

Law, lack of respect for, 376-378.

Lawyers, virtually a ruling class, 300-302.

Lecky, W. E. H., on the purpose of the framers, 129.

Liberty, class control of industry destructive of, 306; democratic conception of, 293; eighteenth century economic conditions favorable to, 304; eighteenth century view of, negative, 291; survival of the old view in our legal literature, 301-303.

Lincoln, Abraham, on the right of the majority to overthrow minority government, 335; a minority president, 334.

Lowell, A. Lawrence, on the importance of the judiciary in our scheme of government, 65.

Madison, James, on the evils of American government, 42; on the power of a state to oppose the Federal government, 170; on the danger of government by a majority, 205.

Maine, Henry S., on the success of the Senate in opposing democracy, 337.

Mallock, W. H., on the benefits and justice of minority control, 389, 392, 394.

Marshall, John, on the judicial veto, 93, 322.

Martin, Luther, on the precautions against publicity in the Federal Convention, 34 note.

McMaster, J. B., on the character of the framers, 32; on the political immorality of the fathers, 50.

Miller, S. F., on the relation of the people to the government, 31.

Morality, change in the standard of, 361; effect of change in theological beliefs on, 364; influence of class rule on, 366-378.

Municipal government, a creature of the legislature, 252; attitude of the courts toward, 254; evils of, attributed to the rule of the masses, 251, 284; examples of legislative interference, 258-263; extension of legislative authority over, 254; fear of majority rule in, 277; financial powers of, limited, 271-273; franchise granting power in,

416

THE JOHN HARVARD LIBRARY

*The intent of
Waldron Phoenix Belknap, Jr.,
as expressed in an early will, was for
Harvard College to use the income from a
permanent trust fund he set up, for "editing and
publishing rare, inaccessible, or hitherto unpublished
source material of interest in connection with the
history, literature, art (including minor and useful
art), commerce, customs, and manners or way of
life of the Colonial and Federal Periods of the United
States . . . In all cases the emphasis shall be on the
presentation of the basic material." A later testament
broadened this statement, but Mr. Belknap's interests remained constant until his death.*

*In linking the name of the first benefactor of
Harvard College with the purpose of this later,
generous-minded believer in American culture the
John Harvard Library seeks to emphasize the importance of Mr. Belknap's purpose. The John Harvard
Library of the Belknap Press of Harvard University
Press exists to make books and documents
about the American past more readily
available to scholars and the
general reader.*